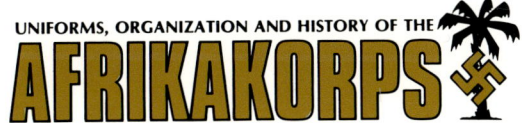

UNIFORMS, ORGANIZATION AND HISTORY OF THE
AFRIKAKORPS

UNIFORMS, ORGANIZATION AND HISTORY OF THE AFRIKAKORPS

BY
ROGER JAMES BENDER
AND
RICHARD D. LAW

1st EDITION

ISBN NO. 0-912138-09-2

COPYRIGHT © 1973 BY
ROGER JAMES BENDER
AND
RICHARD D. LAW
SECOND PRINTING--DECEMBER 1976
THIRD PRINTING--DECEMBER 1986

PRINTED IN THE UNITED STATES OF AMERICA

DESIGNED AND ILLUSTRATED
BY
ROGER JAMES BENDER

ALL RIGHTS RESERVED. THIS BOOK, OR PARTS THEREOF, MAY NOT BE REPRODUCED IN ANY FORM WITHOUT PERMISSION OF THE AUTHORS.

R. JAMES BENDER PUBLISHING
P.O. Box 23456, San Jose, Calif. 95153 (408) 225-5777

Table of Contents

Acknowledgements 6
Foreword. 7
Introduction 9
Preparations for North Africa. 22
Army Commands in North Africa 27
   Deutsches Afrikakorps 28
   Panzergruppe Afrika/Panzerarmee Afrika/
      I. italienische Armee 34
   Stab Nehring/XC. Korps. 39
   Panzer-Armeeoberkommando 5. 41
   Heeresgruppe Afrika. 46
German Divisions in North Africa 49
   5. leichte Division. 50
   10. Panzer-Division. 56
   15. Panzer-Division 60
   21. Panzer-Division. 66
   90. leichte Afrika-Division 72
   164. leichte Afrika-Division. 78
   334. Infanterie-Division 82
   999. leichte Afrika-Division. 84
   Division von Broich/von Manteuffel. 88
   Division "Hermann Göring" 92
Battle Groups (Kampfgruppen) in North Africa 94
Knight's Cross Holders: Africa 1941-1943 131
Special Units in North Africa 145
   Military Field Police 146
   Secret Field Police 147
   SS/SD Einsatz-Kommando Tunis 148
   The Brandenburger 149
   The Ramcke Parachute Brigade. 151
   The German Red Cross 156
   Field Post Service 158
Tropical Uniforms and Insignia 161
   Tropical Rank Insignia 164
   Waffenfarben. 172
   Shoulder Strap Insignia 173
   Specialty Patches 173
   Tropical Uniforms. 174
   Tropical Belts and Buckles 183
   Tropical Footwear. 185
   Tropical Headgear. 188
   Cuff Titles 196
   The Italo-German Medal 201
Field Equipment used in North Africa. 205
Army Flags and Pennants utilized in North Africa 221
   Command Flags 222
   Staff Flags 224
   Vehicle Pennants. 225
Vehicle Markings and Camouflage. 229
   Vehicle Markings 230
   Vehicle Camouflage 240
Miscellaneous 242
Bibliography 250

Acknowledgements

We would like to take this opportunity to thank the following individuals for giving so freely of their time, energy, resources and knowledge during the production of this book. Our special thanks go to Walther Nehring and Friedhelm Ollenschläger for their scrupulous editing of our complex manuscript, and to John R. Angolia and George A. Petersen for supplying a great portion of the never-before published photographs, which have made this book truly unique.

    Rudy D'Angello
    Major John R. Angolia
    Bernhard Bäter (Bundesgeschäfts-
        führer, Verband Deutsches Afrika-Korps)
    Helmut Damerau
    Mrs. Hanna Davis
    Steve Dukes
    Robert S. Eddy
    Hartvig Fleege
    Charles J. Hinz
    Clement Kelly
    Ken Lazier
    Andrew Mollo
    Richard L. Mundhenk
    Gen. d. Pz.-Truppe a. D. Walther Nehring
    Scott van Ness
    Warren Odegard
    Friedhelm Ollenschläger
    George A. Petersen
    Guenther G. Schoen
    Andy Southard
    Peter Stahl
    Merrill Stiggy
    Hugh Page Taylor
    Jerry Weiblen
    Gen. d. Kavallerie a. D. Siegfried Westphal
    owner/employees of Bayou Books, Gretna, La.

Institutions:
    Hoover Library/Stanford University
    The United States National Archives
        Modern Military Records: George Wagner and Robert Wolfe
        Microfilm Reading Section
        Audio-Visual Department

Foreword by
GENERAL DER PANZERTRUPPE a. D.
Walther K. Nehring

Much has been written in books and essays concerning details of the campaigns and battles between the German Army and its adversaries in North Africa. For this reason, Mr. Bender and Mr. Law have not attempted to rewrite this familiar subject once again, but have gone into the background events leading up to German involvement in Africa. They have also taken great pains to gather accurate historical data on the Afrikakorps and the units which evolved to form Heeresgruppe Afrika in 1943. Thus, one is justified in describing it as completely unique in its presentation.... a "liber sui generis".

The authors have spent many months of diligent research evaluating the available documents on all German units, both large and small, which had been involved in North Africa. The result is a detailed, organizational study of the divisions, corps, armies, their commanders and staffs, and their orders-of-battle. Also new in their unique approach to this subject, is the compilation of all documented Battle Groups (Kampfgruppen), their structure, list of commanders, assignments, as well as the point of time of their operations. Doubtless, this is in itself a great achievement.

Of additional interest, is the complete listing of Knight's Cross holders who served in North Africa, the date of award, plus their assignment and unit. A further impressionable supplement to this section are the numerous photographs of Knight's Cross recipients, which include ranks from Generalfeldmarschall Erwin Rommel to Grenadier Günther Halm.

Then, an especially detailed section follows on tropical uniforms and insignia, which completely discusses and describes such items as headgear, cuff titles, the Italo-German Medal, etc. This section by itself promises to be of great value to the uniform and insignia aficionado. The section on special units, which includes the German Red Cross, Secret Field Police, the Brandenburger, Ramcke Parachute Brigade, etc., is also of profound interest.

Considering all of the above, this book must be regarded as a reliable source of accurate information concerning the organization, personnel, plus materiel matters which pertained to the German units in the African campaign. Its study is therefore highly recommended.

General der Panzertruppe a.D.
Commanding General in
Libya, Egypt and Tunisia (1942)

Introduction

The signing of the armistice by France on June 22, 1940, left Germany and Italy only one active foe remaining in Europe.. ...Great Britain. The Germans could resort to one of two alternatives for defeating the island nation: One choice was a total blockade by air and sea, constant aerial attacks on military targets, and finally, an invasion of the island itself. The other choice was to permit German attacks against any part of the Empire which was geographically feasible, thus nations seeking the Empire's destruction would be potential allies (i.e. Spain, Russia and Japan).

Hitler decided on the first choice, however, and on July 16, issued Directive No. 16, "Operation Lion" (later "Sealion"). This directive called for the preparation of the Wehrmacht to invade England. While these measures were being implimented, England was being bombed daily by the Luftwaffe and blockaded at sea by U-Boats. All tentative work and planning was halted in September 1940, however, when Hitler postponed the invasion until the following spring.

As the war became stalemated in mid-1940, the German leaders sought a way out of the impass. On July 22, a five point program for expanding the Mediterranean theater of war was proposed by Generalfeldmarschall von Brauchitsch. It called for:

(a) attacking Gibralter via Spain,
(b) supporting Italy in North Africa with armor,
(c) attacking the British at Haifa,
(d) attacking the Suez Canal itself, and
(e) causing Russia to attack the Persian Gulf area.

It was believed that if these proposals could become reality, Germany could literally wage war against England indefinately. A further Army proposal of July 31, which covered the possibility of sending an expeditionary force to Africa, was carefully examined by the German National Defense Branch. It was decided that armored forces could be spared until September 1941, and that the chances of success were good, especially if an attack could be launched against Gibralter at the same time. If all succeeded, the British power in the Mediterranean would be crushed.[1]

At Oberkommando der Wehrmacht (OKW), the plans for the proposed African campaign were initiated at an unenthusiastic pace. Generalmajor Walter Buhle, Chief of the Organization Branch of OKH, on August 21, reported that sufficient vehicles and equipment could be made available for one armored corps. Personnel would be drawn from the 3. and 5. Panzer-Division and the 13. Division (mot).

By late August, the OKH (Oberkommando des Heeres) was still struggling with the many unanswered questions poised by the looming African adventure. It was therefore decided, to get a first-hand account of the situation in that theater. General Ritter von Thoma was chosen for the reconnaissance trip, his task being to report on whether German forces were actually essential to the Italians' campaign against the British in Egypt. Hitler, on September 14, held a conference and reemphasized that an armored corps must be readied for use in North Africa, as he now felt that the British would soon establish air bases there for bombing of the Italian mainland.[2]

A major problem overlooked until this time were the difficulties of unloading operations in North African ports. The ports in Cyrenaica and Benghazi were too shallow for transports and the British fleet was menacingly close, being stationed only 660 miles away at Alexandria. If the unloading was attempted in Tripoli, the vehicles faced a long march to the front, causing great wear and tear on them in addition to consuming a vast amount of precious fuel. There was also but one decent road in the whole coastal area....the Via Balbia, which stopped at the Libyan border. This British-built road was merely a layer of asphalt spread on the ground which occasionally collapsed under the weight of heavy vehicles.[3]

---

[1]Helmuth Greiner, Ministerialrat a. D., Aid to the Italians during 1940-1941, (Office of the Chief of Military History, MS# C-065c).

[2]Franz Halder, The Halder Diaries in English, Microfilm Publication T34, roll 191, EAP 21g 16/4K vol. IV, September 14, 1940.

[3]Heinz Hegenreiner, Oberst a. D., The Operations of Marshall Graziani prior to the Arrival of German Troops, (Office of the Chief of Military History, MS# O-216).

While the OKH studied the pros and cons of the North African intervention, the Navy was also reviewing the Mediterranean situation. The Naval Staff was convinced that the Italo-German control of the Mediterranean would have a great influence on the course of the war. With key ports of the British Empire under direct assault or threat of attack, it was imagined that Britain might be compelled to abandon further resistance, especially if her position could be made untenable before American aid could prove effective. In a report dated September 19, 1940, the Naval Staff put forth the fear the OKW would allow the Italians to control the war in the Mediterranean. The Staff suggested that Germany must immediately reinforce the Italians, for the North African theater was now the primary front in the stalemated European war. They felt so strongly about their observations that they decided they must convince Hitler and the OKW into accepting their strategic views. Grossadmiral Raeder, Oberkommando der Kriegsmarine (OKM), met with Hitler on September 6 and again on the 26th. In the latter meeting, he pointed out to Hitler that the English had always considered the Mediterranean as the pivot point of the Empire and that was where a major portion of her strength was situated. Raeder went on to call for the conquest of Gibralter, the Canary Islands and the Suez Canal. With the Canal in German hands, Germany could advance as far as Turkey and would secure Italy's colonies in East Africa.[4] Raeder had hoped to dissuade Hitler from his planned attack on Russia but the Führer was not to be swayed from this path of action.

GROSSADMIRAL Dr. h. c. RAEDER

GENERALFELDMARSCHALL V. BRAUCHITSCH
(HERE AN GENERALOBERST)

---

[4]Erich Raeder, Führer Conferences on Naval Affairs, Brassey's Naval Annual 1948, ed. Rear-Admiral H. G. Thursfield (New York: The Macmillan Co., 1948), p. 111.

At a joint meeting between Hitler and Mussolini on October 3, the Duce promised to re-open the long-stalled Egyptian offensive on the 12th or 13th. In turn, Hitler promised support for the operation to the sum of approximately a Panzer brigade. Along with the brigade, the VIII. Fliegerkorps would be sent as aerial support.

On October 17, a preliminary report was received from General von Thoma concerning the military situation in North Africa. "Stab Thoma" (von Thoma's reconnaissance staff in Libya) reported that the situation was in a state of confusion with neither the Italians nor the Germans knowing what was expected of them. The report stressed a greater allied unification in order to function with some semblence of efficiency. The lack of port facilities and the vast distances to be covered in Libya were also emphasized.[5]

General Ritter von Thoma returned to Germany on October 24, to report directly to Hitler on his Libyan reconnaissance mission. He explained that the Libyan conditions were extremely poor for warfare by reason of topography alone. He concluded with the fact that the major problem was supplying an army, not only because of the desert but also because of the British control of the Mediterranean. He stressed that nothing less than four Panzer divisions could ensure success in the campaign and no more than four divisions could be supplied in a cross-desert drive on the Nile Delta. Hitler flatly rejected his proposals and stated that only one Panzer division could be spared at this time. At this, von Thoma suggested that the whole operation should then be abandoned as one Panzer division could do little in the existing situation. Hitler became angry and pressed his belief that the Italians could hold their own against the British and that his whole reason for sending aid was to keep Mussolini loyal to the Axis. Von Thoma knew better, however, for he had just witnessed the Italians in action and had fought alongside them for three years during the Spanish Civil War. Despite his knowledgeable arguments, von Thoma was not able to change Hitler's mind.[6]

The long-awaited Italian offensive against the British in Egypt was continually delayed, now under the premise that Graziani was waiting for the supply road construction to be completed. The British, however, had been heavily reinforced in the meantime which indicated that more German troops and material could be required from Germany than previously planned. It also meant that Alexandria, the port of British dis-

---

[5] The Halder Diaries, October 21, 1940, p. 291.

[6] Ritter von Thoma as cited in B.H. Liddell Hart's, The German Generals Talk, (New York: William Morrow & Co., 1948).

embarkation, would have to be siezed, and that the Axis would have to control the eastern Mediterranean and Crete.

During these undecisive weeks, the Army continued its planning for the African operation and the National Defense Branch worked to coordinate the operation with other plans.... arranging the transportation, setting up staff organizations, etc. It was estimated at this time, that the first army components would be ready for shipment on December 1, 1940.

All of the reports, meetings, planning and preparations were in vain, however, when on October 28, the Italians invaded Greece without informing their German allies. In part, Mussolini had launched this attack in retaliation for Hitler's unannounced occupation of Rumania Mussolini had felt that his prestige had been lessened by the German move and the attack on Greece was meant to present Hitler with a surprise in turn.[7]

Hitler was enraged and rumors were soon rampant that the Führer had had a change of attitude and no aid would be sent to the Italians in Libya. On November 4, Hitler held a major conference with Keitel, Jodl, Halder, von Brauchitsch, Oberstleutnant Willy Deyle (Jodl's personal representative), Major Gerhard Engel (one of Hitler's adjutants), and Raeder in attendance. There, Hitler stated that the Libyan operation had been postponed for several reasons, among which were:
- (a) the Italians were reluctant to continue their offensive,
- (b) von Thoma's unsatisfactory impression of the Italian headquarters in Libya,
- (c) the Italian request that the Germans use Tunis for a supply base while retaining Tripoli for their own use,
- (d) and finally, he did not want to send troops over an enemy-controlled sea.

He did conclude that his aerial commitment would be met and that the National Defense Branch should continue its planned use against Egypt, and for the mining of Alexandria and the Suez Canal. On November 9, Generalmajor Warlimont, Chief of the National Defense Branch (Chef L), sent a situation report to Generalleutnant Enno von Rintelen, German Military Attache in Rome, in which he stated that the Italians could expect only a Luftwaffe commitment in Egypt and this would come only when Marsa Matruh (western Egypt) had been taken.

Meanwhile, the German Naval Staff had been busy once again preparing a memorandum on their views regarding Libya which Raeder delivered to Hitler on November 14. In it, the Staff called for the following plan of action: First, OKW must realize that no further support or relief will

---

[7]Count Galeazzo Ciano, edited by Hugh Gibson, The Ciano Diaries, 1939-1943, (New York: Doubleday & Company, Inc., 1946), p. 300.

GENERALFELDMARSCHALL KESSELRING, GENERAL VON RINTELEN (GERMAN MILITARY ATTACHE IN ROME), AND CROWN PRINCE UMBERTO.

be coming from the Italians; second, the entire Greek peninsula should be cleared of the British; and finally, the British must be forced out of the Mediterranean at any cost. At this point, Raeder again tried to dissuade Hitler from attacking Russia. He argued that the Russian campaign could be postponed for a short time until the defeat of Britain was at hand and then, perhaps, there would be no need for military action at all in the east.[8] As before, Hitler did not listen, but did, however, on that date issue Führer-Weisung Nr. 18 for delivery to OKH. In it, Hitler decreed that aerial support would be given the Italians once they took Marsa Matruh and provided air bases were made available. Additionally, the Army was to keep a Panzer division in readiness for use in North Africa if necessary.[9] He also ordered the commitment of Luftwaffe units against the dangerous British naval forces, plus naval and air bases in the eastern Mediterranean. The British Alexandria Squadron (four battleships and two aircraft carriers) was operating in the Malta area in

---

[8] Erich Raeder, pp. 154-156.

[9] Microfilm Publication T-77, roll 774, American Historical Association Committee for the Study of War Documents, (Records of the Headquarters, OKW, Führer Directives and other Top-Level Directives of the German Armed Forces, 1939-1945).

conjunction with air units from that beleagured island and southern Greece. These strong British forces had harassed Axis shipping traffic between Italy and Libya to the extent that the Italian offensive against Egypt could not be contemplated for some time.[10] The committed Luftwaffe unit was ordered to Italy on December 10, the day the British launched their surprise counter-offensive in Egypt.

In the space of one week, the Italian Army had been overrun by numerically inferior British armored and mechanized units, advancing in an enveloping movement. Sollum fell, the Egyptian-Libyan border was crossed, Bardia was encircled and approximately 26,000 men and four generals were captured. Marshal Graziani now intended to fight delaying actions both at Bardia and Tobruk while a new defensive line could be established at the eastern edge of the Djebel-el-Akdar, at Derna and to the south of it. And if he could not hold this area, the Italians were to fall back to Tripolitania and there establish a final defense around Tripoli.

In all fairness, it must be pointed out that although the Italians were strong in numbers, they had less than 2,000 motor vehicles of all kinds and no modern anti-tank or anti-aircraft artillery, no motorized General Headquarters artillery and no armored reconnaissance vehicles. The air force, also numerically adequate, consisted of mainly obsolete aircraft, and the Italian Fleet has been neutralized by the British Fleet and the Royal Air Force. In short, the Italians were in a very exposed position and would need immediate help to extricate themselves.

On December 19, Commando Supremo (the Italian High Command) reversed their previous requests for raw materials and equipment only and now asked for German troops. The Italians received their first visible assistance when the X. Fliegerkorps, under General der Flieger Hans-Ferdinand Geissler, was transferred from Norway in late December, to Sicily. This force's mission was to make Malta ineffectual, disrupt British naval strength and sea transportation and secure air and sea lanes from Italy and Sicily to North Africa.

**GENERAL DER FLIEGER
HANS-FERDINAND GEISSLER**

---

[10]Greiner, MS# C-065F, pp. 1-2.

On January 7, news was received that Bardia had fallen and that the Italian Army Group Libya had the strength of no more than five divisions, which included the 61st. "Sirte" Reinforced Division. The only bright sign was that reinforcements for Libya consisted of the 132nd "Ariete" Armored Division and the 102nd "Trento" Motorized Division.

At a Berghof conference on January 9, 1941, Hitler decided to send a German unit to Libya for the following reasons:

> "The loss of the Libyan area must be prevented under all circumstances. The loss of this colony would not entail very far-reaching military consequences, because it would neither substantially increase the danger of air attacks on Italy nor affect the situation in French North Africa. However, the British forces committed in Egypt would then be freed for other tasks and, above all, the effect on Italian morale would be extremely unfavorable. Obviously, the Italians are not able to resist the British without our support. This is due not so much to their inferiority as soldiers as to their lack of modern defensive weapons against British armor". (11)

Hitler knew that an armored blocking force (Sperrverband) must be made available for the Libyan theater which could both block the British advance and make local counterthrusts. Thus, it would consist of anti-tank and engineer units with large numbers of mines; a small number of modern tanks (i.e. the Pz. Mark III (Model G) with the new 50mm cannon); and an anti-aircraft unit. A unit of this size could be transferred much faster and be in action before the restrictive hot season set in. German plans for intervention in Libya now took concrete form and it appeared that by February 15, the troops would be enroute.

On January 22, however, the fortified city of Tobruk fell to the British Western Desert Forces, a disaster which threatened to upset the entire operation. In addition to Tobruk, the Italians lost the XXII Infantry Corps H.Q., the 61st. "Sirte" Reinforced Division, and 700 officers and men of the cruiser San Giorgio. Because of the critical Libyan situation, the program was now greatly accelerated and the first elements of the Fifth Light Division (5. leichte Division) departed for Naples on January 31.[12]

Hitler called another conference at the Berghof on February 3, to discuss the measures Germany could take in support of the Italians. At this time, von Brauchitsch, Commander-in-Chief of the Army, was asked if a Panzer division could be sent in addition to the 5. leichte Division. His reply was that if one was taken from "Marita" (the upcoming invasion of

---

[11] Greiner, MS# C-065F, p. 8.

[12] The Fifth Light Division (5. leichte Division) was made up primarily of cadres from the 3. Panzer-Division.

Greece), it would not be available for "Barbarossa" (the invasion of Russia), because units from "Marita" were to be used later in the Russian campaign.[13] Von Brauchitsch suggested, however, that the blocking force be reinforced with a Panzer regiment, with the other elements of the parent Panzer division being transferred at a later date. He also proposed that all German and Italian motorized forces in Libya be placed under the command of a German corps headquarters. Hitler was in agreement with these proposals and ordered:

1. The Luftwaffe is to immediately examine the possibilities for the commitment of dive bomber and twin-engine bomber formations in North Africa; for having the X. Fliegerkorps protect North African-bound transports; and for the elimination of the British Air Base at Malta.
2. The Army is to accelerate the shipment of the planned blocking force, to reinforce this immediately with a Panzer regiment, and prepare the follow-up of one Panzer division, which is to be drawn from the second build-up wave of "Operation Marita"..., the placing of all German and Italian mobile forces in Libya under a single German command, should be requested of the Italian High Command and a corps H.Q. should be formed for this purpose. (14)

As commander of the German ground forces in Libya, Hitler personally requested that Generalleutnant Erwin Rommel be given command with Oberstleutnant von dem Borne, as his Ia (Chief of Operations). Hitler had known Rommel since 1937, when the latter published his book, <u>Infanterie greift an</u>, which was

GENERALMAJOR ERWIN ROMMEL

HITLER, BORMANN AND ROMMEL IN POLAND (NOTE "FÜHRERHAUPT-QUARTIER" CUFF TITLE).

[13]Greiner, MS# C-065K, p. 141.

[14]Ibid.

based on his experiences in World War I at which time he won the Pour le mérite at Caporetto. Due to Hitler's admiration of the book, Rommel was shortly thereafter made commander of the escort battalion (Führer-begleit-Bataillon) responsible for the Führer's safety during the Sudetenland takeover. He remained in this position during the march into Czechoslovakia and was then attached to Hitler's headquarters (Führerhauptquartier) as the officer responsible for Hitler's safety. After serving in this capacity during the Polish campaign, Rommel was given command of the 7. Panzer-Division at Godesberg.[15] In the French campaign of 1940, he was once again drawn to Hitler's attention by his exceptional handling of his division.

On February 5, Hitler issued a top secret directive to commanders whose destination was North Africa. It was entitled "Conduct of German troops in Italian Theaters of War", with the preamble exhorting the German troops...

> ...fighting shoulder to shoulder with our allies in the Mediterranean must be conscious of their lofty military and political mission. They have been selected for a purpose of rendering valuable assistance in both a psychological and military way, to our allies, who in every theater are struggling against an enemy greatly superior in numbers and who, on account of the limited productive capacity of Italy's war economy, are insufficiently equipped with modern weapons.

This prologue was ended with an order for German troops to treat their allies as equals, not act as superiors, and to show the Italians, by example, how good soldiers behave.[16]

Rommel had been informed of his new assignment by von Brauchitsch on February 6, and spent the next week learning all he could about his appointed task. He was told by Hitler that he had been chosen as the man who could best adapt himself most quickly to the entirely different conditions in Africa. He was also informed, that Hitler's Chief Adjutant, Oberst Schmundt, would accompany him on the first stage of reconnaissance.

Rommel and his party arrived in Rome on February 11 where they immediately went to the German Embassy, then to Commando Supremo where Rommel conferred with Mussolini, General Guzzoni,[17] and General Mario Roatta.[18] That afternoon, Rommel, General Roatta and por-

---

[15] Desmond Young, <u>Rommel, the Desert Fox</u>, (New York: Berkeley Publishing Corporation, 1961), pp. 39-44.

[16] Microfilm Publication T-77, roll 774, National Defence Branch Nr. 44075/41, Chef/geheime Kommandosache.

[17] Undersecretary of War and Deputy Chief of the Italian General Staff.

[18] Chief of the Italian General Staff.

tions of Rommel's staff flew to Catania, Sicily. There, Rommel met with General Geissler, commander of X. Fliegerkorps, who relayed the latest news from Libya. Lieutenant-General Sir Richard O'Connor's Western Desert Force had taken Benghazi and was now moving into Tripolitania.

Rommel, accompanied by Schmundt, von dem Borne, and the other members of his staff (Aufklärungsstab Rommel) landed at Castel Benito on February 12.[19] There, they were met by Major Heggenreiner, General von Rintelen's representative in Africa, who briefed Rommel on the most recent reports from the disintigrating front. All of Cyrenaica had fallen to the British on February 8. All that now stood between the British and Tripoli were 7,000 Italian troops, mostly headquarters troops, who had evaded capture and now formed small pockets of ineffective resistance.

On February 14, the first German combat troops arrived at Tripoli harbor and were personally reviewed by Rommel and von dem Borne. After a march past, the newly arrived forces continued marching, arriving at Misurata late that same day. The advance units of 3. Aufklärungs-Abteilung reached Sirte, where they were ordered to remain as a mobile reserve for the time being.

ROMMEL REVIEWING HIS TROOPS IN TRIPOLI.

---

[19]Castel Benito was Tripoli's airfield, located approximately fifteen miles south of the city.

At approximately this time, Rommel ordered the construction of dummy tanks to be mounted on Volkswagens. He reported that they looked "deceptively real" and with these dummies he intended to make the Germans appear as strong as possible and induce caution in the British.[20]

On February 19, a directive was issued from the Führer's Headquarters, which stated:

> "The Führer has made the following decisions on February 18:
> 1. The German forces in Africa under Generalleutnant Rommel will be known as the "German Africa Corps" (Deutsches Afrika-Korps), effective immediately.
> 2. In order to reinforce the German Africa Corps, the OKH should transfer a full Panzer division to Tripolitania in addition to the Fifth Light Division, with its Panzer regiment. (21)

The D. A. K. made its first contact with the British Western Desert Forces on February 24. "Advance Unit Wechmar" ran into two troops of armored cars of the Dragoon Guards and a troop of Australian anti-tank guns. The Germans opened fire destroying one armored car, one truck, two armored reconnaissance cars, and disabled another armored car which

---

[20]Erwin Rommel, The Rommel Papers, (New York: Harcourt, Brace and Company, 1953), p. 103.

[21]Microfilm Publication T-78, roll 774, folder "Lybien" from WFSt./Abt. L (10) Nr. 44 189/41 g. k. Chefs of 19.2.41.

the Germans were able to tow away. Only one soldier was killed, an English armored car crewman, and the Germans suffered no losses.[22]

With this minor encounter, the Afrikakorps began a two year career of classic armored warfare in the wastes of the North African desert. The leader of this force, Erwin Rommel, went on to become the most famous and respected German commander of the war. He and his grossly neglected and always undernourished Africa Corps were to write a chapter in military history which, in the final analysis, would place them with the ranks of Hannibal and his legions, and Robert E. Lee and his Army of Virginia ....all defeated, but never outfought nor outgeneralled.

[22] KTB DAK Ia, frame #815, February 24, 1941.

Preparations for North Africa

> "It has probably never happened before in modern warfare that an operation of this kind was undertaken with so little preparation"...Generalfeldmarschall Rommel (1)

This section has been included to illustrate the multitude of complex problems encountered by the German Army in planning for their African adventure. The breakdown of thought on some problems and the complete lack of thought on others, placed the Afrikakorps at a distinct disadvantage from the very beginning of their involvement.

The German Army High Command had been taken almost completely by surprise when the necessity arose to dispatch troops for warfare in the desert. In any event, the Command had no time to make thorough preparations for this type of combat employment. For this reason, all preparatory work which was possible in the short amount of time available had to be restricted mainly to the following measures:

1. Medical examination of all troops to determine their fitness for service in the tropics, with the application of very severe standards.
2. Equipping of all soldiers with tropical clothing.
3. Adaptation of a training program for combat in open terrain.
4. Camouflage of all vehicles with a coat of desert-colored paint.
5. Organization of special units to handle water supply problems.
6. Familiarization of the troops with the hygienic measures necessary in tropical climates.
7. Orientation of the troops on the military/geographical conditions of the new theater of war and on the peculiarities of Germany's allies and enemies.

As early as July 1940, Generalleutnant Heinrich Kirchheim had proposed the formation of a special staff to inspect the varied conditions in North Africa. Its task was to determine the type of troops needed in case Germany would ever have to come to the support of the Italians there. In August 1940, OKH approved his plan and the staff was formed. Commando Supremo, however, refused the staff and stated that they preferred to use

---

[1] MS#P-129, German Experiences in W.W. II: Desert Warfare, p. 1.

its services at a later date. The staff was therefore disbanded, but reformed again later that year due to the disintegrating situation in North Africa. It disembarked for Africa on February 24, 1941.[2]

Kirchheim's Special Staff Libya (Sonderstab Lybien) was composed of a number of officers who had served in Africa during W.W. I, among which were veterans of mounted artillery units, mounted infantry units, the Cameroon colonial troops and the Camel Corps. When Kirchheim and his staff arrived in Africa, however, Rommel obtained permission from OKH to dispose of the staff as he saw fit, due to the prevailing lack of officers in that theater. Thus, the potential benefit of this Staff for future reinforcement and replacement troops was lost forever.

The first contingents of German troops sent to North Africa received no specialized training for their employment, other than some research in the Army library, a number of lectures by specialists in tropical medicine, and by officers who had a vague knowledge of conditions from traveling in that region. Even units which were transferred to Africa later in the campaign received no real specialized training, due to the fact that their transfer orders usually came so unexpectedly that there was no time for it.

> NOTE:
> At a later date, Grafenwöhr in North Bavaria, was used during the summer months as a troop replacement area with emphasis on hot weather training. Also, German troops stationed in Italy or the Balkans did receive some acclimatization since their climates were similar to that of the coastal areas of North Africa.

Once committed to the African campaign, the problem arose of proper rations for the troops. The staple food for them on the continent had been bread and potatoes, but these were believed unsuitable in North Africa. Potatoes were eliminated altogether from the soldiers' diet because they would spoil in storage and were therefore replaced by legumes. It was also believed that bread would go moldy in shipment, so Zwieback was substituted. Since butter was needed but spoiled easily, olive oil and tinned sardines were substituted.[3]

The Italians were able to provide some foods but not the delicacies like ham, eggs, bacon, butter, condensed milk or cheese. They did supply coffee beans to the German troops, 3 ounces of grated cheese per man

---

[2] It is interesting to note that Rommel, his staff and the 5. leichte Division had already arrived in North Africa.

[3] Nehring, MS#T-3, p. 41.

per day, 6 ounces of cooking oil per man per day, and marmalade.[4] The Afrikakorps members, therefore, had sufficient carbohydrates and oils with some protein, but they lacked fresh fruit, vegetables or any kind of fresh food. As Hans von Esebeck, the German war correspondent, later told Desmond Young, the biographer of Rommel:

> "One of the reasons we had so much sickness, especially jaundice, was that our rations were too heavy for the desert. Our black bread in a carton was handy but how we used to long to capture one of your field bakeries and eat fresh, white bread! And your jam! For the first four months we got no fresh fruit or vegetables at all. We lived all the time on Italian tinned meat.. The tins had a big "A. M." on them: the troops used to call it "asinus Mussolini"(5) or "Alter Mann".

By mid-March 1941, Bakery Company 531 had begun operations and fresh bread was then available. Another example of early haphazard planning was the fact that the bakery's ovens used wood as fuel as did the field kitchens of the regular units...thus, fuel oil or logs had to be shipped from Italy since wood was particularly precious in the desert.

The water situation was good since the General Staff had over-estimated the requirements. Special water procuring and/or filtration companies and a special water transporting company were established for employment in the desert and accompanied the 5. leichte Division to Africa (6):

1. Water supply companies were under the command of engineering officers. They were assigned to the Corps and operated under the Water Supply Branch of the Corps Supply and Administration Officer. These companies had equipment for the drilling of deep wells as well as pumps, while some of them had installations for the distillation of water.
2. Water supply transporation columns were organized in the same way as ordinary supply transporation columns, but employed solely in the transportation of water to the troops. They had no tank trucks or tank trailers as was customary with the British units so they had to transport the water in 20-liter cans. (7) This method of transportation proved extremely tiresome, quite apart from the considerable loading space required.

The first German tanks in Africa lacked the proper air and oil filters and reinforced cooling systems for the desert, thus, their engine life was 600-900 miles whereas the British were getting 1200-1800 miles. Other vehicles were also plagued by frequent engine breakdowns caused by heat,

---

[4]Microfilm Publication T-77, Roll 774, p. 40.

[5]Desmond Young, <u>Rommel, the Desert Fox</u>, (New York: Harper & Brothers, 1950), pp. 111-112.

[6]Toppe, MS#P-129.

[7]These were the "Jerry" cans. Gasoline and water were carried in the same type cans, the only difference being that water cans had a large white cross painted on them.

dust and sand. Until the above problems could be eliminated with the development of the proper filtering and cooling devices, German tanks moved up mainly at night and made frequent stops. Rommel also complicated these problems for he seldom allowed sufficient time for repairs and maintenance during his rapid advances.

Rommel, himself, was not allowed any preparatory time before leaving for Africa. Generalfeldmarschall von Brauchitsch informed him of his new assignment on February 6, 1941, he reported to Mussolini and General Guzzoni in Rome on February 11, and he and his staff took off for Tripoli on the 12th. The task of gathering information on the terrain and on the peculiarities of the desert which he required for the conduct of operations, would have to be done by himself. [8]

In spite of the many early problems of the campaign, the Afrikakorps under Rommel was still a formidable force as was evident by its successes in the field. The Germans were quick to learn and by the fall of 1941, ingenuity and hard work had eliminated many of the initial difficulties.

The German soldier performed well in this theater of the war for the ranks usually consisted of battle-hardened veterans and volunteers. [9] What the Afrikakorps lacked in collective desert experience, it made up in individual courage and the application of advanced mobile warfare.

---

[8] Generalmajor Freiherr von Funck had originally been destined to lead the German blocking force in North Africa. He had been allowed some preparatory time, however, and had left for Africa on January 15, 1941. He had submitted his first report to Rome on January 25, and had returned from Africa on February 1. It was because of the negative tone of his written and verbal reports that Hitler decided to replace him with Rommel (see Greiner, MS#C-065f).

[9] All German troops, during their tour of duty in North Africa, received the following extra pay per day:
Enlisted Men - 2RM
NCOs - 3RM
Officers - 3RM

Microfilm Publication T315, Roll 1474, Frame 001031.

Army Commands in North Africa

Deutsches Afrikakorps (D.A.K.)

Prior to the official establishment of the "Deutsches Afrikakorps" on February 19, 1941, the headquarters staff for the German Army in Africa was "Aufklärungsstab Rommel"[1]. This Staff was formed shortly after Rommel was advised of his new command on February 6, and it remained as such until the Führer himself announced the formation of the "Afrikakorps".

STAFF COMMANDER

February 6, 1941 - February 19, 1941 _____ Generalleutnant Rommel
    (before Feb. 19, his official title was "Befehlshaber der deutschen Truppen in Libyen)

    Ia: Oberstleutnant von dem Borne
    Ic: Hauptmann von Plehwe
    Luftwaffen-Verbindungsoffizier: Major i.G. Grunow
    Pionier-Offizier: Oberstleutnant Hundt
    Kommandant Stabsquartier: Oberstleutnant d.R. Behrendt

On February 19, 1941, Hitler announced that the German forces in Africa subordinated to Generalleutnant Rommel would receive the title....
.."Deutsches Afrikakorps", with immediate effect. "Aufklärungsstab Rommel" was automatically absorbed by this new command.

KORPS COMMANDERS

February 19, 1941 - August 15, 1941 _____ Generalleutnant Erwin Rommel
    (promoted to General d. Pz. Tr. on July 1, 1941)

August 15, 1941 - March 8, 1942 _____ Generalleutnant Ludwig Crüwell (2)

March 9, 1942 - August 31, 1942 _____ Generalleutnant Walther K. Nehring (promoted to Gen. d. Pz. Tr. on June 22 at Tobruk, and wounded on August 31)

---

[1] M. Warner Stark, The Creation of the German Africa Corps, (unpublished thesis), p. 140; also see KTB DAK Ia, for February 9, 1941.

[2] Generalleutnant Crüwell was later shot down in his Storch and captured on May 29, 1942, while commanding the Italian front and leading the attack on the Gazala line.

August 31, 1942 - August 31, 1942 _____ Oberst i.G. Fritz Bayerlein (temporary)(3)

August 31, 1942 - September 17, 1942 ___ Generalmajor Gustav von Vaerst

September 17, 1942 - November 4, 1942 __ General der Panzertruppe Wilhelm Ritter von Thoma (captured)

November 4, 1942 - November 19, 1942 __ Oberst Fritz Bayerlein (temporary)

November 19, 1942 - January 16, 1943 ___ General der Panzertruppe Gustav Fehn (wounded)

January 16, 1943 - February 17, 1943 ___ Generalmajor Kurt Freiherr von Liebenstein (wounded)

February 17, 1943 - March 5, 1943 _____ Generalleutnant Heinz Ziegler (temporary)

March 5, 1943 - May 12, 1943 _____ General der Panzertruppe Hans Cramer (permanent)

KORPS STAFF

Stabschef: Oberstleutnant i.G. von dem Borne
      Oberst i.G. Bayerlein
      Oberst i.G. H.W. Nolte

Ia: Major i.G. Ehlert
    Major i.G. Wüstefeld
    Major i.G. Westphal
    Major i.G. Trevert

Qu (Logistik):[4] Major i.G. Otto
         Major i.G. Willers
         Walter Schmidt
         Oberstleutnant
           Dr. Müller(5)

Ic: Hauptmann Graf Baudissin (captured)
    Major i.G. F.W. von Mellenthin
    Hauptmann Laubinger+
    Hauptmann Liebl

IIa: Major Schräpler+
     Oberst Schulte-Heuthaus

IVb(Arzt): Oberstarzt Dr. Barnewitz

GENERALLEUTNANT ROMMEL

---

[3] See <u>KTB DAK</u>, August 31, 1942.

[4] The Ib (chief supply officer) at Corps level was titled Quartiermeister, abbreviated "Qu".

[5] Afrikakorps-Kraftfahrtransportoffizier.

GENERALLEUTNANT CRÜWELL

GENERAL DER PANZERTRUPPE NEHRING

OBERST BAYERLEIN

GENERALMAJOR VON VAERST

GENERAL DER PANZERTRUPPE VON THOMA

GENERAL DER PANZERTRUPPE FEHN

JOHN R. ANGOLIA COLLECTION

GENERALMAJOR FREIHERR VON LIEBENSTEIN

GENERAL DER PANZERTRUPPE CRAMER

SONDERFÜHRER DR. FRANZ (ROMMEL'S TRANSLATOR, LEFT)

ORDER-OF-BATTLE

Stab des Korps
  (Generalkommando)
5. leichte Division
  (later 21. Panzer-Division)
15. Panzer-Division

Individual Units:

Korpskartenstelle (mot) 576

Oasen-Bataillon z. b. V. 300

Panzerjäger-Abteilung (mot) 605

I./Flak-Regiment (mot) 18 (Luftwaffe)

I./Flak-Regiment (mot) 33 (Luftwaffe)

Flak-Abteilung (mot) 606 (later assigned to Panzerarmee Afrika)

Nachrichten-Abteilung (mot) 475
  leichte Nachrichtenkolonne
  Funkleitstand-Zug 10
  Panzer Funk-Zug
  Funk-Zug
  Fernkabel-Zug

Nachschub-Bataillon (mot) 572
  grosse Kraftwagenkolonne (1-6)
  grosse Kraftwagenkolonne für Betriebsstoff
  Kraftwagenwerkstatt-Zug
  Munitionsverwaltung-Kompanie 588

Wasserversorgungs-Bataillon (mot) 580
  Wasserversorgungs-Kompanie (SW) 659
  Wasserdestillations-Kompanie (mot) 655
  grosse Wasserkolonne 641
  grosse Wasserkolonne 645
  grosse Wasserkolonne 651
  Filterkolonne 877
  Wehrgeologenstelle (mot) 8
  Wehrgeologenstelle (mot) 12

Aufklärungs-Kompanie (mot) 580 (later assigned to 90. leichte Afrika Division)

Feldersatz-Bataillon 598

Feldersatz-Bataillon 599

Bäckerei-Kompanie (mot) 554

Korps-Verpflegungslager (mot)

Feldgendarmerie-Trupp (mot) 498

Feldpostamt (mot)

Panzergruppe Afrika/Panzerarmee Afrika /1. italienische Armee

Rommel's command was raised to the status of a Panzergruppe on August 15, 1941. It included the "Afrikakorps" (5. leichte Division (retitled 21. Panzer-Division) and the 15. Panzer-Division) and the 90. leichte Division. Six Italian divisions were also placed under Rommel.... the "Ariete" and "Trieste" (forming the XX.Korps); the "Pavia", "Bologna" and "Brescia" (forming the XXI.Korps) and the "Savona". The Gruppe's HQ was stationed in Beda Littoria. "Panzerarmee Afrika" evolved from this Panzergruppe on January 30, 1942, and was also known as the "deutsch-italienische Panzerarmee". One year later, on February 23, the use of this title was discontinued in favor of the newly adopted title of "1. italienische Armee".

GRUPPE/ARMEE COMMANDERS

August 15, 1941 - March 9, 1942	General der Panzertruppe Erwin Rommel (sick leave)(1)
March 9, 1942 - March 19, 1942	Generalleutnant Ludwig Crüwell (acting CO)
March 19, 1942 - September 22, 1942	Generaloberst Erwin Rommel (sick leave)
September 22, 1942 - October 24, 1942[2]	General der Kavallerie Georg Stumme (acting CO)
October 24, 1942 - October 25, 1942[3]	Generalleutnant Wilhelm Ritter von Thoma
October 25, 1942 - February 23, 1943	Generalfeldmarschall Erwin Rommel (transfer)(4)
February 23, 1943 - May 13, 1943	Generale di Armata Messe (surrendered)(5)

[1]Rommel was promoted to Generaloberst on February 1, 1942.

[2]It is presumed that General d. Kav. Stumme suffered a heart attack and fell dead from his moving vehicle.

[3]Generalleutnant von Thoma was acting as CO while General d. Kav. Stumme was still missing and Rommel was returning from Europe.

GENERAL DER KAVALLERIE STUMME **GENERALE DI ARMATA MESSE**

GRUPPE/ARMEE STAFF

Stabschef: Generalmajor Alfred Gause
        Oberst i.G. Fritz Bayerlein
        Oberst i.G. Siegfried Westphal
        Oberst i.G. Fritz Bayerlein(6)

Ia: Oberstleutnant i.G. Siegfried Westphal
    Major i.G. F.W. von Mellenthin
    Major i.G. Richard Feige

OQu: Major i.G. Otto
     Major i.G. Schleusener

> **NOTE:** The Ib (chief supply officer) at Armee level was titled Oberquartiermeister, abbreviated "OQu".

Ic: Major i.G. F.W. von Mellenthin
    Major i.G. Josef Zolling
    Major Liebl

IIa: Major Schräpler+

IVb(Arzt): Oberstabsarzt/Gen. Arzt Dr. Asal

Verbindungsoffizier zum Reichspresschef: Leutnant der Reserve Alfred I. Berndt

Heeres-Nachrichtenoffizier: Oberst Büchting
                              Leutnant Heinze

Pionieroffizier: Oberst Hecker
               Oberst Bülowius

---

[4] Rommel was promoted to Generalfeldmarschall on June 22, 1942.

[5] Generale di Armata Messe took command and for the first time during the war, German divisions came under Italian field command. Maresciallo d' Italia Messe was promoted to Field Marshal on May 13, 1943, the last day of the campaign in Africa.

[6] One of Rommel's last official acts was to transfer Oberst Bayerlein to the 1. italienische Armee as Stabschef.

ORDER-OF-BATTLE (AUGUST 15, 1942)

Stab der Armee (Armeeoberkommando)

Deutsches Afrikakorps
   15. Panzer-Division
   21. Panzer-Division

90. leichte Division

164. Infanterie-Division

Fallschirmjäger-Brigade Ramcke

X. Korps
   Infanterie-Division "Brescia"
   Infanterie-Division "Pavia"

XX. Korps (mot)
   Panzer-Division "Ariete"
   Panzer-Division "Littorio"
   motorisierte Division "Trieste"
   Fallschirmjäger-Division "Folgore"

XXI. Korps
   Infanterie-Division "Trento"
   Infanterie-Division "Bologna"

} Italian

Individual Units:

Brigade Stab z.b.V. (mot) 15

Kampfstaffel (mot)

Armee-Kartenstelle (mot) 575

Stab Koluft Libyen (Koluft = Kommandeur der Luftwaffe)

Sonderverband (mot) 288

Aufkl. Staffel 2 (Heer)/14. Pz. Div.

Panzerjäger-Abteilung (mot) 605

Artilleriekommando 104 (Arko 104)
   Stab Artillerie-Regiment 221
   Stab schwerste Artillerie-Abteilung 408
      2. u. 3. Batterie/408
      5./Artillerie-Regiment 115
      Artillerie-Abteilung 364
   Stab schwerste Artillerie-Abteilung 528
      2. u. 3. Batterie/528
   Artillerie-Batterie 362
   Artillerie-Batterie 533
   Artillerie-Batterie 902
   Stab I./Artillerie-Regiment 115
      4./Artillerie-Regiment 115
      6./Artillerie-Regiment 115
      4./Armee-Küstenartillerie-Batterie 149

Artillerie-Vermessungs-Trupp (mot) 721 - 730

Beobachtungs-Abteilung (mot) 11
   Stabs-Batterie
   Schallmess-Batterie
   Lichtmess-Batterie

Flak-Abteilung (mot) 606

Flak-Abteilung (mot) 612

Flak-Abteilung (mot) 617

Flak-Regiment (mot) 135 (Luftwaffe)

Heeres-Bau-Dienst-Stelle (mot) 73
Bau-Bataillon 85
1./Landesschützen-Bataillon 278
Nachrichten-Regiment (mot) 10
Kurierstaffel (Luftwaffe)
V. Heeres-Funkstelle
VI. Heeres-Funkstelle
XIII. Heeres-Funkstelle
"Tripolis" Heeres-Funkstelle
Funk-Trupp z.b.V. "Afrika"
Nachrichten-Zug 937
Nachschub-Regiment 585
Stab Nachschub-Bataillon (mot) 619
Entlade-Stab z.b.V. (mot) 681
Stab Nachschub-Bataillon z.b.V. (mot) 792
Stab Nachschub-Bataillon z.b.V. (mot) 798
Nachschub-Bataillon (mot) 148[7]
Nachschub-Bataillon (mot) 149[8]
Nachschub-Bataillon (mot) 529
Nachschub-Bataillon (mot) 532
Nachschub-Bataillon (mot) 533
Nachschub-Bataillon (mot) 902
Nachschub-Bataillon (mot) 909
Kraftfahrzeuginstandsetzungs-Abteilung (mot) 548
    Panzer-Berge-Zug (mot)
    Reifenstaffel (mot) 13
    Reifen- und Ersatzteillager (mot) 548
    Reifeninstandsetzungsstaffel (mot) 573
    Kraftwagenwerkstatt-Zug (mot) 434
    "Volkswagen"-Kraftwagenwerkstatt-Zug (mot)
    "Bosch"-Kraftwagenwerkstatt-Zug (mot)
Munitionsverwaltungs-Zug (mot) 542 - 547
Betriebsstoffuntersuchungs-Trupp (mot) 12
Heeres-Betriebsstoffverwaltungs-Zug (mot) 5
Betriebsstoffverwaltungs-Zug (mot) 979 - 981
Geräte-Verwaltungsdienste (mot)
Heeres-Kraftfahr-Park (mot) 560
Heeres-Kraftfahr-Park (mot) 566
Feldzeugdienst-Zug (mot) 1 - 3

OBERST BAYERLEIN AND OBERST VON MELLENTHIN, THE ARMY Ia

---

[7] This was an Italian unit.

[8] This was an Italian unit.

1./Bäckerei-Kompanie (mot) 554
Schlächterei-Kompanie (mot) 445
Verpflegungsamt (mot) 317
Verpflegungsamt (mot) 445
Verpflegungsamt "Afrika" (mot)
Stab Kdt. V. A. 556
2./Sanitäts-Kompanie (mot) 592
1./Krankentransport-Kompanie (mot) 705
"Tripolis"-Kriegslazarett (mot)
5./Kriegslazarett (mot) 542
Kriegslazarett (mot) 667
Leichtkrankenkriegslazarett (mot)
Sanitätspark (mot) 531
Geheime Feldpolizei (mot)
Haupt-Streifendienst (mot)
Feldgendarmerie-Trupp (mot)
Wach-Bataillon "Afrika"
Ortskommandant "Misurata" 615
Ortskommandant "Barce" 619
Ortskommandant "Tripolis" 958
Ortskommandant "Benghazi" 959
Ortskommandant "Derna"
Tripolis-Lager Kdr. (km 5)
Kriegsgefangenen-Durchgangslager 782
13./Lehr-Regiment "Brandenburg" 800
Feldpostamt z. b. V. (mot) 659
Feldpostamt z. b. V. (mot) 762
Feldpostamt z. b. V. (für die Luftwaffe) (mot)
Feldpostamt z. b. V. anstelle Armee-Briefstelle (mot)

NOTE OF INTEREST:
KTB Panzerarmee Afrika, dated September 17, 1942, contained the following order: O. K. H. ordered that the method of constructing "mineboxes", which were employed in the Alamein positions, were to be used in the Russian theater of operations (O. K. H. Operation Section Order, General of Engineers and Fortification Troops, #987/42 (Secret) of September 9, 1942).

Stab Nehring/XC. Korps

General der Panzertruppe Walther Nehring, previously commander of the "Afrikakorps" until being wounded in the arm on August 31, 1942, was ordered back to Africa in November 1942. There, he assumed command of the German forces in Tunisia. "Stab Nehring"[1] was provisionally formed on November 14, for the purpose of planning the "establishment of a bridgehead extending to the west at least as far as necessary for freedom of maneuver, and if possible as far as the Tunisian-Algerian border.[2] General Nehring situated his HQ in Tunis and formed two "bridgeheads": the first at Tunis under Oberst Harlinghausen and the second at Bizerte under Oberst Lederer.

One day later, on November 15, OKH ordered that a combined command be formed in Tunisia. This order was transmitted to "Stab Nehring" by OB Süd on November 19, at which time the command's title was changed to XC. Korps.

On December 9, 1942, Hitler announced that Panzer-Armeeoberkommando 5 (Pz. A. O. K. 5) was being formed in order to strengthen the command structure in Tunisia, thus absorbing the short-lived XC. Korps. On the evening of December 8, Generaloberst von Arnim and Generalleutnant Ziegler arrived in Tunis to assume their new command.

KORPS COMMANDER

November 14, 1942 - December 9, 1942 ＿ General der Panzertruppe Walther Nehring

---

[1] This Staff included General der Panzertruppe Nehring and one staff officer, Major Moll (see The Mediterranean and Middle East, Volume IV, p. 72). It is doubtful that a complete staff was ever formed for XC. Korps due to the short duration of its existence. "The equipment of the Korps headquarters with motor vehicles was at first zero. By and by, cars were hired. The commanding general, for instance, was driving around, up to his departure on December 9, 1942, in a rented limousine with one driver, who was a French Captain in reserve, but of Italian extraction."(MS D-147. The 1st Phase of the Battle in Tunisia).

[2] George F. Howe, Northwest Africa: Seizing the Initiative in the West, (Washington: U.S. Government Printing Office, 1957), p. 261.

KORPS STAFF

Stabschef: Oberst Pomtow[3]
Ia: Major Moll
  Leutnant Junker
Ib: Hauptmann Kirsten
IIa: Major von Seubert
Korpsarzt: Stabsarzt Dr. Herzberger

OBERST i. G. POMTOW

Tunis Bridgehead:[4]
  November 11, 1942 - November 18, 1942 — Oberst Harlinghausen
  November 18, 1942 - December 8, 1942 — Oberstleutnant Koch

Bizerte Bridgehead:[5]
  November 12, 1942 - November 16, 1942 — Oberst Lederer
  November 16, 1942 - November 18, 1942 — Oberstleutnant Stolz
  November 18, 1942 - December 8, 1942 — Oberst Freiherr von Broich

South Sector:
  late November - December 8, 1942 ———— General Imperiali

ORDER-OF-BATTLE

Stab XC. Korps

Tunis Bridgehead:
  3./Tunis Feld-Bataillon 1
  Fallschirmjäger-Regiment 5 (advance detatchment)
  one Fallschirmjägerkompanie
  14./Panzergrenadier-Regiment 104
  one Flakbatterie

Bizerte Bridgehead:
  1./Tunis Feld-Bataillon 1
  4./Panzer-Abteilung 190
  4./Artillerie-Regiment 2
  5./Artillerie-Regiment 190
  Sturmgeschütz-Abteilung 557 (6)
  Panzerjäger-Abteilung 136 (7)

South Sector:
  several Italian Divisions (Superga, Imperiali)

---

[3] Oberst Pomtow, who had been appointed to this post, still performed as Ia of his former Panzer Division in the Caucasus Mountains, where snow made it impossible for him to leave by any means of transportation. Therefore, he arrived in Tunis in late November.

[4] This was one of the major elements of XC. Korps.

[5] This was one of the major elements of XC. Korps.

[6] This was an Italian unit.

[7] This was an Italian unit.

Panzer-Armeeoberkommando 5 (Pz.-A.O.K. 5)

The creation of Pz.-A.O.K. 5 was ordered on December 8, 1942, through the extension of XC. Korps, in order to strengthen the command structure in Tunisia. The XC. Korps commander, General der Panzertruppe Nehring, was carried on the Pz.-A.O.K. 5 "Kriegsrangliste" as commanding general from December 8 to 9, 1942, at which time Generaloberst von Arnim assumed command.

A.O.K. COMMANDERS

December 8, 1942 - December 9, 1942 — General der Panzertruppe Walther Nehring

December 9, 1942 - March 9, 1943 — Generaloberst Jürgen von Arnim

March 9, 1943 - May 9, 1943 — General der Panzertruppe Gustav von Vaerst

A.O.K. STAFF

Stabschef: Generalleutnant Ziegler (also deputy to the Army commander)
   Generalmajor von Quast

Ia: Oberst i.G. Pomtow
   Oberst i.G. Markert

Ib: Major i.G. Josef Moll

Ic:[1] Hauptmann Kirsten

---

[1] The Pz.-A.O.K. 5 "Gliederung der Abt. Ic" of February 19, 1943, listed the following individuals and offices:

   Fliegerverbindungsoffizier (Flivo)
   Geschäftszimmer
   Zeichner
   Melder
   Ital. Dolmetscher
   Engl. Dolmetscher
   Schreiber
   Franz. Dolmetscher
   Schreiber
   Wehrbetreuung

GENERALOBERST VON ARNIM

IIa: Major Max-Heinrich von Seubert
IIb: Major Halser
IVb (Korpsarzt): Oberstarzt Dr. Wilhelm Schulz
Abwehroffizier:[3] Oberleutnant Fiedler
Propagandaoffizier:[4] Oberleutnant Haupt

ORDER-OF-BATTLE (DECEMBER 17, 1942)

Stab der Panzerarmee (A.O.K.)
10. Panzer-Division
Division von Broich
20. Flak-Division ⎫
I./Flak-Regiment 54 ⎬ Luftwaffe
II./Flak-Regiment 54 ⎭

---

[3] Pz.-A.O.K. 5 "Abwehrgruppe" contained the following sections as of February 19, 1943:

    Abwehr I
    Abwehr II
       Abw.-Tr. 250
       Abw.-Tr. 251
       Abw.-Tr. 252
    Abwehr III
       Abw.-Tr. 350
    Dienststelle Wido

[4] Pz.-A.O.K. 5 "Propaganda-Zug Tunis" contained the following sections as of February 19, 1943:

    Dienststelle (95 Rue Courbet, Tel: 80 189)
    Geschäftszimmer
       Rechnungsführer
    Aktivpropaganda
       Amerika
       Frankreich
       Arabien
       Franz. Presse u. Rundfunk
       Arab. Presse u. Rundfunk
       Lautsprecherwagen
       Prop. Granat-Werfertrupp
       Kriegsberichter
          Wortberichter
          Bildberichter (f. Illustrierte)
          Filmberichter
          Rundfunkberichter
             deutsch
             englisch
             spanisch
             irisch
             afrikans
       Techniker
    Frontzeitung
    Truppenbetreuung
    Propaganda-Verbindungs-Kp.-Prop. Meldekopf Tunis
    Militarisches Personal
    Zivilfahrer

Abwehrgruppe 210

Propaganda-Zug Tunis

Armee Reserve
    Panzer-Abteilung 190
    schwere Panzer-Abteilung 501 (Tiger)
    Panzer-Aufklärungs-Abteilung 190

Division Imperiali (Italian)

ORDER-OF-BATTLE (MARCH 1, 1943)

Stab der 5. Panzerarmee

10. Panzer-Division
    Pz.-Gren.-Rgt. 69 mit 1 Bataillon
    Pz.-Gren.-Rgt. 86 mit 1 Bataillon
    Kradschützen-Btl. 10
    Pz.-Rgt. 7 mit 1 Abt.
    Pz.-Jg.-Abt. 90
    Teil Artl.-Rgt. 90
    Pi.-Btl. 49

21. Panzer-Division
    Pz.-Gren.-Rgt. 104
    Pz.-Rgt. 5
    Artl.-Rgt. 155
    2./Flak-Abt. 25 (Luftwaffe)
    Nachr.-Abt. 200
    Aufkl.-Abt. 580
    Pi.-Btl. 220

334. Infanterie-Division
    Gren.-Rgt. 754
    Gren.-Rgt. 755
    Geb.Jäg.-Rgt. 756
    Artl.-Rgt. 334
    schnelle Abt. 334

Division von Manteuffel
    Rgt. Barenthin
    Feldabt. T3
    Marschbtl. A30
    IV/Artl.Rgt. 2
    Fallsch.-Pi.-Btl. 11
    Rgt. 10/Bersaglieri (Italian)

19. u. 20. Flak-Division
    3 Flak-Rgter
    3 Flak-Gruppen

Armee direkt unterstellt
    schwere Pz.-Abt. 501 (Tiger)
    Nachr.-Abt. 190
    Aufkl.-Abt. 190
    le. Vermessungs- und Kartenabt.

Kampfgruppe Buhse
    Gren.-Rgt. 47
    I/Artl.-Rgt. 22

Kampfgruppe Schmid
    Fallschirm-Rgt. 5 (Koch)
    je 1 Btl. Rgt. 69 u. 86
    Teil Artl.-Rgt. 90

II./Artil. Rgt. 190
Marsch-Btl. A24 u. A33

Abschnitt Benigni
  Inf.-Rgt. 91
  Marsch-Btl. A28 } Italian
  Artl.-Abt. 57 u. 65

Abschnitt Brandenburg

Abschnitt deutsch-arab. Truppen
  5 Btle.

Abschnitt Fullriede
  Gren.-Rgt. 165

Abschnitt Nord
  Rgt. Ballerstedt
  Rgt. San Marco (Italian Marines)

Abschnitt Tunis
  Gren.-Rgt. 160

Division Superga (Italian)
  Inf.-Rgt. 92
  Feld- u. Marsch-Btl. T5, A22, A25, A26
  Pz.-Jg.-Abt. 1, 101, 136
  Artl.-Rgt. 5

Brigade Imperiali (Italian)
  6 Btl. (II/Lodi, II/92, 10. Bers., 5/CCNN, 22/5 Bers., C.p.d.f.)
  Pz.-Abt. 15/M41
  Pz.-Jg.-Abt. 557
  Artl.-Abt. 35, 58, 77

Heeresgruppe Afrika

"After the deutsch-italienische Panzerarmee had arrived in Tunisia, the forces involved were too strong for one Army headquarters to control them in their varied tasks. The fact alone, that this theater was detached and involved working with the Italian units, demanded a major German headquarters....a Heeresgruppe".[1] On February 23, 1943, an order was received from Commando Supremo which stated that due to the urgent need for a unified command in North Africa, "Heeresgruppe Afrika" was to be formed under the command of Generalfeldmarschall Rommel. The Heeresgruppe consisted of the deutsch-italienische Panzerarmee (1. italienische Armee) under Generale di Armata Messe and the Pz.A.O.K. 5 under Generaloberst von Arnim.

At noon on May 12, 1943, Generaloberst von Arnim, then commander of the Heeresgruppe, capitulated on behalf of the two staffs of "Heeresgruppe Afrika" and the "Afrikakorps".

HEERESGRUPPE COMMANDERS

February 23, 1943 - March 9, 1943 ____ Generalfeldmarschall Erwin Rommel (sick leave)(2)

March 9, 1943 - May 13, 1943 _____ Generaloberst Jürgen von Arnim (surrendered)

HEERESGRUPPE STAFF

Stabschef: Oberst Bayerlein[3]
        Generalleutnant Heinz Ziegler (also permanent deputy to the Heeresgruppe commander)

---

[1] Air Historical Branch Translation No. VII/106 - <u>The War in the Mediterranean (Part II)</u> by Generalfeldmarschall Kesselring, p. 15.

[2] Rommel's sick leave at Wiener-Neustadt, Austria, which had been interrupted by the British offensive at El'Alamein, was now long overdue. The recurrence of ailments forced him to leave Tunisia on March 9, 1943, never to return. He was succeeded by Generaloberst von Arnim, who in turn, yielded his command of Pz.-A.O.K. 5 to General der Panzertruppe Gustav von Vaerst.

[3] Oberst Bayerlein was transferred to 1. italienische Armee as the deutscher Stabschef.

Ia: Oberst i. G. Pomtow
　　Oberst i. G. Markert
Ib:
Ic: Major i. G. Josef Moll

GENERALFELDMARSCHALL ROMMEL

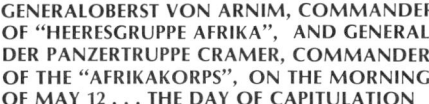

GENERALOBERST VON ARNIM, COMMANDER OF "HEERESGRUPPE AFRIKA", AND GENERAL DER PANZERTRUPPE CRAMER, COMMANDER OF THE "AFRIKAKORPS", ON THE MORNING OF MAY 12 . . . THE DAY OF CAPITULATION

THE FIRST GERMAN TROOPS AND EQUIPMENT BEING UNLOADED IN TRIPOLI ON FEBRUARY 14, 1941.

German Divisions in North Afrika

5. leichte Division

When it was decided to send a "blocking force" to North Africa to contain the drive of the British Western Desert Forces, the 3. Panzer-Division was chosen to supply both troops and equipment. The 5. leichte Division (5th Light Division), which the "blocking force" was entitled, consisted primarily of cadres from the 3. Panzer-Division plus its Panzer-Regiment 5. The first contingents of the 5. leichte Division arrived in Tripoli on February 14, with its armor arriving by February 20.[1] The following six months saw this Division engaged in the major battles against British armored and mechanized units. The 5. leichte Division was reorganized, strengthened and retitled 21. Panzer-Division on October 1, 1941.

PzKw I's BEING UNLOADED IN TRIPOLI (NOTE THE BEFEHLS-PANZER).

*leichte Division symbol

---

[1] Panzer-Regiment 5 had 120 tanks, 60 of which were Pzkw. III and IVs.

PzKw II's

PzKw I's, II's and IV's

ARMORED MARCH-PAST IN DOWNTOWN TRIPOLI.

DIVISIONAL COMMANDERS

February 20, 1941 - July 22, 1941 _____ Generalmajor Johannes Streich (relieved)(2)

July 23, 1941 - October 1, 1941 _____ Generalmajor Johann von Ravenstein

DIVISIONAL STAFF

Ia: Major i.G. Hauser
Ib:
Ic: Hauptmann von Kluge
IIa:
Arzt:

**GENERALLEUTNANT STREICH
(HERE A GENERALMAJOR)**

GENERALMAJOR VON RAVENSTEIN

---

[2]Generalleutnant Streich had been promoted on February 13 and appointed to command the 5. leichte Division by Halder.

ORDER-OF-BATTLE (FEBRUARY 1941)[3]

Stab der Division

Stab z.b.V. 200

Panzer-Regiment 5
  (reassigned to 21. Panzer-Division)

1./Panzerjäger-Abteilung (mot) 33
  (reassigned to 15. Panzer-Division)

Panzerjäger-Abteilung (mot) 39
  (reassigned to 21. Panzer-Division)

Machinengewehr-Bataillon (mot) 2
  (reassigned to 15. Panzer-Division)

Machinengewehr-Bataillon (mot) 8
  (reassigned to 21. Panzer-Division)

I./Artillerie-Regiment (mot) 75

Flak-Abteilung (mot) 605
  (reassigned to Panzerarmee Afrika)

Flak-Abteilung (mot) 606
  (reassigned to Deutsches Afrikakorps)

Aufklärungsstab 2 (Heer)/14. Panzer
  (reassigned to Panzerarmee Afrika)

Aufklärungs-Abteilung (mot) 3
  (reassigned to 21. Panzer-Division)

Fernsprech-Kompanie/Nachrichten-Abteilung "Libyen"

one Kompanie/Pionier-Bataillon (mot) 39
  (reassigned to 15. Panzer-Division)

Nachschubstab z.b.V. (mot) 668
  (retitled/reassigned to 21. Panzer-Division as Nachschubstab z.b.V. (mot) 200 (4))

Nachschub-Bataillon (mot) 532
  (retitled/reassigned to 21. Panzer-Division as Nachschub-Kompanie (mot) 200 (4))

Nachschub-Bataillon (mot) 533
  (reassigned to Panzerarmee Afrika)

3./Nachschub-Bataillon (mot) 39

Nachschub-Bataillon (mot) (ohne Nr.)

Wasserkolonne (mot) 797
  (retitled/reassigned to 21. Panzer-Division as 3./Wasserkolonne (mot) 200 (4))

Wasserkolonne (mot) 801
  (retitled/reassigned to 21. Panzer-Division as 5./Wasserkolonne (mot) 200 (4))

Wasserkolonne (mot) 803
  (retitled/reassigned to 21. Panzer-Division as 6./Wasserkolonne (mot) 200 (4))

---

[3]M.W. Stark, "The Creation of the German Africa Corps", p. 194-195.

[4]Microfilm Publication T313, roll 437, frame 8730219, (Umbenennung von Versorgungstruppen der 21. Pz.-Div. - Nr. 3761/41 geh., 28.9.41). The date of reorganization was October 1, 1941.

WATER SUPPLY UNITS IN FEBRUARY 1941.

Wasserkolonne (mot) 822
 (retitled/reassigned to 21. Panzer-Division as 8./Wasserkolonne (mot) 200 (2))

Wasserkolonne (mot) (ohne Nr.)

Filterkolonne (mot) 800
 (retitled/reassigned to 21. Panzer-Division as 4./Filterkolonne (mot) 200 (2))

Filterkolonne (mot) 804
 (retitled/reassigned to 21. Panzer-Division as 7./Filterkolonne (mot) 200 (4))

grosse Wasserkolonne (mot) 641
 (reassigned to Panzerarmee Afrika)

grosse Wasserkolonne (mot) 645
 (reassigned to Panzerarmee Afrika)

Reifenstaffel (mot) 13
 (reassigned to Deutsches Afrikakorps)

Reifenstaffel (mot) 210
 (reassigned to Deutsches Afrikakorps)

Kraftwagenwerkstatt-Kompanie (mot) 122
 (retitled/reassigned to 21. Panzer-Division as 2./Kraftwagenwerkstatt-Kompanie (mot) 200 (4))

Kraftwagenwerkstatt-Kompanie (mot) 129
 (retitled/reassigned to 21. Panzer-Division as 3./Kraftwagenwerkstatt-Kompanie (mot) 200 (4))

1./Sanitäts-Kompanie (mot) 83
 (retitled/reassigned to 21. Panzer-Division as Sanitäts-Kompanie (mot) 200 (4))

4./Kriegslazarett (mot) 572
 (retitled/reassigned to 21. Panzer-Division as Feldlazarett (mot) 200 (4))

Krankenkraftwagen-Zug (mot) 631
 (retitled/reassigned to 21. Panzer-Division as 1./Krankenkraftwagen-Zug (mot) 200 (4))

Krankenkraftwagen-Zug (mot) 633
 (retitled/reassigned to 21. Panzer-Division as 2./Krankenkraft-
 wagen-Zug (mot) 200 (4))

Bäckerei-Kompanie (mot) 531
 (retitled/reassigned to 21. Panzer-Division as Bäckerei-Kompanie
 (mot) 200 (4))

Feldgendarmerie-Trupp (mot) 309
 (retitled/reassigned to 21. Panzer-Division as Feldgendarmerie-
 Trupp (mot) 200 (4))

Feldpostamt z.b.V. (mot) 735
 (retitled/reassigned to 21. Panzer-Division as Feldpostamt (mot)
 200 (4))

DIVISIONAL SYMBOL

The vehicles and armor of the short-lived 5. leichte Division did not carry a specific divisional symbol. The exception to this was the symbol of the 3. Panzer-Division which was carried on vehicles and armor originating from that Division. This symbol was utilized in the early desert battles of 1941.

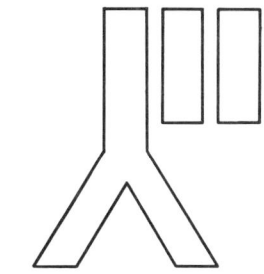

3. PANZER-DIVISION SYMBOL (YELLOW)

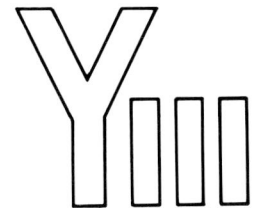

10. Panzer-Division

Before being committed to the North African campaign, the 10. Panzer-Division had already proven itself in the Polish, French and Russian campaigns. In May 1942, it was transferred to France, Amiens area, for rest and refitting. Three months later, the Division served as a reserve force for countering the Allied landing at Dieppe and in November, participated in the occupation of Southern France. In late November of 1942, the Division was transferred to Tunisia where it was assigned to XC. Korps, under General der Panzertruppe Nehring.

The Division was immediately committed to battle during XC. Korps attempt to widen the Tunis Bridgehead, and although it had initial success, the attack was slowed and finally halted on December 10. In late December, the Division held a defensive sector of the line between Division von Broich and Division Superga.

The 10. Panzer-Division, along with Fallschirmjäger-Regiment 5 and Kampfgruppe Burk, executed a secondary drive in the direction of Bou Arada in mid-January 1943, in support of von Arnim's attempt to drive the French forces from the Eastern Dorsal (10. Pz.-Div. was put under von Arnim's Pz.A.O.K.5 when it was formed in December 1942). Although losses were considerable, Pz.A.O.K.5 gained control of the vital passes by late January.

During "Unternehmen Frühlingswind" (battles of Sidi Bou Zid, Feb. 14-15, 1943), 10. Panzer-Division was organized into Gruppe Gerhardt, Gruppe Reimann and a reserve Gruppe and was ordered to attack along the Faid-Sbeitla road. At Sbeitla, Gruppe Gerhardt assisted in forcing the Allies to retreat, abandoning key positions. During the ensuing weeks, 10. Panzer-Division was either on the defensive or held in reserve. On March 21, it was released from its reserve roll and put under control of Cramer's D.A.K. for a counterattack toward Yafsa. It pushed northwards against the Allied southern flank until stopped by American artillery and tank destroyers. This, plus a second attack, took a heavy toll of the Division's armor.

By April 8, the Division had joined the general Axis withdrawal from the hills east of Maknassy. It was initially positioned west of Tunis to serve as mobile Pz.A.O.K.5 reserve against the expected Allied thrust against Tunis. By April 21, after fierce fighting, the Division was reduced in strength to 25 operational tanks. The mauled Division continued its defensive actions until it was finally pushed into the hills north of Bizerte. At 1250 hours on May 9, 1943, the battered remnants of the Division surrendered.

DIVISIONAL COMMANDERS

August 2, 1941 - February 1, 1943 _____ Generalleutnant Wolfgang Fischer (killed)[1]

February 1, 1943 - May 12, 1943 _____ Generalmajor Fritz Freiherr von Broich (captured)

DIVISIONAL STAFF

Ia: Oberstleutnant i.G. Bürker (wounded)
Oberstleutnant i.G. Graf Stauffenberg (wounded)[2]

Ib: Oberleutnant von Hagen
Hauptmann Sinkel

Ic: Hauptmann Buchstein
Hauptmann Dr. Menges

IIa: Hauptmann Mengels

Arzt:

ORDER-OF-BATTLE (JANUARY 1, 1943)

Stab der Division

Divisions-Kartenstelle (mot)

Panzer-Regiment 7

Panzerjäger-Abteilung (mot) 90

Infanterie-Regiment (mot) 69

Infanterie-Regiment (mot) 86

Sturmregiment "Hermann Göring" (mot)(Luftwaffe)

Infanterie-Bataillon (mot) A4

Artillerie-Regiment (mot) 90

---

[1] Generalleutnant Fischer was killed, and his Ia, Oberstleutnant Bürker seriously wounded, when their staff car drove into a minefield which had been installed by the Italians but not adequately marked by them.

[2] Oberstleutnant Graf Stauffenberg was badly wounded when his armored truck was strafed by a British fighter-bomber. Ironically, this incident was to allow him the chance to play a further role in Germany's war-time history (July 20, 1944), for he was quickly evacuated, thus escaping capture.

Flak-Gruppe Böhmer (Luftwaffe)
Kradschützen-Bataillon (mot) 10
Panzer-Nachrichtten-Abteilung (mot) 90
Pionier-Bataillon (mot) 49
Divisions-Nachschub-Bataillon (mot)
Divisions-Verpflegungsamt (mot)
Bäckerei-Kompanie (mot)
Sanitäts-Kompanie (mot)
Krankenkraftwagen-Zug (mot)
Kraftwagenwerkstatt-Zug (mot)
Feldgendarmerie-Trupp (mot)
Feldpostamt (mot)

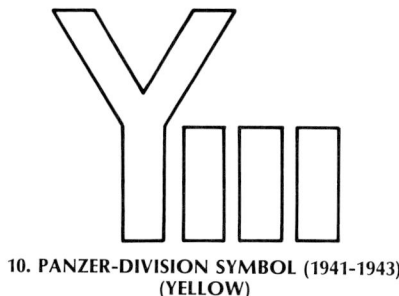

**10. PANZER-DIVISION SYMBOL (1941-1943)
(YELLOW)**

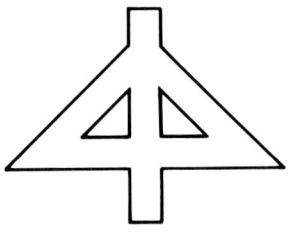

15. Panzer-Division

This Division was originally formed as the 33. Infanterie-Division on April 1, 1936, and participated in the French campaign under the command of Generalleutnant Hermann Ritter von Speck. On November 1, 1940, it was reorganized as a Panzer division, designated 15. Panzer-Division and stationed in Germany until early 1941.

Portions of the Division arrived in Africa in late April 1941, with some of the units participating in the April 30th attack against the Tobruk fortress. By mid-June, the Division's transfer to Africa had been completed. Within two weeks, it was heavily engaged against strong British armored units during the British offensive "Battleaxe". Operating alongside the 5. leichte Division, the 15. Panzer-Division was able to push through the British forces, but was unable to halt the escape of most of the British remnants.

The Division saw considerable action once again during the British offensive "Crusader", which began on November 18, 1941. By December 26, Rommel had decided to disengage due to the enemy's increasing strength and retreated to the Gazala positions and then back to El Agheila. After his divisions were sufficiently refitted, Rommel again took to the offensive on January 21. The 15. Panzer-Division, attached to the DAK, served as the striking force during the battles at Gazala, which began on May 26 ("Unternehmen Venezia"). After the successful battles for Got el Ualeb and Bir Hacheim, the German forces once more stood before Tobruk on June 16, 1942. By June 21, Tobruk had fallen. The next day, Rommel was informed by wireless from the Führerhauptquartier that he had been made a Generalfeldmarschall as reward for this significant victory. The 15. Panzer-Division was not to rest after this victory, for shortly thereafter, all of the German and Italian forces joined "the pursuit into Egypt". By June 30, advance elements of the Division had reached a point beyond El Daba. The DAK mounted its first major attack against the El Alamein line on July 1, but with little success. The next serious assault against the British positions was on August 30, and again on September 1. Rommel now realized the in-depth strength of the British and therefore called off the attack on September 2. His divisions then went on the defensive.

The 15. Panzer-Division saw daily combat, with the unleashing of the massive British offensive on October 23, 1942, until November 3, when the Division was ordered to withdraw to the west. From November 8 to November 25, all of Rommel's forces were in full retreat. By fighting numerous flank and rearguard actions, however, much of his Panzerarmee escaped the pursuing British. On February 13, 1943, the last units of the Panzerarmee entered Tunisia...the Libyan campaign had come to an end.

The Division was placed under the command of the I. italienische Armee when it was formed in February 1943, and served as Armee reserve in the Mareth Line, with an armored strength of 50 tanks. It, plus the 21. Panzer-Division, was later put into the Heeresgruppe Afrika reserve.

When the Germans went on the offensive at Medenine on March 6, 1943, the 15. Panzer-Division had an armored strength of 62 tanks. The initial gains made by the Division in this sector were eliminated, however, by a British counterattack which cost the Division 24 irreplaceable tanks.

On March 22, the 15. Panzer-Division was pulled out of reserve again in order to thwart the main British attach at Wadi Zigaou. After destroying two-thirds of the heavily outgunned British Valentine tanks and pushing the exhausted British infantry back across the Wadi, the Division once again went into reserve.

It was the Division's mission to hold up the full exploitation of the massive Allied breakthrough on March 27, near El Hamma, but was only able to muster 10 tanks against the advancing New Zealanders. Throughout the remainder of March and all of April, the Axis forces were slowly forced into withdrawal after withdrawal. By May 8, 1943, the remaining forces of Pz. A. O. K. 5 were isolated in two major pockets: the 15. Panzer-Division was in the northernmost one, along with the remnants of Division von Manteuffel and elements of the 10. Panzer-Division. At 1250 hours, on May 9, the 15. Panzer-Division surrendered to British forces.

DIVISIONAL COMMANDERS

March 22, 1941 - April 10, 1941 _____Generalmajor Heinrich von Prittwitz und Gaffron (killed)(1)

April 15, 1941 - July 25, 1941 _____Oberst Hans-Karl Freiherr von Esebeck (promoted to Generalmajor on April 15, 1941) (wounded in front of Tobruk)

July 25, 1941 - December 6, 1941 ____ Generalmajor Neumann-Silkow (wounded)(2)

December 6, 1941 - December 8, 1941 _ Oberst Erwin Menny (temporary)

December 9, 1941 - May 26, 1942 ____ Generalleutnant Gustav von Vaerst (wounded)

May 26, 1942 - July 8, 1942 _____ Oberst Eduard Crasemann (temporary)

July 8, 1942 - August 31, 1942 _____ Generalleutnant Gustav von Vaerst (transferred)(3)

September 1, 1942 - September 17, 1942 _ Generalmajor Heinz von Randow (transferred)

September 17, 1942 - November 11, 1942 _ Generalleutnant Gustav von Vaerst (sick leave)

November 11, 1942 -   ____ Oberst Eduard Crasemann (temporary)

                - December 12, 1942 _ Generalleutnant Gustav von Vaerst

December 12, 1942 - May 13, 1942 ____ Oberst Willibald Borowietz (captured)(4)

GENERALMAJOR FRHR. VON ESEBECK

OBERST MENNY

GENERALMAJOR NEUMANN-SILKOW

---

[1] "At about midday, Count Schwerin reported to me (Rommel) at a point some 25 miles west of Tobruk that General von Prittwitz had been killed a few hours earlier by a direct hit from an anti-tank gun." The Rommel Papers, p. 122. Generalmajor von Prittwitz was the first German General killed in the African campaign.

[2] Generalmajor Neumann-Silkow was seriously wounded on December 6, 1941, by a shell which burst beside his command vehicle, KTB Deutsches Afrikakorps and KTB 15. Panzer-Division. He was evacuated to a Benghazi hospital where he died on December 8.

**GENERALLEUTNANT
VON VAERST**

**OBERST CRASEMANN
(HERE A GENERALMAJOR)**

GENERALLEUTNANT BOROWIETZ

---

[3]Generalleutnant von Vaerst took over temporary command of the Afrikakorps when General der Panzertruppe Nehring was wounded by a direct hit on his armor-plated vehicle near the front on August 31, 1942.

[4]Oberst Borowietz was promoted to Generalmajor on January 1, 1943, and to Generalleutnant on May 1, 1943. He later died in U.S. captivity.

DIVISIONAL STAFF

Ia: Oberst i.G. Rainer Kriebel
Oberst i.G. Heinrich Müller

Ib: Major Frey
Oberleutnant Dittmann

Ic: Hauptmann Gerhard Kircher

IIa: Major Riese
Major Stollbrock

Arzt: Oberfeldarzt Dr. Oskar Pelizaeus

ORDER-OF-BATTLE

Stab der Division

Divisions-Kartenstelle (mot) 33

Kradmelde-Zug

Panzer-Regiment 8

Panzerjäger-Abteilung (mot) 33

Schützen-Brigade (mot) 15 (5)
    Infanterie-Regiment (mot) 115
    Infanterie-Regiment (mot) 200 (6)
    Maschinengewehr-Bataillon (mot) 8
    Kradschützen-Bataillon (mot) 15

Artillerie-Regiment (mot) 33

Aufklärungs-Abteilung (mot) 33

Nachrichten-Abteilung (mot) 33

Pionier-Bataillon (mot) 33

Feldersatz-Bataillon 33

Nachschub-Bataillon (mot) 33
    Nachschubkolonne (1-11) 33
    Panzer-Ersatzteilkolonne (mot) 33
    Filterkolonne (mot) 581
    Kraftwagenwerkstatt-Kompanie (mot) 33
    Nachschub-Kompanie (mot) 33

Sanitäts-Kompanie (mot) 33

Feldlazarett (mot) 33

Krankenkraftwagen-Zug (mot) 33

Bäckerei-Kompanie (mot) 33

Schlächterei-Kompanie (mot) 33

Divisions-Verpflegungsamt (mot) 33

Feldgendarmerie-Trupp (mot) 33

Feldpostamt (mot) 33

---

[5] Stab Schützen-Brigade 15 was later attached to Panzerarmee Afrika. The Order-of-Battle chart for 15. Panzer-Division of April 15, 1942, listed only Infanterie-Regiment 115.

[6] This unit was later transferred to 90. leichte Afrika-Division, and only included two Infanterie-Bataillonen.

DIVISIONAL SYMBOL

The 15. Panzer-Division symbol below was carried on all divisional vehicles in either yellow or white. When the vehicle was in a tan camouflage, however, the symbol was generally in black or dark grey (see photo below of knocked out Mark IV with small divisional symbol on back of rear turret box plus a sub-unit symbol from within the Division.

U.S. ARMY PHOTOGRAPH

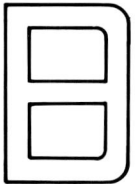

21. Panzer-Division

This Division was formed from the reorganized and strengthened 5. leichte Division on October 1, 1941, and its first major engagement was during the British "Crusader" offensive of November 18-23, 1941. During the early phases of this battle, 21. Panzer-Division faced the British 7th Armored Brigade and by November 22, had reduced the British force to ten tanks.[1] Shortly thereafter, the Division joined with "Ariete" Division, fought, and finally "routed the 5th South African Infantry and the 22nd Armored Brigade".[2] Despite these initial successes, Rommel decided to disengage as British superiority grew continuously stronger on both the ground and in the air. The German forces then withdrew to defensive positions at Gazala which they had prepared the previous May, and after further British pressure, back to El Agheila. Tobruk was thus relieved after an eight month, German siege.

In early 1942, Rommel took the offensive once again after his divisions had been sufficiently replenished. During this push from El Agheila (January 21, 1942 - February 8, 1942), the 21. Panzer-Division served as part of the DAK. Rapid advances led to the fall of Benghazi on January 29, and within a two week period, Rommel had advanced approximately 350 miles. The offensive was finally slowed, however, by stiffened British resistance as they dug in at Gazala-Bir Hacheim. The 21. Panzer-Division participated in the battle of Gazala which began on May 26, 1942. At Tobruk, the Division was situated between the 15. Panzer-Division and the 90. leichte Division, with orders to proceed to Tobruk itself when the British perimeter had been breached, which it did. After the fall of Tobruk, Rommel's forces pushed on to El Alamein where they were stopped at Alam Halfa on July 31, 1942.

The 21. Panzer-Division moved into the static El Alamain line alongside the "Ariete" Division. It was here that the 21. Panzer-Division, as well as the remainder of the Panzerarmee, suffered heavy losses during the

---

[1] D. W. Braddock, B.A., The Campaign in Egypt and Libya 1940 - 1942, (Aldershot: Gale Polden Limited, 1964), p. 58.

[2] Ibid, p. 60.

British operations "Lightfoot" (October 23, 1942) and "Supercharge" (November 1, 1942). By November 7, the retreating Division had been badly mauled by British armor in the Fuka sector, and only four of its thirty tanks, which had survived the El Alamein battle, were intact.[3] During the withdrawal towards Tunisia, the Division acted as rearguard for most of the retreating Axis forces. Upon crossing the Tunisian frontier, it was put under the command of Pz.A.O.K. 5. During the Faid-Maknassy actions (January 30, 1943 - February 3, 1943), the Division was organized into two Kampfgruppen: "Kampfgruppe Pfeiffer" and "Kampfgruppe Grün" (see details of these actions in the Kampfgruppen section). The Division had built its strength back to 91 tanks for the battle of Sidi Bou Zid (February 14-15), at which time the major units of the Division were organized into "Gruppe Stenkhoff" and "Kampfgruppe Schuette". At the battle of Sbeitla, one day later, the Division was again represented by "Kampfgruppe Pfeiffer" and "Gruppe Stenkhoff". After capturing Sbeitla on February 17, the 21. Panzer-Division was put under Rommel's command with orders to participate in his attack against Kasserine Pass. The Division's attack started north to Sbeitla on February 19, with its objective being a road junction at Ksour. The advance was halted, however, at Sbiba. The remaining weeks of defensive actions in Africa consisted of many minor actions for "Kampfgruppe Pfeiffer", which finally surrendered to the British on May 11. The remainder of the Division, which was attached to the I. italienische Armee, fought on until May 13, when it surrendered as a subunit of that Army.

DIVISIONAL COMMANDERS

October 1, 1941 - November 29, 1941	Generalmajor Johann von Ravenstein (captured)
November 29, 1941 - November 30, 1941	Oberstleutnant Gustav-Georg Knabe (temporary)
November 30, 1941 - January 30, 1942	Generalleutnant Karl Böttcher
January 30, 1942 - July 17, 1942	Generalmajor Georg von Bismarck (wounded)
July 21, 1942 -	Oberst Alfred Bruer (temporary)
- August 31, 1942	Generalmajor Georg von Bismarck (killed)(4)

---

[3] Paul Carell, The Foxes of the Desert, (New York: E. P. Dutton & Co., 1961), p. 310.

[4] KTB Deutsches Afrikakorps, August 31, 1942. 21. Panzer-Division reported that the divisional commander, Generalmajor von Bismarck, had been killed by enemy mortar fire while advancing with the foremost battalion of the Division.

August 31, 1942 - September 18, 1942 _____ Oberst Carl-Hans Lungershausen (transferred)

September 18, 1942 - December 21, 1942 _ Generalmajor Heinz v. Randow (killed near Tripoli)

January 1, 1943 - April 25, 1943 _____ Oberst Hans-Georg Hildebrandt (sick leave)

April 25, 1943 - May 13, 1943 _____ Generalmajor Heinrich-Hermann von Hülsen (surrendered)(5)

GEORGE PETERSEN COLLECTION

GENERALMAJOR VON RAVENSTEIN

OBERSTLEUTNANT KNABE

GENERALMAJOR VON BISMARCK

---

[5]Oberst von Hülsen was appointed temporary commander on April 25, 1943, while Oberst Hildebrandt was on sick leave. He was promoted to Generalmajor on May 1 and later captured by the British in Tunisia.

OBERST BRUER AND MAJOR
VON HEUDUCK, THE DIVISIONAL Ia.

GENERALMAJOR VON HÜLSEN
(HERE AN OBERST)

DIVISIONAL STAFF

Ia: Major i.G. von Heuduck
   Major i.G. Frhr. von Süsskind und Schwendi
   Oberst i.G. Stempel

Ib: Hauptmann Böhles

Ic: Oberleutnant Rickert

IIa: Hauptmann d.R. Garke

Arzt: Oberfeldarzt Dr. Franz-Josef Pott

ORDER-OF-BATTLE

Stab der Division

Divisions-Kartenstelle (mot) 200

Kradmelde-Zug

Panzer-Regiment 5

Panzerjäger-Abteilung (mot) 39

Infanterie-Regiment (mot) 104
   (III. Bataillon was Maschinengewehr-Bataillon (mot) 8)

Artillerie-Regiment (mot) 155

Aufklärungs-Abteilung (mot) 3

Nachrichten-Abteilung (mot) 200
   Panzer-Nachrichten-Kompanie

Panzer-Funk-Kompanie
leichte Nachrichten-Kolonne

Pionier-Bataillon (mot) 200

Feldersatz-Bataillon 200

Nachschub-Bataillon (mot) 200
    kleine Kraftwagenkolonne (1-11) (mot) 200
    Panzer-Ersatzteilkolonne (mot) 200
        (formerly Panzer-Ersatzteil-Staffel 1)
    Filterkolonne (mot) 200
    grosse Kraftwagenkolonne für Betriebsstoff (mot) 200
    Werkstatt-Kompanie (mot) 200
    Kraftfahrzeuginstandsetzungs-Kompanie (mot) 200
    Nachschub-Kompanie (mot) 200

Sanitäts-Kompanie (mot) 200

Feldlazarett (mot) 200

Krankenkraftwagen-Zug (mot) 200

Bäckerei-Kompanie (mot) 200

Schlächterei-Kompanie (mot) 200
    (formerly Schlächterei-Kompanie (mot) 503)

Divisions-Verpflegungsamt (mot) 200
    (formerly Divisions-Verpflegungsamt (mot) 341)

Druckerei-Trupp (mot) 200

Feldgendarmerie-Trupp (mot) 200

Feldpostamt (mot) 200

DIVISIONAL SYMBOL

This symbol was either in yellow or white and was utilized on all vehicles of the Division. It was generally displayed in conjunction with the white "Afrikakorps" symbol (palm tree and swastika).

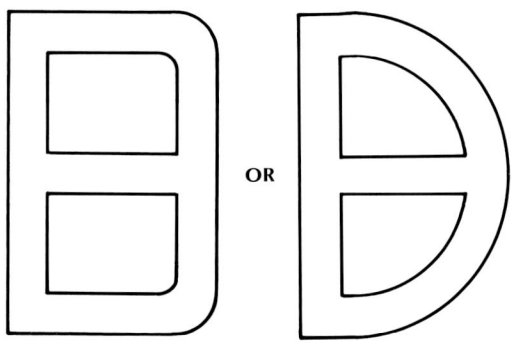

A TWIN MG 34 ANTIAIRCRAFT TRUCK MOUNT (NOTE DIVISIONAL SYMBOL ON TAILGATE).

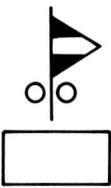

90. leichte Afrika-Division

This Division was initially organized as Afrika-Division z.b.V.[1] in August 1941, and consisted of various independent units which were already serving in Africa, plus troops which were ferried across the Mediterranean by air transport. The Division's first major action came with the German assault on Tobruk on November 21, 1941. During the Sidi Rezegh battles (November 19 - December 1, 1941), the Division was used to halt a sortie by the Tobruk garrison on November 21, which was repulsed after bitter and costly fighting.

On November 27, a new designation was given the Division...90. leichte Division. This new title was not, however, officially used in orders/dispatches until late afternoon on November 28.[2]

In March 1942, the Division was reorganized and was now designated 90. leichte Afrika-Division. During Rommel's attack on Gazala (May 26 - June 14, 1942), the Division was heavily engaged in the siege of both Got el Valeb and Bir Hacheim. The Division, with the Italian Division "Trieste", moved against Got el Ualeb on May 30, and captured the strong point on the 31st. Two days later, Bir Hacheim was attacked but did not fall until June 10. On June 29, the Division assisted in the capture of Mersa Matruh...the last British fortress in the western desert.

During the first assault on the El Alamein positions on July 1, the Division suffered very heavy losses. On July 8, shortly before the main battles in front of El Alamein, Rommel assessed the Division's strength as follows:[3]

> four Infantry Regiments (overall strength of 1500 men)
> 30 anti-tank guns
> and two batteries

---

[1] Afrika-Division z.b.V. = Afrika-Division for special purposes.

[2] KTB, 90. leichte Division, Appendix 134 and 135, and Battle Report Ia on the Operations of Panzerarmee Afrika (November 18, 1941 - February 6, 1942), November 28, 1941.

[3] The Rommel Papers, p. 251.

The Division later participated in the Alam Halfaya battles of August 30-September 5, 1942.

When the British launched their massive offensive at El Alamein on October 23, 90. leichte Afrika-Division was holding the northernmost sector of the line, next to the coast. German losses were staggering during this offensive and by early January 1943, when Panzerarmee Afrika was retreating into Tunisia, the divisional strengths "were down to about half strength. They had approximately 1/3 of their full tank strength (129 tanks, of which less than half were operational), 1/3 of their complement of armored personnel carriers, about 1/4 of their anti-tank guns and 1/6 of their artillery strength."[4]

During the British offensive at Mareth which began on March 26, 1943, Panzergrenadier-Regiment Afrika was sent to assist 10. Panzer-Division near El Guettar. At this time, the Division was only 50% mobilized. The British 30th Corps attacked at Wadi Akarit on April 5, and heavily engaged the weakened Division. On April 6, the remainder of the Armee was ordered to withdraw with units of the 90. leichte Afrika-Division acting as "perpetual rearguard". At this time, the Division's strength was estimated at about 5700 men.[5]

The Division was forced to retreat once more after heavy defensive fighting during the British offensive of April 19-21, and the night attacks at Djebel Terhouna and Djebel Es Srafi (April 23-24, 1943). This time it withdrew towards Enfidaville. On May 12, after a fruitless attempt at getting terms, 90. leichte Afrika-Division finally surrendered unconditionally.[6]

DIVISIONAL COMMANDERS

July 17, 1941 - December 10, 1941 _____ Generalmajor Max Sümmermann[7]

December 11, 1941 - December 27, 1941 ____ Oberst Johann Mickl

December 28, 1941 - April 28, 1942 _____ Generalmajor Richard Veith

April 29, 1941 - June 14, 1942 _____ Generalmajor Ulrich Kleemann

June 14, 1942 - June 18, 1942 _____ Oberst Werner Marcks

June 18, 1942 - June 19, 1942 _____ Oberst Erwin Menny

June 19, 1942 - June 21, 1942 _____ Oberst Werner Marcks

---

[4]Northwest Africa: Seizing the Initiative in the West, p. 371.

[5]Maj. Gen. W.G. Stevens, Bardia to Enfidaville, (Wellington: Dept. of Internal Affairs, New Zealand, 1962), p. 309.

[6]Ibid, p. 366.

June 21, 1942 - September 8, 1942	Generalmajor Ulrich Kleemann[8]
September 8, 1942 - September 17, 1942	Generalmajor Bernhard Hermann Ramcke
September 17, 1942 - September 22, 1942	Oberst Hermann Schulte-Heuthaus
September 22, 1942 - May 12, 1943	Generalleutnant Theodor Graf von Sponeck

GENERALMAJOR SÜMMERMANN

OBERST MARCKS (HERE A GENERALMAJOR)

GENERALMAJOR KLEEMANN

---

[7] On December 10, low flying British aircraft attacked Generalmajor Sümmermann's command vehicle and by 1900 hrs, the divisional commander was dead.

[8] KTB, 90. leichte Division, September 2, 1942. At 0530 hrs, the divisional commander, Generalmajor Kleemann, was wounded when his command car struck a mine. At this time, Generalmajor Ramcke took over temporary command of the Division.

GENERALMAJOR RAMCKE

OBERST SCHULTE-HEUTHAUS

GENERALLEUTNANT GRAF VON SPONECK

DIVISIONAL STAFF

Ia: Major von Ziegler und Klipphausen
    Major i. G. Schumann

Ib: Major Lippmann
    Major Übigau
    Hauptmann Hayessen

Ic: Leutnant d. R. Wiesse
    Oberleutnant d. R. Hiltmann
    Hauptmann Kircher

IIa: Major Kolbeck

IIb: Oberleutnant d. R. Rauert

Arzt: Oberfeldarzt Dr. Werlemann

Divisionsveterinär: Oberstabsveterinär Prof. Dr. Schmidt

ORDER-OF-BATTLE

Stab der Division

Divisions-Kartenstelle (mot) 259 (attached to Staff, Panzerarmee Afrika on January 26, 1942)(9)

Infanterie-Regiment (mot) 155

Infanterie-Regiment (mot) 200 (this unit was formed by combining one Bataillon/Infanterie-Regiment 155, and III./Infanterie-Regiment 347, on March 24, 1942. (10)

Infanterie-Regiment Afrika (mot) 361 (this unit contained many veterans of the French Foreign Legion)

Panzergrenadier-Regiment (mot) Afrika (previously known as Sonderverband 288; reorganized/renamed by Panzerarmee Stab order Ia 5910/42 (secret) on August 6, 1942, but not actually redesignated until October 31, 1942)(11)

Kolbeck-Bataillon (formed on November 25, 1942, from the 90. le. Div. transport and flak transport personnel; reinforced by 500 men from Infanterie-Regiment Afrika 361, who were released from a New Zealand P.O.W. camp and put under the command of Major Kolbeck on November 28, 90. le. Div IIa.

schwerste Infanteriegeschütz-Kompanie 707 (placed under operational command of 164. le. Div. on August 14, 1942)

schwerste Infanteriegeschütz-Kompanie 708 (placed under operational command of 164. le. Div. on August 14, 1942)

Panzerjäger-Abteilung (mot) 190 (formed by combining 3./Panzerjäger-Abteilung 33, 3./Panzerjäger-Abteilung 39, and I./Flak-Abteilung 613 on March 24, 1942)(12)

Artillerie-Regiment (mot) 190 (formed from Artillerie-Regiment 361 on May 27, 1942)(13)

Aufklärungs-Kompanie (mot) 580 (reorganized as Aufklärungs-Abteilung 580 on May 23, 1942)(14)

Nachrichten-Abteilung (mot)

Pionier-Bataillon (mot) 900

Feldersatz-Bataillon

Krankenkraftwagen-Zug (mot) 638

Kraftwagenwerkstatt-Zug 566

Munitionsverwaltungs-Kompanie (mot) 540

Bäckerei-Kompanie (mot) 535

Schlächterei-Kompanie (mot) 517

Divisions-Verpflegungsamt (mot)

Feldgendarmerie-Trupp (mot)

Feldpostamt (mot) 190

DIVISIONAL SYMBOL

As a recognition symbol for the 90. leichte Afrika-Division, a horizontal, white rectangle (6 x 12cm) was to be applied on each of the Division's vehicles. Furthermore, the vehicles of the Regiments and independent Battalions were to be numbered, with the digits (10cm high) positioned below the palm/swastika symbol in white. [15]

The white rectangle was positioned on the left front fender and left rear section of the car or truck body. On motorcycles, the rectangle was positioned on both the front and rear fenders. In most cases, a tactical symbol was positioned directly above this rectangle.

The white palm/swastika symbol was carried on the right front fender and right rear section of car or truck bodies. It was also positioned on both the front and rear of motorcycle sidecars. The white vehicle number was always positioned below this symbol. When a motorcycle was used without a sidecar, the vehicle number was carried directly under the white rectangle on the fenders.

ARM INSIGNIA FOR
SONDERVERBAND 288[16]

[9] KTB, Panzerarmee Afrika, January 26, 1942, Appendix 624.

[10] For a time, this unit included Maschinengewehr-Bataillon 2 and Kradschützen-Bataillon 15. These two battalions were later disbanded.

[11] Sonderverband 288 consisted of 3 Kampfbataillone (2 German and one Arab). The German battalions were composed of ethnic Germans from Palistine, East Africa, Spain, etc., and the Arab battalion from Arabs from North Africa.

[12] Panzerarmee order of March 24, 1942.

[13] War Ministry order of May 27, 1942.

[14] KTB, Panzerarmee Afrika, May 23, 1942.

[15] 90. leichte Afrika-Division special order, dated January 15, 1942.

[16] As illustrated by Günter Schwallach, "Der Orientfeldzug fand nicht statt: Kampf und Untergang des Sonderverbandes 288", Der Frontsoldat erzählt..., Nr. 1, 1956, p. 12.

164. leichte Afrika-Division

This Division was formed in November 1939, as the 164. Lehr-Infanterie-Division. Although it remained in reserve during the western campaigns, it was attached to XXX. Korps and fought in Greece during the summer of 1941. The Division was later assigned to XVIII. Gebirgs-Korps and stationed in Salonika. From here, it was transferred to Crete where it also became known as "Festungsdivision Kreta". In early July, the Division was flown to Africa without its vehicles. There, most of its units were immediately moved to the front to relieve units of 90. leichte Afrika-Division. A short time later, the 164. Lehr-Infanterie-Division was officially redesignated 164. leichte Afrika-Division.

The Division's first action took place on August 30, 1942, during a raid on the Australian positions at El Alamein, which proved to be a costly venture for the Division. Its first major engagement was during the British offensive at El Alamein on October 23, 1942. A general withdrawal from El Alamein was ordered by Rommel on November 3, with the Division and other units acting as a rearguard. During the retreat, surviving units of the Division were distributed among the Panzer formations as additional infantry support.

Before its arrival in Tunisia, the 164. leichte Afrika-Division was sent to Tripoli for a rest and refitting. In early December, however, the Division was moved forward to Buerat where it was put in charge of the defence construction work at that position. "With vehicles gleaned from other German formations," the Division was made fully motorized in early January 1943.

The British launched a major operation against the Mareth Line on March 19, which found the Division attached to the Italian XXI. Korps, along with Divisions "Spezia" (80th) and "Pistoia" (16th). On March 26, the Allies broke through on the costal plain and New Zealand infantry overran two battalions of the Division. After a withdrawal to the Akarit positions, the Division found itself once again completely immobile. Generaloberst von Arnim ordered Generale di Armata Messe to get transportation to the Division on April 6, but before it could be supplied, the Division was forced to retreat once more on foot.

During the month of April, the Division was continually engaged in minor actions alongside the 1. italienische Armee. Its strength was estimated at only 2500 men by late April. Maresciallo d' Italia Messe (promoted on May 13), accompanied by the commander of the 164. leichte Afrika-Division, Generalmajor Freiherr von Liebenstein, surrendered in person to General Freyberg at the Headquarters, 10th Corps, on May 13.

DIVISIONAL COMMANDERS

August 1942 - August 31, 1942 ———— Oberst Carl-Hans Lungershausen (temporarily replaced the fallen Generalmajor v. Bismarck commander of 21. Pz. Div.)

August 31, 1942 - September 18, 1942 — Oberst Hermann-Hans Hecker (temporary)

September 18, 1942 - late November —— Oberst Carl-Hans Lungershausen (promoted to Generalmajor on October 1, 1942)

December 6, 1942 - December 30, 1942 — Oberst Siegfried Westphal (temporary)

January 1, 1943 - January 16, 1943 ———— Generalmajor Kurt Freiherr von Liebenstein(1)

January 16, 1943 - February 17, 1943 — Oberst Becker (temporary)

February 17, 1943 - March 13, 1943 ——— Generalmajor Fritz Krause (temporary)

March 13, 1943 - May 13, 1943 ———— Generalmajor Kurt Freiherr von Liebenstein

GENERALMAJOR LUNGERSHAUSEN

OBERST WESTPHAL (HERE A GENERALLEUTNANT)

[1] Generalmajor von Liebenstein took over as acting commander of the Afrikakorps on January 16, 1943. He was also given command of "Kampfgruppe DAK" on February 10, and held both commands simultaneously. When he was injured in an auto accident on February 17 and evacuated, General d. Pz. Tr. Hans Cramer assumed command of the DAK, Generalmajor Bülowius was given command of "Kampfgruppe DAK" and Generalmajor Krause became the acting commander of 164. leichte Afrika-Division. Generalmajor Krause most probably relieved Oberst Becker (Artillerie-Regiment 220) because the Division was in need of a commander with a higher rank than Oberst, if the commander was to be absent for any extended length of time.

GENERALMAJOR KRAUSE

GENERALMAJOR FREIHERR VON LIEBENSTEIN

DIVISIONAL STAFF

Ia: Oberst Markert
Ib: Hauptmann i. G. Gerhardt
Ic: Oberleutnant Leihner
IIa: Major Werner
Arzt: Oberstarzt Dr. Ziegler

ORDER-OF-BATTLE

Stab der Division

Panzergrenadier-Regiment (mot) 125

Panzergrenadier-Regiment (mot) 382

Panzergrenadier-Regiment (mot) 433

schwerste Infanteriegeschütz-Kompanie 707 (transferred from 90. leichte Afrika-Division on August 14, 1942)

schwerste Infanteriegeschütz-Kompanie 708 (transferred from 90. leichte Afrika-Division on August 14, 1942)

Artillerie-Regiment (mot) 220

Flak-Abteilung (mot) 609

Panzerpionier-Bataillon (mot) 220

Aufklärungs-Abteilung (mot) 220

Nachrichten-Kompanie (mot) 220

Sanitäts-Kompanie (mot) 220
Krankenkraftwagen-Zug (mot) 220
Werkstatt-Kompanie (mot) 220
Divisions-Nachschubführer 220
Bäckerei-Kompanie (mot) 220
Schlächterei-Kompanie (mot) 220
Verpflegungsamt (mot) 220
Feldgendarmerie-Trupp (mot) 220
Feldpostamt (mot) 220

NOTE:
The photo at right was taken at the headquarters of General Freyberg shortly after the surrender of Generalmajor Freiherr von Liebenstein and Maresciallo d'Italia Messe.

DIVISIONAL SYMBOL

Crossed swords over the continent of Africa were introduced in December 1942, as the new divisional symbol for the 164. leichte Afrika-Division. As of the order date, December 7, 1942, the former divisional symbol (crossed swords only) was to be immediately altered by the addition of the African continent. This work was to be done on the divisional vehicles by Werkstatt-Kompanie 220.[2]

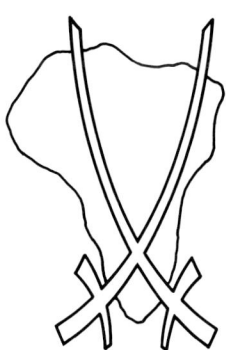

NOTE:
This divisional symbol was to be applied with white paint.

---

[2] 164. leichte Afrika-Division Order, dated December 7, 1942 and signed by the divisional Ib. Microfilm Publication T313, #1474, frame #001208.

334. Infanterie-Division

The 334. Infanterie-Division was formed in the autumn of 1942 at the Grafenwöhr Maneuver Area, and its first units arrived in North Africa in late December 1942, under the command of Oberst Friedrich Weber.[1] Upon its arrival, the Division was immediately assigned to Pz.-A.O.K. 5, and given the sector between Division von Broich and 10. Panzer-Division.

While the major portions of the Division were assembled in the Tunis-Tebourba area, as Army reserve,[2] Infanterie-Regiment 754 participated in the "Christmas Battles" (Dec. 20-23, 1942) as an active element of 10. Panzer-Division. On January 5, 1943, Infanterie-Regiment 755, under the command of Oberst Eder, arrived in Tunisia and was followed on January 15, by the remainder of the Division.

The Division's first major action in Africa occurred during "Unternehmen Eilbote I" (Jan. 18-28, 1943), while operating as part of "Korpsgruppe Weber". Its mission was to act as support for von Arnim's major effort by making a drive towards Bou Arada (Tunisia).

The Division was continually engaged in Northern Tunisia during the period from February 26 to March 15 (still operating as "Korpsgruppe Weber). The fighting there was fierce and costly, for by March 1, Oberst Weber had only six operational tanks remaining in his command.

On April 20-21, "Gruppe Audorff", of the 334. Infanterie-Division, participated in an attack against the heights around Medjez el Bab. Its objective was "Grenadier Hill", but after some initial success the attack was halted. In return, the Allies attempted to seize "Longstop Hill" (Hill 296) which had remained in German hands for four months. Infanterie-Regiment 756 held out against numerous attacks, but after four days of fierce fighting, the Regiment retired from the hill.

The German forces in Tunisia divided on May 6, as the British pressed their attack towards Tunis. By this move, 10. Panzer-Division, 15. Panzer-Division and 334. Infanterie-Division were pulled back from the front

---

[1] MS #D-215: "Battles of 334. Infanterie-Division and of "Gruppe Weber" from the end of December 1942 to May 1943", p. 10. The commander, Ia, Ib, Ic, and IIa, with their subordinate personnel, one Volkswagen and three motorcycles were flown across from Naples to Bizerta on December 25, 1942.

[2] Ibid.

line and moved to the north of the Medjerda. On May 7, however, the 334. Infanterie-Division was immobilized near Chonigui Pass due to lack of fuel. The Division soon became encircled in the hills between Mateur and Tebourba and for one day attempted to escape. It soon proved impossible and on May 8, the Division plus some smaller units surrendered to the British.

DIVISIONAL COMMANDERS

November 13, 1942 - April 15, 1943 — Oberst Friedrich Weber (promoted to Generalmajor on January 1, 1943)

April 15, 1943 - May 8, 1943 — Generalmajor Fritz Krause

DIVISIONAL STAFF

Ia: Major i.G. Strzemicczny
    Hauptmann Lerche

Ib: Hauptmann Lerche
    Oberleutnant Ebertshauser

Ic: Oberleutnant Dr. Rietschel

IIa: Hauptmann Reinhardt
    Major König

Arzt:

ORDER-OF-BATTLE (NOVEMBER 16, 1942)

Stab der Division
Divisions-Kartenstelle (mot)
Infanterie-Regiment (mot) 754
Infanterie-Regiment (mot) 755
Gebirgs-Infanterie-Regiment (mot) 756
Panzerjäger-Abteilung (mot) 334
Artillerie-Regiment (mot) 334
Pionier-Bataillon (mot) 334
Nachrichten-Abteilung (mot) 334
Nachschub-Bataillon (mot) 334
    Nachschubkolonne (1-7)(mot) 334
    Kraftwagenwerkstatt-Kompanie (mot) 334
    Nachschub-Kompanie (mot) 334
Verpflegungsamt (mot) 334
Schlächterei-Kompanie (mot) 334
Bäckerei-Kompanie (mot) 334
Sanitäts-Kompanie (mot) 334
Krankenkraftwagen-Zug (mot) 334
Veterinär-Kompanie (mot) 334
Feldgendarmerie-Trupp (mot) 334
Feldpostamt (mot) 334

GENERALMAJOR FRIEDRICH WEBER

DIVISIONAL SYMBOL

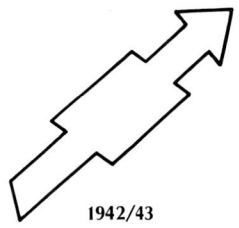

1942/43

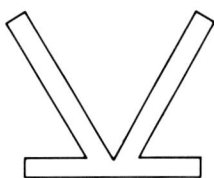

999. leichte Afrika-Division

This unit, which was formed late in 1942 at Neuberg as the 999. Afrika-Brigade, consisted mainly of court-martialed German soldiers to whom combat duty had been authorized for purposes of rehabilitation.[1] Many of the Brigade's personnel had served or were serving long prison sentences, but were not considered habitual criminals.[2] The officers and NCOs were, however, hand-picked from available Army rolls. In March 1943, the Brigade was redesignated 999. leichte Afrika-Division and two of its regiments were transferred to Tunis in late March/early April. During the units' movement to North Africa, the commander of the division, Generalleutnant Kurt Thomas was shot down during his flight and reported as missing on April 1. As a result, a divisional headquarters was never fully organized.

In early April, Afrika-Schützen-Regiment 961 was attached to "Kampfgruppe Fullriede" in the Fondouk area. I./Afrika-Schützen-Regiment 961 saw action near Pichon while II./Afrika-Schützen-Regiment 961 was engaged south of Fondouk, during the British 9th Corps attack against that area on April 7/8, 1943. Afrika-Schützen-Regiment 962 was defending the hills overlooking "Longstop Hill" in mid-April, but was driven from its position by April 15. The bulk of this Division was attached to the D.A.K. on April 24 and fought defensive actions for the next three weeks. Just after midnight on May 12/13, General Cramer, commander of the D.A.K., sent his last message (including a "hail-and-farewell" to Rommel) to Heeresgruppe Afrika and OKH:

> "Ammunition shot off. Arms and equipment destroyed. In accordance with orders received, D.A.K. has fought itself to the condition where it can fight no more. The deutsche Afrikakorps must rise again. Heia Safari. Cramer, General commanding."(3)

NOTE:
All attached units of 999. leichte Afrika-Division marched into captivity with the D.A.K..

---

[1] Northwest Africa, Seizing the Initiative in the West, p. 581.

[2] The offenses included blackmarketeering, etc.

[3] Maj. Gen. C.B. Playfair, D.S.O., The Mediterranean and Middle East: Vol. IV, (London: Her Majesty's Stationery Office, 1966), p. 457.

DIVISIONAL COMMANDERS

December 23, 1942 - April 1, 1943 _____ Generalleutnant Kurt Thomas (missing)

April 2, 1943 - May 13, 1943 _____ Oberst Ernst-Günther Baade

OBERST BAADE (HERE A GENERALMAJOR)

DIVISIONAL STAFF

Ia: Hauptmann Lankheit

Ib: Hauptmann Nels
　　Hauptmann Retzlaff

Ic: Oberleutnant Haarmann

IIa: Hauptmann Hiller

Arzt: Oberstabsarzt Dr. Schnettelker

Divisionsveterinär: Oberstabsveterinär Dr. Voss

999. AFRIKA-BRIGADE ORDER-OF-BATTLE
(JANUARY 11, 1943)

Stab der Brigade

Afrika-Schützen-Regiment (mot) 961

Afrika-Schützen-Regiment (mot) 962

Nachschub-Bataillon (mot) 999
　　　Kraftfahrkolonne (mot) 999
　　　　Kraftwagenwerkstatt-Zug (mot) 999
　　　　Nachschub-Zug (mot) 999

Schlächterei-Kompanie (mot) 999

Bäckerei-Kompanie (mot) 999
Divisions-Verpflegungsamt (mot) 999
Sanitäts-Kompanie (mot) 999
Krankenkraftwagen-Zug (mot) 999
Feldgendarmerie-Trupp (mot) 999

999. LEICHTE AFRIKA-DIVISION ORDER-OF-BATTLE
(MARCH 1, 1943)

Stab der Division
Divisions-Kartenstelle (mot) 999
Musikkorps
Afrika-Schützen-Regiment (mot) 961
Afrika-Schützen-Regiment (mot) 962
Afrika-Schützen-Regiment (mot) 963
Panzerjäger-Abteilung (mot) 999
Artillerie-Regiment (mot) 999
Pionier-Bataillon (mot) 999
Aufklärungs-Abteilung (mot) 999
Astronomischer Messtrupp (mot) 999
Werkstatt-Kompanie (mot) 999
Entgiftungs-Batterie (mot) 999
Nachschub-Bataillon (mot) 999
Schlächterei-Kompanie (mot) 999
Bäckerei-Kompanie (mot) 999
Divisions-Verpflegungsamt (mot) 999
Sanitäts-Kompanie (mot) 999
Krankenkraftwagen-Zug (mot) 999
Veterinär-Kompanie (mot) 999
Feldgendarmerie-Trupp (mot) 999
Feldpostamt (mot) 999

999. LEICHTE AFRIKA-DIVISION ORDER-OF-BATTLE
(ACTUAL UNITS SERVING IN NORTH AFRICA)

Stab der Division
Afrika-Schützen-Regiment (mot) 961
Afrika-Schützen-Regiment (mot) 962
Artillerie-Regiment (mot) 999
Pionier-Bataillon (mot) 999
Astronomischer Messtrupp (mot) 999
Krankenkraftwagen-Zug (mot) 999
Feldgendarmerie-Trupp (mot) 999

DIVISIONAL SYMBOL

A Brigade document, dated January 18, 1943, ordered the immediate creation of a Brigade vehicle symbol.[4] The symbol was in white and was affixed on all Brigade-owned vehicles as well as on directional signs. Its positioning was as follows:

    a. on the right front and right rear fender of all vehicles,
    b. on the front and rear fenders of motorcycles,
    c. and on the rear of motorcycle side-cars.

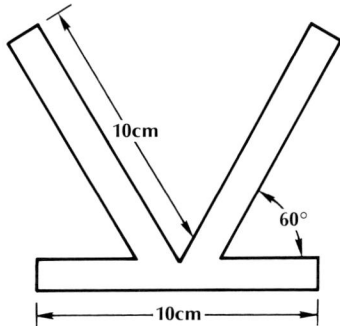

NOTE:
When this Brigade was redesignated as a division in March 1943, the above symbol was retained.

---

[4] 999. Afrika-Brigade, Abt. Ia Nr. 192/43 geh. (dated January 18, 1943).

Division von Broich/von Manteuffel

All German units in Tunisia were officially reorganized under the designation of "Stab Lederer" on November 11, 1942,[1] which was later retitled "Stab Stolz" on November 16. On November 18, Oberst von Broich, who had been made commander of the Bizerte bridgehead, also assumed command of "Stab Stolz". At this time, the command was officially redesignated "Division von Broich". On November 26, shortly after its formation, a small force from the Division was sent towards Tebourba, with the mission of pursueing an aggressive method of defense. The impending action resulted in the first battle between German and American armor in World War II.[2] When Pz.-A.O.K. 5 was organized in December, the Division came under its command and was thereupon assigned to the northernmost sector of the Tunisian front.

When the 10. Panzer-Division commander, Generalleutnant Fischer, was killed in action, Oberst von Broich was sent to replace him on February 5, 1943. Two days later, Generalmajor Hasso von Manteuffel assumed command of "Division von Broich", which was redesignated "Division von Manteuffel". During the German offensive of February 26-March 15, 1943, this Division was split into three Gruppen.... they were:

    (a) 10. Bersaglieri-Regiment (Italian)
    (b) "Gruppe Witzig"   } Fallschirmjägerverbände
    (c) Regiment Barenthin

By March 19, von Manteuffel's Gruppen had advanced to within 2 1/2 miles of Djebel Abiod,[3] fulfilling their mission but too battered to continue the drive. Generalmajor Bülowius took over command of "Division von Manteuffel" on March 31, but with no change in unit designation. During the last phases of the battle for Tunisia, this bloodied Division continued to hold the northern sector of the front.

---

[1] "Stab Lederer" was also referred to as "Division Lederer" on Microfilm Publication T315, roll 2276, frames 000067-000069 and 000295.

[2] *Northwest Africa: Seizing the Initiative in the West*, p. 301.

[3] *Ibid*, p. 505.

"Division von Manteuffel", as part of Panzer-Armeeoberkommando 5, surrendered on May 9, 1943.

EVOLUTION AND TITLES OF DIVISION VON BROICH/VON MANTEUFFEL

November 11, 1942 - November 15, 1942 _____ "Stab Lederer"
November 16, 1942 - November 17, 1942 _____ "Stab Stolz"
November 18, 1942 - February 7, 1943 _____ "Division von Broich"
February 7, 1943 - May 9, 1943 _____ "Division von Manteuffel"

DIVISIONAL COMMANDERS

November 18, 1942 - February 5, 1943 _____ Oberst Fritz Freiherr von Broich
February 7, 1943 - March 31, 1943 _____ Generalmajor Hasso von Manteuffel
March 31, 1943 - May 9, 1943 _____ Generalleutnant Bülowius (captured)

DIVISIONAL STAFF

Ia: Major i.G. Ulrich Boes
    Hauptmann i.G. Prahast

Ib: Hauptmann Beck

Ic: Leutnant Habedank (Kriegsberichter)

IIa: Hauptmann Selig
     Hauptmann Felix

Arzt:

**OBERST FRITZ FREIHERR VON BROICH
(HERE A GENERALMAJOR)**

GENERALMAJOR HASSO VON MANTEUFFEL

GENERALLEUTNANT BÜLOWIUS
(COMMITTED SUICIDE MARCH 31, 1945, IN U.S. CAPTIVITY)

DIVISION VON BROICH
ORDER-OF-BATTLE (JANUARY 30, 1943)

Stab der Division

Fallschirmjäger-Regiment (mot) "Barenthin" (Luftwaffe)
    I. Bataillon (Infanterie)
    II. Bataillon (Infanterie)
    III. Bataillon (Panzerjäger)(4)

Infanterie-Bataillon T3

4. u. 12./Artillerie-Regiment (mot) 2

4./Artillerie-Regiment (mot) 190

Aufklärungs-Kompanie (mot)

Fallschirmjäger-Pionier-Bataillon (mot) 11 (Luftwaffe)

Panzer-Nachrichten-Zug (mot) 190

Bersaglieri-Regiment 10 (Italian)
    Panzerjäger-Zug (mot)
    Infanterie-Bataillon XVI
    Infanterie-Bataillon XXXIV
    Infanterie-Bataillon LXIII
        Fla-Kompanie
        Granatwerfer-Kompanie
        Machinengewehr-Kompanie
    Flak-Zug (mot) (Luftwaffe)
    Kradmelde-Zug (mot)
    Nachrichten-Zug
    Werkstatt-Zug (mot)

Werkstatt-Zug (mot) 215

Verpflegungsamt (mot)

---

[4] By March 18, 1943, all three battalions were Infanterie (Kriegsgliederung der Div. v. Manteuffel - stand 18.3.43).

DIVISION VON MANTEUFFEL
ORDER-OF-BATTLE (MARCH 18, 1943)

Stab der Division

Fallschirmjäger-Regiment (mot) "Barenthin" (Luftwaffe)

Panzergrenadier-Regiment (mot) 160
    Panzergrenadier-Bataillon (mot) A20
    Panzergrenadier-Bataillon (mot) T3
    Panzergrenadier-Bataillon (mot) T4

IV./"Afrika"-Artillerie-Regiment (mot) 2

Flak-Kampftruppe (Luftwaffe)

Fallschirmjäger-Pionier-Bataillon (mot) 11 (Luftwaffe)

Panzer-Nachrichten-Zug (mot) 190

Bersaglieri-Regiment (mot) 10 (Italian)
    Infanterie-Bataillon (mot) XVI
    Infanterie-Bataillon (mot) XXXIV
    Infanterie-Bataillon (mot) LXIII
    Kradmelde-Zug (mot)
    Nachrichten-Zug (mot)
    Werkstatt-Zug (mot)
    Marsch-Bataillon (5)

Kraftwagenkolonne (mot) "Weber"

Werkstatt-Kompanie (mot) 215

Sanitäts-Kompanie (mot) "Burgass"

Verpflegungsamt (mot)

Feldpostamt (mot)

---

[5] Division von Manteuffel order-of-battle chart for 24.3.43 listed this unit as a "Marsch-Kompanie".

Division "Hermann Göring"

Although not an Army formation, this Luftwaffe division did play a major role as a combat unit during the final phases of the Tunisian campaign, and is therefore included in this study. With the Allies advancing into Tunisia in late 1942, the Division was ordered to Italy from where it was to be transported to North Africa as soon as its reorganization as a division had been completed. The I. and III./Jäger-Regiment HG were the first divisional units to be sent to Tunisia in early November to counter the new Allied landings. There, these Battalions were attached to 10. Panzer-Division. During the ensuing weeks of combat, replacements as well as entire units from the Division were received. By early March 1943, the majority of the Division had arrived in Tunisia and was placed under the command of Oberst Schmid. The entire group of Division "Hermann Göring" units in Tunisia was therefore known as "Kampfgruppe Schmid", Vorkdo. Division "Hermann Göring", and fought with distinction on the southern section of the collapsing front. On May 12, 1943, the bulk of the Division surrendered with only a few fragments of the command escaping by air to Sicily. Within the next few months, however, a new division was built in southern France and Italy, with the designation of Panzer-Division "Hermann Göring". This newly formed Panzer-Division and 15. Panzergrenadier-Division were to be the backbone of Axis resistance on Sicily. Panzer-Division "Hermann Göring" was also to be the Allies' fierce opponent at Salerno, Anzio-Nettuno, and numerous other battles before the war's end.

KAMPFGRUPPE COMMANDER

March 1943 - May 9, 1943[1]_____Generalmajor Josef Schmid[2]

---

[1] Reichsmarschall Göring ordered Generalmajor Schmid to fly out of Tunisia on May 9, in order to avoid capture.

[2] Generalmajor Schmid was only in command of the HG units serving in North Africa, and his staff was only an advance HQ. He had been promoted to Generalmajor on March 1, 1943.

**GENERALMAJOR
JOSEF SCHMID**

KAMPFGRUPPE STAFF

Ia: Hauptmann Marvan
Ib:
Ic:
IIa:
Arzt: Oberfeldarzt d. R. Ronher

ORDER-OF-BATTLE (MARCH 13, 1943)

Stab/Kampfgruppe Schmid

I. & III./Grenadier-Regiment "Hermann Göring"

I. & III./Jäger-Regiment "Hermann Göring"
   9./Panzer-Grenadier-Regiment 69
   14./Panzer-Grenadier-Regiment 104
   2. & 4./Panzerjäger-Abteilung 90
   "Afrika"-Bataillon T4

II./Artillerie-Regiment 190

Flak-Regiment "Hermann Göring"

Werfer-Batterie von Bülow

Panzer-Nachrichten-Abteilung "Hermann Göring"

Nachschub-Bataillon "Hermann Göring"

1. Fallschirm-Sanitäts-Kompanie

ORDER-OF-BATTLE (APRIL 4, 1943)

Stab/Kampfgruppe Schmid

I./Panzer-Regiment "Hermann Göring"

II. & III./Grenadier-Regiment "Hermann Göring"

I. & III./Jäger-Regiment "Hermann Göring"
   9./Panzer-Grenadier-Regiment 69
   14. (Pz. Jäg)/Panzer-Grenadier-Regiment 104
   "Afrika"-Bataillon T4
   "Tunisia"-Bataillon 5

I./Artillerie-Regiment 90

2./Artillerie-Regiment 190

I. & II./Flak-Regiment "Hermann Göring"

2./Werfer-Abteilung 1

Aufklärungs-Abteilung "Hermann Göring"
   (only 1., 5. & 6. Kompanie plus Panzerspäh-Kompanie)

Panzer-Nachrichten-Abteilung "Hermann Göring"

Nachschub-Bataillon "Hermann Göring"

1. Fallschirmjäger-Sanitäts-Kompanie

Battle Groups (Kampfgruppen) in North Africa

The German Kampfgruppen in North Africa generally fell into one of three major catagories, which are as follows:

1. Those Gruppen which included only one individual unit and were named after the commander of the unit (i.e. Verband Ablöscher, Gruppe Briel, Gruppe Menton, etc.).
2. Groups of units assembled for special missions, and named after the commanding officer in charge of the entire force (i.e. Angriffsgruppe Weber, Kampfgruppe Funk, Gruppe Haut, etc.). This type of Gruppe could also be named after the sector in which it was to operate (i.e. Kampfgruppe Nord, Kampfgruppe Mitte and Kampfgruppe Süd). The Gruppe could also be assigned numbers instead of sector designations (i.e. Kampfgruppe I, Kampfgruppe II, etc.).
3. Gruppen could also be sub-units (Untergruppen)....one battalion of a regiment, one company of a battalion, etc. (i.e. Gruppe Bach was one battalion of Infanterie-Regiment 104).

There were also Gruppen formed for marches (Marschgruppe), rearguards, etc., but have been included in this Kampfgruppen section only if they saw action as a Gruppe. It was not unusual for a single officer to be given command of more than one Gruppe during his tour of service in Africa (i.e. Vorhut Geissler, Kampfgruppe Geissler).

VERBAND ABLÖSCHER

"November 4, 1942, 0800 hrs: Hauptmann Ablöscher reported to 15. Panzer-Division HQ with a troop of captured guns. "Verband Ablöscher" was attached to the 15. Panzer-Division". (1) This unit was then put under the command of III./Artillerie-Regiment 33.

    2 Batterien (captured guns)

Commander: Hauptmann Ablöscher

Engagements: Battles at El Alamein, November 1942

AFRIKAKORPS STAB KAMPFGRUPPE

This Gruppe was formed on or near April 14, 1942.(2)

    2./Flak-Abteilung 606
    1 Zug/Panzerjäger-Abteilung 39
    1 Panzer-Zug (5 Pzkw II's)
    1 Zug, 1./Pioniere-Bataillon 33
    1 Panzerspähwagen-Zug/Aufklärungs-Abteilung 3

ARTILLERIE GRUPPE BIEL

Formed on or near June 13, 1942, with orders to protect the flank of the 21. Panzer-Division while it attempted to "roll up the Riegel position from the west". (3)

    I./Artillerie-Regiment 155
    II./Artillerie-Regiment 155

Commander:

Engagements: Rommel's second offensive (began May 26, 1942)

ARTILLERIE KOMMANDO 104

This Gruppe was formed in early 1941 to consolidate all of the miscellaneous artillery units of the Panzerarmee. Generalmajor Böttcher was in command until he assumed command of the 21. Panzer-Division on November 29, 1941. Oberst Mickl commanded the Gruppe from December 1, 1941. (4)

    Stab Artillerie-Regiment 221
    Stab schwerste Artillerie-Abteilung 408
        2.u.3. Batterien/408
        Artillerie-Abteilung 364
        5./Artillerie-Regiment 115
    Stab II./Artillerie-Regiment 115
        4./Artillerie-Regiment 115
        4./Armee Küstenartillerie-Batterie 149
        2 Batterien/408
    6./Artillerie-Regiment 115
    Artillerie-Batterie 362
    Stab schwerste Artillerie-Abteilung 528
        2.u.3. Batterien/528
    Artillerie-Batterie 533
    Artillerie-Batterie 902

Commanders: Generalmajor Böttcher
              Oberst Mickl

Engagements: This Gruppe saw action in most of the battles in which the DAK engaged.

KAMPFGRUPPE AUDORFF

Formed on February 22, 1943, as the third Untergruppe of Korpsgruppe Weber. Its mission, during the German offensive in Tunisia of February 26 - March 15, 1943, was to launch holding attacks opposite Madjez el Bab. (5)

    Grenadier-Regiment 754
    1 Bataillon/Panzer-Division "Hermann Göring"

---

[1] KTB 15. Panzer-Division, Nov. 4, 1942.

[2] Panzerarmee message to the War Ministry, April 14, 1942.

[3] KTB 21. Panzer-Division.

[4] KTB Panzerarmee-Afrika, appendicies no. 88/42 Top Secret, August 22, 1942.

[5] Northwest Africa: Seizing the Initiative in the West, p. 504

Commander: Oberstleutnant Paul Audorff

Engagements: German offensive in northern Tunisia (Feb. 26 - Mar. 15, 1943) and the Axis attack on Medjez el Bab (Tunisia, Apr. 20 - 21, 1943)

AUFKLÄRUNGSGRUPPE

This Gruppe was formed on August 22, 1942, and put under the command of Schützen-Brigade 15. The Italian XX. Korps-Aufklärungsgruppe was instructed to cooperate with this Gruppe. (6)

    Aufklärungs-Abteilung 3
    Aufklärungs-Abteilung 33
    Aufklärungs-Abteilung 580
    Flak-Abteilung 612 (- 1./612)

Commander: Oberst Erwin Menny

Engagements: Battles at El Alamein, August 1942

GRUPPE BAADE

This Gruppe was formed on July 17, 1942 for operations during the El Alamein battles. The Australian War History, Tobruk and Alamein, state that "Gruppe Baade" was formed on July 14, 1942 for a counterattack, but the Gruppe failed to get into the battle". (7)

    Stab Panzergrenadier-Regiment 115
    one Bataillon/Panzergrenadier-Regiment 115
    one Panzer-Zug/Panzer-Regiment 5
    one Artillerie-Batterie

Commander: Oberst Ernst-Günther Baade

Engagements: Battles at El Alamein, July 1942

MAJOR BACH

GRUPPE BACH

This name was given to the battalion commanded by Major Bach of the Infanterie-Regiment 104. The Gruppe, plus its commander, was captured at Halfaya Pass on January 17, 1942.(8)

    I./Infanterie-Regiment 104

Commander: Major der Reserve Wilhelm Bach

Engagements: Battles for Halfaya Pass (Libya, 1941 - 1942)

KAMPFGRUPPE BALLERSTEDT

This Gruppe was formed on January 5, 1942.(9)

    K. B. 15
    one Kompanie/Panzerjäger-Abteilung 33
    one leichter Zug, I./Flak-Abteilung 33
    one Kompanie/Panzer-Pionier-Bataillon 33
    one Batterie, II./Artillerie-Abteilung 33
    one Funkstelle

Commander: Oberstleutnant Ballerstedt

Engagements:

GRUPPE BARENTHIN

This was the designation given to the Barenthin Fallschirmjäger-Regiment.

Commander: Oberst Barenthin

GRUPPE BESDE

This Gruppe, also known as "Abschnitt Mitte", for formed on June 25, 1942, from units of the 15. Panzer-Division. The Gruppe, along with "Gruppe Warrelmann" and "Gruppe Dedekind", was under the overall command of Oberst Baade, with orders to hold protective positions near Sidi Mahmud.(10)

    Panzerjäger-Abteilung 33
    Panzer-Pionier-Bataillon 33
    III./Artillerie-Regiment 33

Commander: Major Besde

Engagements: Rommel's second offensive (began May 26, 1942)

---

[6] Barton Maughan, Tobruk and El Alamein, (Canberra: Australian War Memorial, 1966), p. 87, and KTB Panzerarmee-Afrika, appendicies, no. 88/42 Top Secret, August 22, 1942.

[7] Tobruk and El Alamein, pp. 567-568, and KTB 21. Panzer-Division, July 17, 1942.

[8] W. E. Murphy, The Relief of Tobruk, (Wellington: Dept. of Internal Affairs, New Zealand, 1961), p. 514.

[9] Microfilm Publication T315, roll 666, frame 000543.

[10] 15. Panzer-Division Administrative Diary.

GRUPPE BÖTTCHER

This designation was given to Artillerie-Kommando 104 while Generalleutnant Böttcher was in command. Another "Gruppe Böttcher" was formed shortly before the British "Crusader" offensive, after he had turned over command of Arko 104 to Oberst Mickl. (11)

    Infanterie-Regiment 155
    Afrika-Regiment 361
    Pionier-Bataillon 900

Commander: Generalleutnant Karl Böttcher

Engagements:

GRUPPE BRIEL

This was the designation given to Flak-Abteilung 606.

Commander: Hauptmann Briel

Engagements:

KAMPFGRUPPE BUHSE

Formed prior to the German attacks on Sbeitla on February 15-16, 1943. The Kampfgruppe's mission was to pin down the Allies near Sbeitla. (12)

    Grenadier-Regiment 47

Commander: Oberstleutnant Rudolf Buhse

Engagements: German drive on Sbeitla (Tunisia, February 15-16, 1943)

GRUPPE BURK

This Gruppe saw action as an Untergruppe of Kampfgruppe Weber on or about January 18-28, 1943. (13)

    5./Panzer-Regiment 7
    7./Panzer-Regiment 7
    one Zug, 8./Panzer-Regiment 7
    3(Fla)./Panzerjäger-Abteilung 90
    one Zug, 3./Panzer-Pionier-Bataillon 49

Commander:

Engagements: Battles for the eastern Dorsal Passes (Tunisia, January 18-25, 1943)

KAMPFGRUPPE BURCKHARDT

This Kampfgruppe designation was given to XI. Fliegerkorps-Fallschirmjäger-Lehreinheit (demonstration unit). (14)

---

[11] The Relief of Tobruk, pp. 235, 265.

[12] Northwest Africa: Seizing the Initiative in the West, p. 426.

[13] Northwest Africa: Seizing the Initiative in the West, p. 376, and Microfilm Publication T315, roll 570, frame 000305.

[14] KTB Panzerarmee-Afrika, January 23-24, 1942.

GRUPPE CRÜWELL

This Gruppe was formed by Rommel for the attack on the Gazala positions in May 1942. Generalleutnant Crüwell, former commander of the DAK*, commanded the Gruppe until May 29, when he was forced to land his Storch behind British lines and was captured. Generalfeldmarschall Kesselring, who was visiting the front at that time, agreed to take over Crüwell's Gruppe for a few days since there was no one else available at the time. It is interesting to note that although Kesselring outranked Generaloberst Rommel, he placed himself under Rommel's command.

*Generalleutnant Crüwell had commanded the DAK from August 15, 1941 to March 8, 1942, at which time he took over temporary command of Panzergruppe Afrika (March 9) when Rommel went to the continent on a short sick leave. Upon Rommel's return, Crüwell, who was then suffering from jaundice (a common illness among the Germans in Africa because of the lack of fresh food or fruit), was sent to the continent for convalescence. His early return was doubtful, therefore, Rommel gave the command of the DAK to Generalleutnant Nehring. When Crüwell did return in May, Nehring retained command of the DAK, while Crüwell was ordered to take over the Italian front plus Oberst Menny's 15. Schützen-Brigade.

X. italienisches Korps
    Infanterie-Division "Pavia"
    Infanterie-Division "Brescia"
XXI. italienisches Korps
    Infanterie-Division "Trento"
    Infanterie-Division "Sabrata"
15. Schützen-Brigade
Armee-Artillerie

Commanders: Generalleutnant Crüwell (May 25 - May 29, 1942)
              Generalfeldmarschall Kesselring (May 29 - June 3, 1942)

GENERALLEUTNANT CRÜWELL

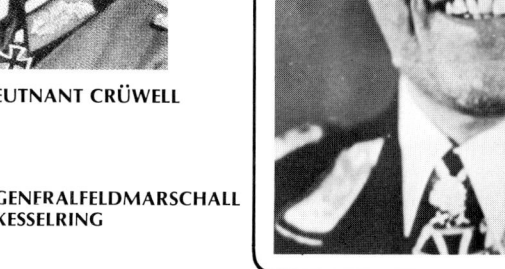

GENFRALFELDMARSCHALL KESSELRING

Engagements: "Unternehmen Venezia", the German attack on Gazala (Libya, May 26-June 15, 1942).

KAMPFGRUPPE DAK

This Kampfgruppe was formed on February 10, 1943. Its first mission was to move against Gafsa during the Battle of Sidi bou Zid. The Kampfgruppe was a "composite German-Italian force in divisional strength consisting of infantry and armored units, and supported by artillery, Flak and miscellaneous other units". When the commander, Oberst von Liebenstein, was wounded on February 17, 1943, the command was passed on to Generalmajor Bülowius. (15)

    Stab DAK
    one Panzer-Abteilung/Panzer-Regiment 8
    Panzer-Grenadier-Regiment Afrika
    Panzerjäger-Kompanie
    Luftwaffen-Jäger-Brigade 1
    Stab, I./Artillerie-Regiment Afrika 1
    I./Artillerie-Regiment 190
    three Batterien/Werfer-Regiment 71
    Stab Flak-Regiment 135 (Luftwaffe)
    Aufklärungs-Abteilung 33
    one Kompanie/Pionier-Bataillon 200
    italienisches Panzer-Bataillon
    italienisches Infanterie-Bataillon
    italienisches Infanterie-Bataillon
    italienisches Bersaglieri-Bataillon
    italienisches Artillerie-Bataillon
    italienisches Artillerie-Bataillon
    italienische Sturmgeschütz-Batterie

Commanders: Oberst Freiherr von Liebenstein
              Generalmajor Bülowius

GRUPPE DEDEKIND

This Gruppe, also known as "Abschnitt West", was formed on June 25, 1942, from units of the 15. Panzer-Division. The Gruppe, along with "Gruppe Warrelmann" and "Gruppe Besde", were under the overall command of Oberst Baade, with orders to hold protective positions near Sidi Mahmud. (16)

    Infanterie-Regiment 115 (- III./115 and two Kompanien, I./115)
    I./Artillerie-Regiment 33
    leichte Flak

Commander: Major Dedekind

Engagements: Rommel's second offensive (began May 26, 1942)

GRUPPE DJEDEIDA

Originally formed as a pursuit unit during the operations of XC. Korps after December 1, 1942. The Gruppe was to pursue the Allies if they pulled back from the armored battles north of Tebourba. Under the leadership of Generalmajor Fischer, the Gruppe attacked the Allies west of Djedeida, but was held up far short of its objective. (17)

---

[15] Northwest Africa: Seizing the Initiative in the West, pp. 409, 425.

[16] 15. Panzer-Division Administrative Diary.

[17] Northwest Africa: Seizing the Initiative in the West, pp. 313-314.

three Pzkw III's
two Pzkw VI "Tiger"
one Panzerjäger-Kompanie
one Fallschirmjäger-Kompanie
one Infanterie-Kompanie
one Flak-Batterie
eighteen 20mm guns
one Zug/ Kradschützen-Kompanie

Commander: Generalmajor Wolfgang Fischer

Engagements: Axis counter-attack in the Tunis North Sector, December 1-3, 1942

GRUPPE ECKARDSTEIN

This designation was given to Infanterie-Regiment 104.

Commander: Oberst Eckardstein

Engagements:

KAMPFGRUPPE EDER

Formed on December 8, 1941, as the rearguard for the Afrikakorps, which was planning to withdraw from the area around Bir Hatiet el Genadel. The Gruppe was under orders "not to withdraw until attacked by the enemy in superior strength". Although originally formed as a rearguard, the Kampfgruppe was retained throughout December 1941 and possibly longer.(18)

one Panzerjäger-Kompanie
one Infanterie-Bataillon
one Artillerie-Batterie
plus one wireless-transmitter vehicle

Commander:

Engagements: Saw action during the British "Crusader" offensive which began on November 18, 1941.

GRUPPE EDER

Formed as the second Untergruppe of "Korpsgruppe Weber" on February 22, 1943. Its mission was to advance across Djebel el Ang, turn south and destroy Allied units in the mountains near Chaouach and Toukabeur, and cut the nearby main highway. (19)

Grenadier-Regiment 755

Commander:

Engagements: German offensive in northern Tunisia (February 26 - March 15, 1943).

GRUPPE EWERT

Infanterie-Regiment 104

---

[18] KTB Deutsches Afrikakorps, December 8, 1941.

[19] Northwest Africa: Seizing the Initiative in the West, p. 504.

KAMPFGRUPPE FISCHER

Formed on November 3, 1942, to cover the 15. Panzer-Division while it withdrew to new positions. (20)

    Panzerjäger-Abteilung 605
    III./Artillerie-Regiment 33
    I./Flak-Regiment 33 ⎫ Luftwaffe
    II./Flak-Regiment 33 ⎭

Commander: Hauptmann Fischer

Engagements: Minor actions at El Alamein (November 1942).

KORPSGRUPPE FISCHER

Generaloberst von Arnim organized this Kampfgruppe on January 4, 1943, because Pz.-A.O.K. 5 was operating with a minimum staff at the time (without a lower "Korpsstab"). This Staff was made necessary when the 334. Infanterie-Division was placed in the front lines between Division von Manteuffel and 10. Panzer-Division. "Korpsgruppe Fischer" was to fill in where a staff was needed, and was assigned the task of capturing Medjez el Bab, which Generalfeldmarschall Kesselring had assigned to Pz.-A.O.K. 5 on January 2, 1943. (21)

    10. Panzer-Division
    one Kompanie/Panzer-Abteilung 190
    Fallschirmjäger-Regiment 5
    II./Artillerie-Regiment 190
    Marsch-Bataillon A24

Commander: Generalleutnant Fischer

Engagements: Battle for the eastern Dorsal Passes (Tunisia, January 18-25, 1943).

GRUPPE FRANZ

Formed in May 1943, this unit defended a section of cliff and beach at Hamman Lif and repulsed all Allied attacks for two days, even though it was heavily outnumbered.(22)

    a Panzerjäger unit
    an Artillerie unit

GENERALMAJOR GOTTHARD FRANZ

---

[20]KTB 15. Panzer-Division, November 3, 1942.

[21]Northwest Africa: Seizing the Initiative in the West, p. 371, and Microfilm Publication T315, roll 570, frame 000295.

[22]Northwest Africa: Seizing the Initiative in the West, p. 662.

Commander: Generalleutnant Gotthard Franz

Engagements: Battle at Hamman Lif (Tunisia, May 7-9, 1943).

KAMPFGRUPPE FULLRIEDE

Formed on or near February 26, 1943, as a replacement unit for Grenadier-Regiment 47, which had been pulled from its position and employed in Generaloberst von Arnim's offensive in Tunisia on February 26. This unit successfully defended its positions along the road from El Ala to Pichon and Fondouk.(23)

>Infanterie-Regiment 961, plus several small German and Italian units

Commander: Oberstleutnant Fritz Fullriede

Engagements: Allied attack on Fondouk (Tunisia, March 27, 1943).

KAMPFGRUPPE FUNK

Formed as the third force for an operation on April 22, 1943. This Kampfgruppe was part of "Kampfgruppe Schmid" and its mission was to protect the southern flank.(24)

>I./Jäger-Regiment "Hermann Göring"

Commander: Major Funk

Engagements: Axis attack on Medjez el Bab (Tunisia, April 20-21, 1943)

VORHUT GEISSLER

Formed on December 2, 1941, this Gruppe was to be the advance guard for a push up the via Balbia to relieve the Sollum front and "Gruppe Bach". Its orders were "to join forces with the Sollum front and occupy the area on either side of the via Balbia, acting as escort for supply transport to the front". The Gruppe, acting in cooperation with "Vorhut Knabe", suffered very heavy casualties on December 3, 1941, at Menastir, with its leading elements being nearly annihilated.(25)

>one and one-half Kompanien/Panzerjäger-Abteilung 33
>Stab Infanterie-Regiment 200
>one and one-half Batterie/Artillerie-Abteilung 33
>Kradschützen-Bataillon 15

Commander: Oberstleutnant Erich Geissler

Engagements: Battles around Ed Duoa (Libya, November/December 1941).

KAMPFGRUPPE GERHARDT

Formed on February 8, 1943, as one of three "Sturmgruppen" of 10. Panzer-Division. The Gruppe participated in "Unternehmen Frühlingswind". (26)

---

[23] Ibid, p. 509.

[24] Ibid, p. 609.

[25] The Relief of Tobruk, pp. 475-478, and KTB 15. Panzer-Division, December 2, 1941.

[26] Northwest Africa: Seizing the Initiative in the West, p. 407, and Microfilm Publication T315, roll 570, frame 000358.

II./Panzer-Regiment 7
II./Panzer-Grenadier-Regiment 69
one Zug, 1./Panzerjäger-Abteilung 90
one Zug, 3./Panzerjäger-Abteilung 90
one Zug, 3./Panzer-Pionier-Bataillon
one leichte Feldhaubitzen-Batterie/Panzer-Artillerie-Regiment 90

Commander: Oberst Gerhardt

Engagements: Battle of Sidi Bou Zid (Tunisia, February 14-15, 1943) and in the German advance on Pichon (Tunisia, February 17, 1943).

KAMPFGRUPPE GRÄF

This Gruppe was formed on June 1, 1942, as a "pursuit" Gruppe. The Gruppe was given all the fuel remaining in the 21. Panzer-Division, and ordered to advance in order to capture as much fuel and material as possible. The remainder of the Division was to remain in its positions. (27)

one Kompanie/Panzerjäger-Abteilung 39
one Bataillon/Infanterie-Regiment 104
one Batterie/Artillerie-Regiment 155
one Batterie (8.8cm) Flak
one Kompanie/Pionier-Bataillon 200

Commander: Major Gräf

Engagements: On July 15, 1942, a second "Kampfgruppe Gräf" was formed but only included I./Artillerie-Regiment 155. This Kampfgruppe was under orders to operate in a south-westerly direction in the El Alamein area.

KAMPFGRUPPE GRÜN

This Kampfgruppe was formed shortly before the Faid-Maknessy actions of January 30 - February 3, 1943. It was a part of the 21. Panzer-Division, which formed both "Kampfgruppe Grün" and "Kampfgruppe Pfeiffer", for the coming battles. "Kampfgruppe Grün" was under orders to "make a long encircling march through Maizila Pass", enabling it to attach the French garrison at Faid Village and then "join in the seizing of the Pass". During the battle, the Gruppe was held up for five hours but was later able to drive off an American armored force which had approached from the northwest. "By 1400 on January 31, the Germans had succeeded in capturing Faid Pass." (28)

I./Panzer-Regiment 5

Commander: Hauptmann Werner Grün

Engagements: Faid-Maknassy Battles (Tunisia, January 30 - February 3, 1943).

GRUPPE HAIN

On September 16, 1942, at 2000 hrs, the Panzerarmee Ia sent the following message to the "Afrikakorps": "Feldersatz-Bataillon 33, Feldersatz-Bataillon 200 and the 90. leichte Division Versorgungsführungs-Bataillon will be tactically subordinated to the Armee as "Gruppe Hain", under the command of Major Hain, C.O. of the 90. leichte Division

---

[27] KTB 21. Panzer-Division, June 1, 1942 and July 15, 1942.

[28] Northwest Africa: Seizing the Initiative in the West, pp. 390-392.

Draft Conducting Bataillon, and will be transferred with all units and vehicles to upper (Fort Sollum) and lower (harbor area) Sollum. The Italian garrison (12. Küstenartillerie-Batterie - 7.6cm guns) will be subordinated to "Gruppe Hain"."(29)

 Feldersatz-Bataillon 33
 Feldersatz-Bataillon 200
 90. leichte Division Versorgungsführungs-Bataillon
 12. Küstenartillerie-Batterie

Commander: Major Hain

Engagements: Battle at Sollum (Libya, September 1942).

GRUPPE HAUT

Formed on or near February 25, 1943, as an Untergruppe of "Gruppe Lang" (Gruppe Lüder was the other Untergruppe).(30)

 1./Panzer-Grenadier-Regiment 86
 Artillerie-Abteilung 190

On March 20, 1943, the Gruppe was strengthened and reorganized as follows:

 Feldbataillon T3
 Feldbataillon T4
 Marschbataillon A30
 Fallschirmjäger-Pionier-Bataillon 11
 IV./Afrika-Artillerie-Regiment 2
  4./Afrika-Artillerie-Regiment 2
  11./Afrika-Artillerie-Regiment 2
  12./Afrika-Artillerie-Regiment 2
  4./Artillerie-Regiment 90
  two Züge, Pakkomp.(mot) Luftwaffen-Regiment Barenthin
 1./Flak-Abteilung 1

Commander:

Engagements: Saw actions in Northern Tunisia (February 26 - March 15, 1943).

GRUPPE HOLZINGER

This was the designation given to Gebirgsjäger-Regiment 756.

KAMPFGRUPPE HUDEL

Formed on or near November 30, 1942. This Kampfgruppe was to operate alongside "Gruppe Lüder" in an attack on Tebourba and was to block the Tebourba gap if the Allies pulled back.(31)

 two Panzer-Kompanien
 two Panzerjäger-Kompanien
 one Kradschützen-Kompanie/Kradschützen-Bataillon 10

---

[29] KTB Panzerarmee-Afrika, September 16, 1942.

[30] Microfilm Publication T315, roll 2277, frame 000822, 001126.

[31] <u>Northwest Africa: Seizing the Initiative in the West</u>, p. 312.

Commander: Major Hudel

Engagements: Axis counterattack in Tunis North Area (Tunisia, November 28 - December 2, 1942).

GRUPPE INFANTERIE-REGIMENT 104

Formed on or near June 1, 1942. This Gruppe contained most of the combat formations of the 21. Panzer-Division, with the exception of Panzer-Regiment 5. The Division was under orders from the Afrikakorps to "occupy Eluet El Tamir and to prepare hedgehog defences for the whole area, which would prevent the British from breaking through from the west.(32)

>Panzerjäger-Abteilung 39
>I./Infanterie-Regiment 104
>III./Infanterie-Regiment 104
>I./Artillerie-Regiment 155
>III./Artillerie-Regiment 155
>3./Flak-Regiment 18 (Luftwaffe)
>2./Flak-Regiment 617
>Pionier-Bataillon 200

Commander: Oberst Ewert (Kdr. Inf. Rgt. 104)

Engagements: Rommel's second offensive (began May 26, 1942).

KAMPFGRUPPE IRKENS

This Kampfgruppe, also known as Panzer-Brigade Irkens, was formed by Generaloberst von Arnim on April 24, 1943, when he merged nearly all of his remaining armored units into one composite force. On April 28 and 29, the Gruppe which was under the personal supervision of the Pz.-A.O.K.5 commander, General von Vaerst, once more wrested the initiative from the British, regained control of the dominating heights of Djebel Bou Aoukaz and stopped the British 5th Corps advance. Although the Germans had stopped the Allies, they had immobilized their Panzer units by using all available fuel.(33)

>Panzer-Regiment 5
>Panzer-Regiment 7
>Panzer-Regiment 8
>Panzer-Abteilung (Tiger) 501
>Grenadier-Regiment 47
>Artillerie-Abteilung
>italienische Artillerie-Abteilung
>two Flak-Abteilungen
>Gruppe Audorff

Commander: Oberst Irkens

Engagements: Axis offensive against Medjez el Bab (Tunisia, April 20-26, 1943, and the Allied offensive in Tunisia (May 3-13, 1943).

KAMPFGRUPPE KAISER

This Kampfgruppe was formed on June 17, 1942 for actions against the British strongpoints at Belhamed and Sidi Rezeg.(34)

---

[32]KTB 21. Panzer-Division, June 1, 1942.

[33]Northwest Africa: Seizing the Initiative in the West, p. 612.

[34]KTB 90. leichte Afrika-Division.

one Kompanie/Panzerjäger-Abteilung 190
I./Infanterie-Regiment 155
one Batterie/Artillerie-Regiment 361

Commander: Hauptmann Kaiser

Engagements: Battles of Belhamed, Sidi Rezeg (Libya, June 1942).

KAMPFGRUPPE KAUTENFELD

Formed on or near December 11, 1941. This Kampfgruppe, cooperating with "Kampfgruppe Eckardstein" on its left, took up defensive positions in the El Cheina area.(35)

two Kompanien/Maschinengewehr-Bataillon 8
one Batterie/schwerste Artillerie-Abteilung 408
Pionier-Bataillon 200

Commander:

Engagements: Saw action during the British "Crusader" offensive which began on November 17, 1941.

KAMPFGRUPPE KIRCHHEIM

Formed on or near April 30, 1941, for participation in the May assault on Tobruk.(36)

Panzer-Regiment 5
Panzerjäger-Einheit
Maschinengewehr-Bataillon 2
Maschinengewehr-Bataillon 8
Artillerie-Einheit
Flak-Einheit
two Pionier-Kompanien

Commander: Generalmajor Heinrich Kirchheim

Engagements: April 1941 assault on Tobruk and resulting battles.

KAMPFGRUPPE KNABE

Formed in late November 1941, by 21. Panzer-Division, for operations during the British offensive to relieve Tobruk.(37)

Infanterie-Regiment 104
Pionier-Bataillon 200

On December 1, 1941, the Gruppe was reorganized, strengthened and redesignated "Vorhut Knabe". This Kampfgruppe operated alongside "Vorhut Geissler", under the same orders. Because of its armored support, it did not suffer as much as did "Vorhut Geissler".

three tanks
one Kompanie/Panzerjäger-Abteilung 33
II./Infanterie-Regiment 104

---

[35] KTB 21. Panzer-Division.

[36] Tobruk and El Alamein, p. 223.

[37] The Relief of Tobruk, pp. 87, 475-478.

Commander: Oberstleutnant Gustav-Georg Knabe

Engagements: British offensive to relieve Tobruk (Libya, November 1941, and the battles at Sidi Rezegh (Libya, December 1941).

VORHUT KNABE

See "Kampfgruppe Knabe".

KAMPFGRUPPE KOCH

Formed on or near December 1, 1942. This Kampfgruppe was to assist General Fischer's counterattack to regain lost ground in front of the Tunisian bridgehead. "Kampfgruppe Koch" was to the south and its mission was to tie down the Allies by attacking El Bathan.(38)

    Fallschirmjäger-Regiment 5 (Koch)
    2./Panzerjäger-Abteilung 90
    Infanterie-Bataillon A24
    3./T.1
    11./Panzer-Artillerie-Regiment 90
    one leichte Flakbatterie (2cm)

Commander: Oberstleutnant Koch

Engagements: Axis counterattack in Tunis North Sector (November 30 - December 3, 1942), and the German offensive in northern Tunisia (February 26 - March 15, 1943).

KAMPFGRUPPE KOST

This Gruppe was formed on June 17, 1942, for operations against the Belhamed and Sidi Rezeg strongpoints.(39)

    one Kompanie/Panzerjäger-Abteilung 90
    II./Infanterie-Regiment 155

Commander: Major Kost

Engagements: Rommel's second offensive (began May 26, 1942).

KAMPFGRUPPE LANG

Formed shortly before February 8, 1943, as the reserve force for "Unternehmen Frühlingswind".

    one Panzerjäger-Zug
    Kradschützen-Bataillon 10
    one Pionier-Zug
    two 88mm guns

During the German offensive in northern Tunisia (February 26 - March 15, 1943), the Kampfgruppe was reorganized and its strength increased. It was attached to "Korpsgruppe Weber" with the mission of breaking through the Allied position at Sidi Nsir and driving on to Bedja. By March 22, the Kampfgruppe reached its full strength and later saw action at Maknassy from March 27 - April 8, and at Faid-Sfax from April 8-9.(40)

---

[38]Northwest Africa: Seizing the Initiative in the West, p. 312, and Microfilm Publication T315, roll 570, frame 000320.

[39]KTB 90. leichte Afrika-Division.

    Stab des Regiments
    I./Panzer-Grenadier-Regiment 69
    I./Panzer-Grenadier-Regiment 86
    Panzer-Abteilung 501
    Afrika-Bataillon 26
    thirty men from Kampfstaffel O. B. (Luftwaffe)
    one Kompanie/Kesselring-Stabswache (Luftwaffe)
    9./Artillerie-Regiment 90
    two Werferbatterien (21cm)
    one Flak-Zug (20mm)
    two 88mm guns
    one Batterie, (italienisch)

Commander: Oberst Rudolf Lang

Engagements: Battle of Sidi bou Zid (Tunisia, February 14-15, 1943), German offensive in northern Tunisia (February 26 - March 15, 1943), Battles of Gafsa, Maknassy and El Guettar (Tunisia, March 17-25, 1943), Battle at Fondouk (Tunisia, April 1943), and the Battle of Faid, Sfax (Tunisia, April 8-9, 1943).

KAMPFGRUPPE LATINI

This Kampfgruppe was formed on or near February 25, 1943, for operations in the Tunisian battles of February 1943.(41)

    two Kompanien/Fallschirmjäger-Pionier-Bataillon 11
    one Pak-Zug, 10./Luftwaffen-Regiment Barenthin
    4./Artillerie-Regiment 90
    6./Flak-Abteilung 53
    Bersaglieri-Regiment 10 (LXIII. Batl.)(italienisch)
    Feld-Batl. T4 (Stab, three Kompanien)

Commander: Oberstleutnant Latini

Engagements: Saw action in Tunisia, February 1943.

KAMPFGRUPPE VON LIEBENSTEIN

Formed shortly before March 27, 1943. This Kampfgruppe, operating with the Italian XXI. Korps, covered the withdrawal of the non-motorized elements of the Italian XX. Korps when it moved to the Chott position during the battle for the Mareth Line.(42)

    elements of 164. leichte Afrika-Division

Commander: Generalmajor Kurt Freiherr von Liebenstein

Engagements: Allied offensive at the Mareth Line (Tunisia, March 1943).

KAMPFGRUPPE LINDEMANN

See "Kampfgruppe Nord" (January 11, 1943).

---

[40] Northwest Africa: Seizing the Initiative in the West, p. 556.

[41] Microfilm Publication T315, roll 2277, frame 000830.

[42] Northwest Africa: Seizing the Initiative in the West, p. 537.

KAMPFGRUPPE LÖVEN

Formed on May 27, 1942, for operations during the battle for Tobruk. On June 14, 1942, due to the many casualties suffered in the May and June battles, "Kampfgruppe Löven" and "Marcks" were amalgamated under the command of Oberst Löven.(43)

> II./Infanterie-Regiment 155 (- one Kompanie)
> two Batterien/Artillerie-Regiment 361
> two Kompanien/Flak-Abteilung 606

Commander: Oberst Löven

Engagements: Rommel's second offensive (began May 26, 1942).

AUFKLÄRUNGSGRUPPE LUCK

This Gruppe was formed on March 5, 1943, with its mission being to make a swift thrust forward into the Medenine-Mareth Line area, and to observe and hold up any enemy force threatening the 10. Panzer-Division's flank. If hard pressed by superior enemy forces, the Kampfgruppe was to retire to the mountain passes from which it had emerged. (44)

> Kampfstaffel Rommel
> one s. Flak-Batterie/I./Flak-Regiment 53 (Luftwaffe)
> Aufklärungs-Abteilung 3
> Aufklärungs-Abteilung 33

Commander: Major Luck

Engagements: The battles at Mareth (Tunisia, March 1943).

GRUPPE LÜDER

Formed prior to Oberst Fischer's operation of November 30 December 16, 1942. "Gruppe Lüder's" mission was to attack Tebourba from the west. (45)

> one Kompanie/Panzer-Abteilung 501
> II./Panzer-Grenadier-Regiment 69
> Pionier-Zug
> Flak-Zug

Commander: Major Lüder

Engagements: Axis counterattack in Tunis North Area (Tunisia, November 1942) and the battles for the eastern Dorsal Passes (Tunisia, January 18-25, 1943).

GRUPPE MARCKS

The first "Gruppe Marcks" was formed in early 1941.

> Infanterie-Regiment 155
> Maschinengewehr-Bataillon 2
> Flak-Gruppe Hecht

---

[43] KTB 90. leichte Afrika-Division, May 28, 1942.

[44] Microfilm publication T315, roll 570, frame 000391.

[45] Northwest Africa: Seizing the Initiative in the West, p. 312.

"Gruppe Marcks" was reformed on June 6, 1942, as "Kampfgruppe Marcks", when 90. leichte Afrika-Division reorganized for the assault on Bir Hacheim. (46)

    Panzerjäger-Abteilung 605
    Flak-Abteilung 606
    Aufklärungs-Abteilung 580

Commander: Oberst Werner Marcks

Engagements: The battle for Bir Hacheim (Libya, June 1942).

KAMPFGRUPPE MENNY

"Kampfgruppe Menny" was formed prior to, or shortly after the opening phazes of the assault on the Gazala Line (December 13-16, 1941). A second "Kampfgruppe Menny" was formed around April 2, 1943. (47)

    2./Panzer-Regiment 8 (one Zug of Pzkw IVs)
    3./Panzerjäger-Abteilung 33
    Panzer-Aufklärungs-Abteilung 33
    Teile Panzer-Nachrichten-Abteilung 78
    II./Schützen-Regiment 115
    I./Artillerie-Regiment 33
    III./Artillerie-Regiment 33
    1./Flak-Abteilung 18 (Luftwaffe)
    3./Flak-Abteilung 617
    one Panzer-Abteilung von Division Ariete ⎫ Italian
    one Batterie Sfl. von Division Ariete ⎭
    one Kr.K.W.-Zug
    one Horch-Zug

Commander: Oberst Erwin Menny

Engagements: German assault on the Gazala Line (Libya, December of 1941).

KAMPFGRUPPE MENTON

This was the name given to "Sonderverband 288", which was under the command of Oberst Menton. When the unit was reorganized and renamed "Panzergrenadier-Regiment Afrika", it still retained the designation "Kampfgruppe Menton". (48)

    two Bataillone/Panzergrenadier-Regiment Afrika
    Korps-Artillerie (in support only)
    Flak (in support only)

Commander: Oberst Menton

Engagements: The Gruppe took part in most battles of the 90. le. Div. battle for Kasserine Pass.

NOTE:

Also see "Sonderverband 288.

---

[46] KTB 90. leichte Afrika-Division.

[47] Microfilm Publication T315, roll 666, frame 001272, and The Relief of Tobruk, pp. 499-500.

[48] Northwest Africa: Seizing the Initiative in the West, p. 449.

GRUPPE MICKL

The first "Gruppe Mickl" was Infanterie-Regiment 155, which Oberst Mickl commanded until his capture on November 28,
nant Mickl, released on November 30, 1941, was given command of Artillerie-Kommando 104 which was later redesignated Gruppe Mickl. (49)

Commander: Oberst Johann Mickl

Engagements:

RESERVE-GRUPPE MILDEBRATH

At 0615 hrs on July 27, 1942, 15. Panzer-Division received orders from Afrikakorps to hold in readiness a reserve Gruppe under the command of Oberstleutnant Mildebrath. This Gruppe consisted of:

I./Infanterie-Regiment 115
one leichte Artillerie-Abteilung (less one Batterie)
one schwerste Flak-Batterie
one Panzer-Zug (50)

Commander: Oberstleutnant Werner Mildebrath

Engagements: Saw action at the El Alamein positions (Egypt, July 1942).

KAMPFGRUPPE MITTE (OCT. 23, 1942)

This Gruppe was formed on October 23, 1942, along with two other Gruppen, for defensive operations during the British offensive of October 23, 1942. The other Gruppen were "Nord" and "Süd". On October 24, 1942, the units assigned to "Kampfgruppe Nord" were attached to this Gruppe. (51)

II./Panzer-Regiment 8
Stab/Panzer-Grenadier-Regiment 115
III./Panzer-Grenadier-Regiment 115
13./Panzer-Grenadier-Regiment 115 (Sturmgeschütz)
15./Panzer-Grenadier-Regiment 115 (captured guns)
III./Artillerie-Regiment 33
Stab/italienisches Panzer-Regiment 133
IV./italienisches Panzer-Regiment 133
23./Bersaglieri-Regiment 12
29./Artillerie-Regiment 3
italienisches Sturmgeschütz-Bataillon 556

Commander: Major Schemmel

Engagements: Saw action during the British offensive which began on October 23, 1942 (El Alamein, Egypt).

KAMPFGRUPPE MITTE (JAN. 11, 1943)

This was one of four defensive Kampfgruppen formed on January 11, 1943, to deal with four possible plans of attack in the area of Faschia, Tunisia. The other Gruppen were "Kampfgruppe Süd, Nord and Irkens". (52)

---

[49] The Relief of Tobruk, pp. 373, 385 and 412.

[50] KTB Deutsches Afrikakorps.

[51] Microfilm Publication T315, roll 666, frame 00054 and KTB 15. Panzer-Division.

[52] KTB 15. Panzer-Division.

three 50mm cannon/Panzer-Grenadier-Regiment 115
Stab I./Flak-Regiment 43 ⎫
I./Flak-Regiment 43   ⎬ Luftwaffe
5./Flak-Regiment 43   ⎭
one 20mm cannon/Flak-Abteilung 617

Commander: Major Schneider-Eicke

Engagements:

KAMPFGRUPPE NORD (OCT. 23, 1942)

Formed on October 23, 1942, as one of three Gruppen of 15. Panzer-Division, for defensive operations during the British offensive of October 23, 1942. The other Gruppen were "Mitte" and "Süd". This Gruppe was disbanded on October 24, 1942, and its units attached to "Kampfgruppe Mitte". (53)

    I./Panzer-Grenadier-Regiment 115
    Stab, Stabsbatterie/Artillerie-Regiment 33
    3./Flak-Abteilung 617
    51./italienisches Panzer-Bataillon 133

Commander: Oberst Crasemann

**OBERST EDUARD CRASEMANN
(HERE A GENERALMAJOR)**

Engagements: Saw action during the British offensive of October 23, 1942 (El Alamein, Egypt).

KAMPFGRUPPE NORD (NOV. 3, 1942)

Formed on November 3, 1942, the Gruppe was to operate alongside "Kampfgruppe Süd" during the retreat from El Alamein. (54)

    remnants of Panzer-Regiment 8
    Panzer-Pionier-Bataillon 33
    I./Artillerie-Regiment 33
    1. und 2./Flak-Abteilung 43 (Luftwaffe)

Commander: Hauptmann Siemens

Engagements: The Axis retreat from El Alamein (Egypt, November 1942).

KAMPFGRUPPE NORD (JAN. 11, 1943)

"Kampfgruppe Nord" was one of four Kampfgruppen formed on January 11, 1943, for defensive operations. Its orders were: (a) block Wadi el

---

    [53] Microfilm Publication T315, roll 666, frame 000054, and <u>KTB 15. Panzer-Division</u>.

    [54] 15. Panzer-Division report on the Battle of El Alamein and the retreat to Mersa el Brega.

Chief by fire day and night...and prevent the enemy from infiltrating the Wadi by night; (b) prevent the enemy from infiltrating unseen through the gap between the Germans and "Division Centauro", north of Garet Abd el Rahman. (55)

    III./Panzer-Grenadier-Regiment 115 (less 10. Kompanie and three
    2./Panzerjäger-Abteilung 33   50mm guns)
    III./Panzer-Artillerie-Regiment 33
    2./Flak-Abteilung 33
    2./Flak-Abteilung 43
    Stab/Flak-Abteilung 617
    1. und 2./Flak-Abteilung 617

Commander: Major Lindemann

Engagements: Saw action in Tunisia, January 1943.

KAMPFGRUPPE PFEIFFER

On October 31, 1942, Afrikakorps informed 21. Panzer-Division that it was to form "a Kampfgruppe comprising approximately half of its tanks, anti-tank guns (self-propelled), medium field howitzers (self propelled) and 2cm Flak guns. 21. Panzer-Division designated Major Pfeiffer, commander of Panzerjäger-Abteilung 39, as commander of the Kampfgruppe. Since the Division had no serviceable medium field howitzers available, it was ordered to incorporate one light and one heavy battery into the Kampfgruppe. The "Pfeiffer Kampfgruppe" was to launch a counter-attack north of the El Alamein railway line in an attempt to relieve the encircled Panzer-Grenadier-Regiment 125". (56a)

A second "Kampfgruppe Pfeiffer" was formed on November 13, 1942, after the Afrikakorps had received "orders to form a strong bridgehead on the western edge of the Gazala position minefields, so that the 21. Panzer-Division could be passed through in the event of an enemy outflanking move from the south". (56b)

On January 30, 1943, Major Pfeiffer was again put in charge of a Kampfgruppe. The Gruppe was one of the two major Gruppen of 21. Panzer-Division ("Kampfgruppe Grün" was the other). The Gruppe was "further subdivided into "Nord", "Mitte" and "Süd" task forces". Major Pfeiffer was in actual command of "Gruppe Mitte". These Gruppen took part in the Faid-Maknassy actions of January 30 - February 3, 1943. "The small northern task force was to assume protection of the north flank and hold Sidi Khalif Pass. The central Gruppe was to attack Faid Pass from the east, while the somewhat weaker southern task force was expected to seize and block Ain Rebaou Pass and protect the southern flank against the French on Djebel Ksaira." (56c)

    (a) II./Panzer-Regiment 5
        one Panzerjäger-Kompanie
        2cm Flak-Batterie
        one leichte Artillerie-Batterie
        one schwerste Artillerie-Batterie

    (b) two Bataillone/Panzer-Grenadier-Regiment 104
        Panzer-Pionier-Bataillon 200

---

[55] KTB 15. Panzer-Division.

[56] (a) KTB Deutsches Afrikakorps.
    (b) 15. Panzer-Division report on the Battle of El Alamein and the retreat to Mersa El Brega.
    (c) Northwest Africa: Seizing the Initiative in the West, p. 390.

(c) Nord: Tunis-Bataillon 2
Mitte: III./Panzer-Grenadier-Regiment 104
Süd: II./Panzer-Grenadier-Regiment 104

Commander: Major Pfeiffer

Engagements: Battles at Gazala, Tobruk, El Alemein
Battle at Faid Pass (Tunisia, 1943)
German attack at Sbeitla (Tunisia, February 16-17, 1943)
Allied attacks at El Guettar (Tunisia, March 28 - April 1, 1943)
Last Allied offensive in Tunisia (May 3-13, 1943)

KAMPFGRUPPE REIMANN

Formed on or about February 8, 1943, as one of three assault Gruppen of 10. Panzer-Division. The Gruppe took part in "Unternehmen Frühlingswind" and was ordered to proceed along the Faid-Sbeitla highway and attack Sidi Bou Zid from the northeast. (57)

one Panzer-Kompanie (equipped with "Tiger")
one Bataillon/Panzer-Grenadier-Regiment 86
1./Panzerjäger-Abteilung 90 (one Zug)
one Zug/Panzer-Pionier-Bataillon 90
one Sturmgeschütz-Batterie/Panzer-Artillerie-Regiment 90
12. (Flak)/Panzer-Artillerie-Regiment 90 (one Zug)

Commander: Oberst Reimann

Engagements: Battle of Sidi Bou Zid (Tunisia, February 14-15, 1943).

GRUPPE SCHEMMEL

See "Kampfgruppe Mitte", October 23, 1942.

GRUPPE SCHIRMER

This Gruppe was formed in early April 1943. (58)

Panzer-Regiment 7
Jäger-Regiment "Hermann Göring"
Deckungstruppe

Commander: Oberst Schirmer

Engagements: The Axis attack towards Goubellat (Tunisia, April 20, 1943).

GRUPPE SCHMID

Formed on February 25, 1943, this Gruppe was subdivided into three Unter-Gruppen. The Gruppe was part of "Korpsgruppe Weber", and participated in the German offensive in northern Tunisia from February 26 - March 15, 1943. (59)

---

[57] Microfilm Publication T315, roll 570, frame 000357, and Northwest Africa: Seizing the Initiative in the West, p. 409.

[58] Northwest Africa: Seizing the Initiative in the West, p. 609.

[59] Microfilm Publication T315, Roll 2277, frame 000823, and Northwest Africa: Seizing the Initiative in the West, pp. 502-504.

(a) Gruppe Kleeberg:
  II./Panzer-Regiment 7 (one Kompanie)
  I./Panzer-Grenadier-Regiment 69
  I./Panzer-Artillerie-Regiment 90
  Afrika-Bataillon 33 (A 33)
  2./Pionier-Bataillon 334 (one Zug)

(b) Gruppe Koch:
  II./Jäger-Regiment "Hermann Göring"
  II./Artillerie-Regiment 190

(c) Gruppe Holzinger:
  Gebirgsjäger-Regiment 756
  Bataillon Mickley
  9./Artillerie-Regiment 90
  3./Pionier-Bataillon 334
  II./(ital.) 92

Commander: Oberst Josef Schmid

Engagements: German Offensive in northern Tunisia (February 26 - March 15, 1943).

GRUPPE SCHMIDT

This Gruppe was formed in late April 1943. (60)

  immobile units of 10. Panzer-Division
  immobile units of 21. Panzer-Division

Commander:

Engagements: Axis attack towards Goubellat (Tunisia, April 1943) and the last Allied offensive in Tunisia (May 3-13, 1943).

KAMPFGRUPPE SCHNEIDER-EICKE

See "Kampfgruppe Mitte" (January 11, 1943).

GRUPPE SCHUETTE/KAMPFGRUPPE SCHUETTE

This Gruppe was formed on September 3, 1941, for "Unternehmen Sommernachtstraum". It was to operate alongside "Kampfgruppe Stephan". (61)

  Panzerjäger-Abteilung 605 (less one Kompanie)
  Maschinengewehr-Bataillon 8
  Flak-Abteilung 606 (less one Kompanie)
  one Kompanie/Pionier-Bataillon 200
    plus convoys to salvage captured equipment and material

On February 14-15, 1943, prior to the battle of Sidi bou Zid, a "Kampfgruppe Schuette" was formed.

  one Abteilung/Panzer-Regiment 5
  Stab/Panzer-Grenadier-Regiment 104
  Panzerjäger-Abteilung 39/609 (sfl)
  I./Artillerie-Regiment 155 (1. and 3. Batterie)
  Flakkampftruppe (88mm)

---

[60] Northwest Afrika: Seizing the Initiative in the West, p. 611.

[61] KTB Panzerarmee Afrika, Microfilm Publication T315, roll 570, frame 000371, and Northwest Africa: Seizing the Initiative in the West, p. 409.

Commander: Major Schuette

Engagements: "Unternehmen Sommernachtstraum" (Libya, September 1941, and the battle of Sidi bou Zid (Tunisia, February 14-15, 1943).

GRUPPE SCHWERIN

This was the designation given to Maschinengewehr-Bataillon 8 while it was under the command of Oberstleutnant Graf Schwerin.

KAMPFGRUPPE SIEMENS

Formed on November 3, 1942, for operations during the withdrawal of the 15. Panzer-Division to new positions. (62)

    Panzer-Regiment 8
    Panzer-Pionier-Bataillon 33
    I./Artillerie-Regiment 33
    I./Flak-Regiment 43 ⎫ Luftwaffe
    II./Flak-Regiment 43 ⎭
       plus a few Italian tanks

Commander: Hauptmann Siemens

Engagements: Minor actions at El Alamein (Egypt, November 1942).

GRUPPE STENKHOFF

Formed prior to the battle of Sidi bou Zid, which took place on February 14-15, 1943. "Gruppe Stenkhoff" was one of two Gruppen which the 21. Panzer-Division formed.... "Kampfgruppe Schuette" was the other. (63)

    Stab/Panzer-Regiment 5
    one Abteilung/Panzer-Regiment 5
    Panzer-Grenadier-Regiment 104
    Stab III./Artillerie-Regiment 155
       le. Feldhaubitzen-Batterie
       7. Batterie
       8. Batterie
    two Flakkampftruppe (2 - 88mm)

Commander: Oberstleutnant Stenkhoff

Engagements: Battle of Sidi bou Zid (Tunisia, February 14-15, 1943).

KAMPFGRUPPE STEPHAN

This was the designation given to Panzer-Regiment 5 while it was under the command of Oberstleutnant Stephan. During the Sidi Rezegh battles of 1941, several Artillerie- and Flak-Batterien were attached to the unit.

GRUPPE STOLZ

Formed on or about January 13, 1943, by Generaloberst von Arnim to support his efforts to "obtain control over Djebel Mansour and over the main source of the water supply for Tunis". (64)

    large portions of the Italian 1. Superga-Division

---

[62] KTB 15. Panzer-Division.

[63] Northwest Africa: Seizing the Initiative in the West, p. 409.

[64] Ibid, p. 376.

Commander: Oberstleutnant Stolz

Engagements: Eilbote I (Battle for the eastern Dorsal Passes - Tunisia, January 18-25, 1943).

GRUPPE STOTTEN

This Gruppe participated in the actions around Kasserine Pass. (65)

I./Panzer-Regiment 8

Commander: Major Stotten

Engagements: Battle of Kasserine Pass (Tunisia, February 19-20, 1943).

GRUPPE STREMPEL/KAMPFGRUPPE STREMPEL

Formed on February 2, 1943, by Oberst Hildebrandt. The Gruppe was put under command of Oberst Hildebrandt's Chief of Staff, Oberstleutnant Strempel, with orders to defend positions near Maknassy "at all costs". (66)

Afrika-Bataillon 29
Aufklärungs-Abteilung 334
Aufklärungs-Abteilung 580
    miscellaneous units of Italian 50. Sonder-Brigade

Commander: Oberstleutnant Strempel

Engagements: The Allied attack on Maknassy (Tunisia, February 3 - 4, 1943).

KAMPFGRUPPE SÜD (OCT. 23, 1942)

This Gruppe, formed on October 23, 1942, was one of three formed by 15. Panzer-Division for defensive operations during the British offensive of October 23. The other Gruppen were "Mitte" and "Nord". (67)

II./Panzer-Grenadier-Regiment 115
II./Artillerie-Regiment 3
Stab/Artillerie-Regiment 33
II./Artillerie-Regiment 33
Stab/Bersaglieri-Regiment 12
554. Sturmgeschütz-Abteilung (italienisch)

Commander: Oberst Teege

Engagements: Saw action during the British offensive on October 23, 1942 (El Alamein, Egypt).

KAMPFGRUPPE SÜD (NOV. 3, 1942)

Formed on November 3, 1942, this Gruppe was to operate alongside "Kampfgruppe Nord" and set up new defensive positions during the retreat from El Alamein. (68)

---

[65] Ibid, p. 449.

[66] Ibid, p. 398.

[67] KTB 15. Panzer-Division, and Microfilm Publication T315, roll 666, frame 000053.

[68] 15. Panzer-Division report on the battle of El Alamein and the retreat to Mersa el Brega.

Panzerjäger-Abteilung 605
III./Artillerie-Regiment 33
1. and 2./Flak-Regiment 43 (Luftwaffe)

Commander: Hauptmann Fischer

Engagements: Various actions during the Axis retreat from El Alamein (Egypt, November/December 1942).

KAMPFGRUPPE SÜD (JAN. 11, 1943)

Formed on January 11, 1943, as one of four defensive Kampfgruppen Its orders were to: (a) prevent the enemy from surprising the German positions and rushing the commanding heights on the south bank of Wadi el Chief early in the operation; (b) block Wadi el Chief by fire, day and night; (c) and to keep in permanent close touch with the Aufklärungsgruppe and "Kampfgruppe Nord". (69)

Stab/Panzer-Grenadier-Regiment 115
II./Panzer-Grenadier-Regiment 115
3./Panzer-Artillerie-Regiment 33
5./Afrika-Artillerie-Regiment 1

Commander: Major Wissmann

Engagements: Defensive actions around Wadi el Chief (Tunisia, January 1943).

FLAKGRUPPE TOBRUK

This Gruppe was formed shortly after the capture of Tobruk, and its primary mission was the anti-aircraft defense of the Tobruk area. (70)

Flak-Regiment 114 (Luftwaffe)
Flak-Regiment 914

Commander: Major Hartmann

Engagements: This Gruppe, or elements thereof, saw action at Tobruk until shortly before Tobruk was recaptured in late 1942.

GRUPPE VOSS

Formed in November 1942, during the Panzerarmee's retreat from the El Alamein positions. The Gruppe was formed from units of 21. Panzer-Division as a reconnaissance unit. (71)

Commander: Major Voss

Engagements: Various small actions during the retreat from El Alamein (Egypt, November 1942).

GRUPPE WARRELMANN

This Gruppe, also known as "Abschnitt Ost", was formed on June 25, 1942 from units of 15. Panzer-Division. The Gruppe, along with "Gruppe Baade" and "Gruppe Dedekind", was under the overall command of Oberst Baade, with orders to hold protective positions near Sidi Mahmud. (72)

---

[69] KTB 15. Panzer-Division.

[70] KTB Panzerarmee Afrika.

[71] Walker, Alam Halfa and Alamein, p. 437.

[72] 15. Panzer-Division Administrative Diary.

II./Artillerie-Regiment 33 (less one Batterie)
III./Infanterie-Regiment 115
leichte Flak

Commander: Major Warrelmann

Engagements: Rommel's second offensive (began May 26, 1942).

ANGRIFFSGRUPPE WEBER

This Gruppe was formed on or about January 14, 1943. (73)

schwere Panzer-Abteilung 501
II./Panzer-Grenadier-Regiment 69
Stab/334. Infanterie-Division
Gebirgsjäger-Regiment 756
4./Artillerie-Regiment 334
8./Artillerie-Regiment 334

Commander: Oberst Weber

Engagements: "Unternehmen Eilbote".

KAMPFGRUPPE WEBER

This Kampfgruppe was formed by Generaloberst von Arnim on January 13, 1943, to support his main effort during the battle for the eastern Dorsal Passes (Tunisia, January 18-25, 1943). It was supported by transports from Pz.AOK 5, and was divided into 3 Unter-Gruppen. (74)

(a) two Panzer-Kompanien
Gebirgsjäger-Regiment 756
two Pionier-Züge
plus Artillerie and Flak units

(b) Panzergruppe Lüder
one Panzer-Kompanie
one Panzer-Grenadier-Bataillon
one Pionier-Zug
plus a Flak unit

(c) one Kompanie/Panzer-Abteilung 190
deutsch-italienisches Infanterie-Regiment
four Infanterie-Bataillone

Commander: Oberst Weber

Engagements: German attack on the eastern Dorsal Passes (Tunisia, January 18-25, 1943).

NOTE:
It is believed that the initial designation of "Angriffsgruppe Weber" was shortly changed to "Kampfgruppe Weber" after the introduction of additional units plus the above reorganization.

KORPSGRUPPE WEBER

In late February 1943, the designation "Korpsgruppe Weber" was given to all units which were in Oberst Weber's area of responsibility. The Gruppe was given the task of making "a spoiling attack on the Madjez el

---

[73] Microfilm Publication T315, roll 570, frame 000298.

[74] Northwest Africa: Seizing the Initiative in the West, P. 376.

Bab area" by Generalfeldmarschall Kesselring, shortly before February 22, 1943. "Weber's main objective was to be Bedja. Simultaneously he was to capture Medjez el Bab in a double envelopment operation which would also destroy Allied forces at Bon Aruda." (75)

"Korpsgruppe Weber" was divided into five Unter-Gruppen:
    (a) Panzergruppe Lang (77 tanks of which 14 were "Tiger")
    (b) Gruppe Eder (Grenadier-Regiment 755)
    (c) Gruppe Audorff (Grenadier-Regiment 754)
    (d) Gruppe Schmid (one Bataillon/10. Panzer-Division; Jäger-Regiment "Hermann Göring"; Gebirgs-Regiment 756)
    (e) Reserve-Gruppe (Grenadier-Regiment 47; two Infanterie-Bataillone)

Commander: Oberst Weber

Engagements: German offensive in northern Tunisia (February 22 - March 15, 1943), and the Peninsula Battles (Tunisia, May 3 - 13, 1943).

GRUPPE WECHMAR

"Gruppe Wechmar" was formed on November 15, 1941, when Aufklärungs-Abteilung 3 and 33 were placed under the command of Oberstleutnant Frhr. von Wechmar. The Gruppe's task was to reconnoiter south, past the Trigh el Abd and east, past the frontier wire in order to determine whether enemy forces were advancing past these lines. On November 26, 1941, a detachment of tanks was attached to this Gruppe for an attack against Sidi Omar. (76)

    Aufklärungs-Abteilung 3
    Aufklärungs-Abteilung 33

OBERSTLEUTNANT VON WECHMAR

Commander: Oberstleutnant Irnfried Frhr. von Wechmar

Engagements: The Sidi Rezeg battles (Libya, November 1941), and the assault on Sidi Omar (Libya, November 1941).

---

[75] Northwest Africa: Seizing the Initiative in the West, p. 381.

[76] KTB Deutsches Afrikakorps, and Agar-Hamilton & Turner, The Sidi Rezegh Battles 1941, p. 97.

GRUPPE WEICHSEL

This Gruppe was formed shortly before January 10, 1943. Major Wissmann assumed command on January 10, 1943. (77)

    II./Panzer-Grenadier-Regiment 115
    Stab I./Panzerjäger-Abteilung 33
    1/2 Kompanie/Panzerjäger-Abteilung 39
    one Batterie (88mm Flak)

Commanders: Major Weichsel
               Major Wissmann

Engagements:

GRUPPE WERNEYER

This Gruppe was formed on June 25, 1942, from units of 15. Panzer-Division. Its task was to act as divisional reserve for "Gruppe Warrelmann", "Besde" and "Dedekind". (78)

    one Zug/Panzer-Pionier-Bataillon 33
    I./Infanterie-Regiment 115 (two Kompanien)
    one leichte Batterie/Artillerie-Regiment 33

Commander: Major Werneyer

Engagements: Rommel's second offensive (began May 26, 1942).

KAMPFGRUPPE WISSMANN

See "Kampfgruppe Nord" (January 11, 1943). A second "Kampfgruppe Wissmann" was formed on January 21, 1943, for offensive operations around Jefren, Tunisia. (79)

    one Panzer-Abteilung
    one Kompanie/Panzer-Grenadier-Regiment 115
    two Artillerie-Batterien
    Flak-Batterie (88mm)

Commander: Major Wissmann

Engagements:

GRUPPE WITZIG

Formed on or after November 16, 1942, this Gruppe took part in the early battles of XC. Korps. On November 28, the Gruppe repulsed the Allied advance guard on the coast road and "destroyed 10 carriers, killed 30 men, led to the taking of 86 Allied prisoners and drove the remaining Allied troops back with about 50 others wounded". (80)

    4./Panzer-Abteilung 190
    three Kompanien/Fallschirmjäger-Pionier-Bataillon 11
    5./Artillerie-Regiment 190
    one Kompanie 4/7 Pak-Sfl.
    Flak-Batterie (20mm)

---

[77] KTB 15. Panzer-Division.

[78] 15. Panzer-Division Administrative Diary.

[79] KTB 15. Panzer-Division.

[80] Microfilm Publication T315, roll 2276, frame 00076, and Northwest Africa: Seizing the Initiative in the West, p. 306.

Commander: Major Witzig

Engagements: The Allied drive towards Tunis (Tunisia, November 24 - 28, 1942).

GRUPPE WOLF

Formed on or about March 27, 1943. This Gruppe took part in the battles during the first Allied attack on Fondouk. (81)

>Stab/Afrika-Schützen-Regiment 961
>I./Afrika-Schützen-Regiment 961
>II./Afrika-Schützen-Regiment 961
>>plus Panzerjäger and Artillerie units

Commander:

Engagements: Allied attack on Fondouk (Tunisia, March 27 - April 8, 1943).

KAMPFGRUPPE ZIEGLER

This Gruppe was formed on or about February 14, 1943, for employment in the actions after the battle of Sidi bou Zid. Its mission was to advance past the crossroads near Medenine and the Mareth Line, to cover the eastern flank of 10. Panzer-Division and be ready to push on as the situation developed. (82)

>two Bataillone/164. leichte Division
>one italienische Artillerie-Batterie

Commander: Major Ziegler

Engagements: Battle of Sidi bou Zig (Tunisia, February 14-15, 1943), and the battle of Kasserine Pass (Tunisia, February 18-20, 1943).

KAMPFGRUPPE I

This Kampfgruppe was formed from units of 15. Panzer-Division on November 20, 1941, with orders to "advance on either side of the Trigh Capuzzo, attack the enemy at Sidi Aziz and destroy him during the morning". The other Gruppen formed for similar operations were "II" and "III". (83)

>Panzer-Regiment 8
>I./Panzerjäger-Abteilung 33
>I./Artillerie-Regiment 33
>3./Flak-Regiment 33 (Luftwaffe)
>3./Pionier-Bataillon 33

OBERSTLEUTNANT HANS CRAMER

---

[81] Ibid, p. 580

[82] Ibid, p. 416.

[83] KTB 15. Panzer-Division.

Commander: Oberstleutnant Hans Cramer

Engagements: Various actions during the German offensive of November 1941.

KAMPFGRUPPE II

Formed from units of 15. Panzer-Division on November 20, 1941, and under the same orders as "I" and "III". (84)

    Panzerjäger-Abteilung 33 (less two Kompanien)
    Infanterie-Regiment 115
    III./Artillerie-Regiment 33 (less one Batterie)

Commander: Oberst Erwin Menny

Engagements: Various actions during the German offensive of November 1941.

KAMPFGRUPPE III

Formed from units of 15. Panzer-Division on November 20, 1941, and under the same orders as "I" and "II". (85)

    2./Panzerjäger-Abteilung 33
    Panzer-Pionier-Bataillon 33 (less one Kompanie)
    III./Artillerie-Regiment (less one Batterie)

Commander: Oberstleutnant Geissler

Engagements: Various actions during the German offensive of November 1941.

KAMPFGRUPPE 155

Formed on September 5, 1942, for defensive operations in the El Alamein area. (86)

    Panzer-Grenadier-Regiment 155 (less two Kompanien)
    Stab/Panzerjäger-Abteilung 190
    2./Panzerjäger-Abteilung 190
    one Batterie/Artillerie-Regiment 190
    Flak-Batterie 190

Commander: Major Kost

Engagements: Battles at El Alamein (Egypt, September 1942).

KAMPFGRUPPE 200

Formed on September 5, 1942, for defensive operations in the El Alamein area. (87)

    two Kompanien/Panzer-Grenadier-Regiment 155
    Stab/Panzer-Grenadier-Regiment 200
    1./Panzerjäger-Abteilung 190
    7./Flak-Regiment 25 (Luftwaffe)

---

[84] Ibid.

[85] Ibid.

[86] KTB 90. leichte Afrika-Division.

[87] Ibid.

Commander: Major Briel

Engagements: Battles at El Alamein (Egypt, September 1942).

KAMPFGRUPPE 361

Formed on September 5, 1942, for defensive operations in the El Alamein area. (88)

    I./Panzer-Grenadier-Regiment 200
    Panzer-Grenadier-Regiment 361
    I./Artillerie-Regiment 190 (one Batterie)
    9./Flak-Abteilung 25

Commander: Oberstleutnant Panzenhagen

Engagements: Battles at El Alamein (September 1942).

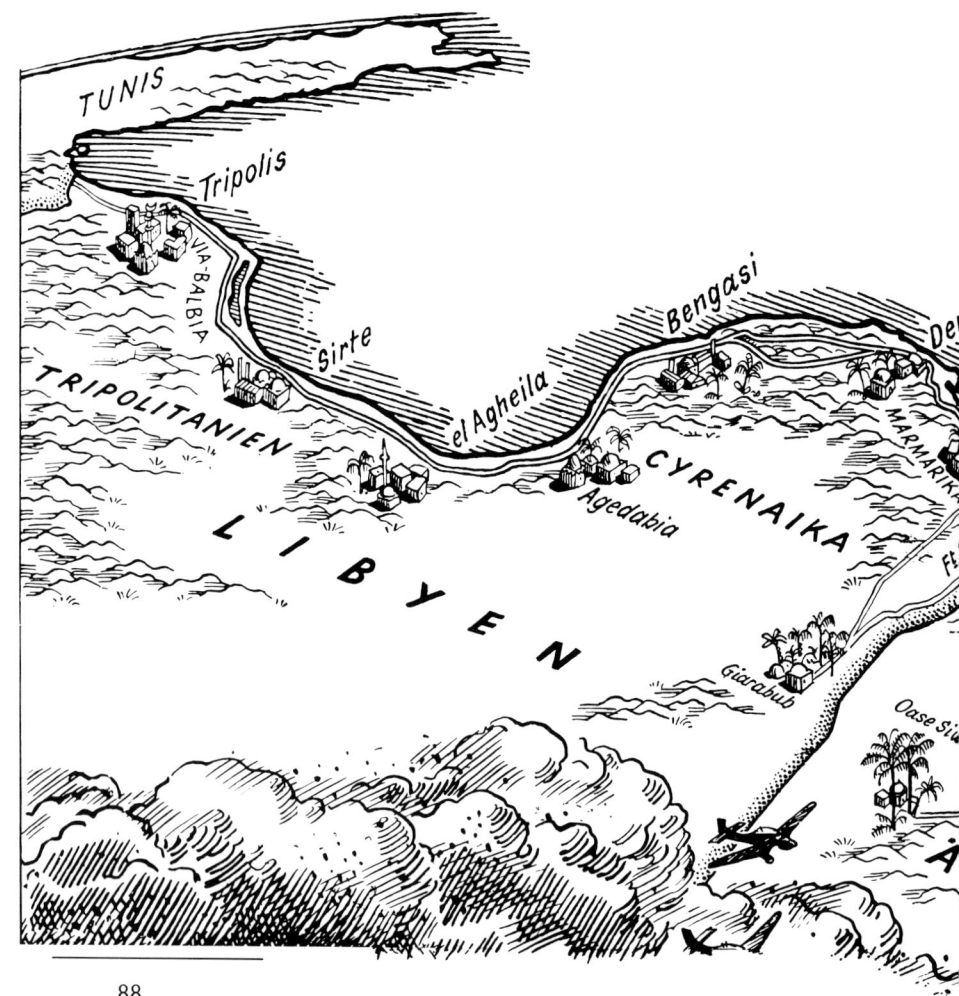

[88]Ibid.

[89]Order of Battle Chart, Panzerarmee Afrika, 15.4.42, and <u>KTB Panzerarmee Afrika</u>, August 28 and October 31, 1942.

SONDERVERBAND 288

Formation date unknown. Although this unit was not renamed "Panzer-Grenadier-Regiment Afrika" until October 31, 1942, its reorganization was approved on August 28, 1942 by Panzerarmee HQ Order Ia 5910/42 (secret). (89)

    Stabskompanie (mot)
        Kradmelde-Zug
        Aufklärungs-Zug
    2/288 (Gebirgs-Kompanie)(mot)
    3/288 (Infanterie-Kompanie)(mot)
    4/288 (Infanterie-Kompanie)(mot)
    5/288 (Panzerjäger-Kompanie)(mot)
    6/288 (Fla-Kompanie)(mot))
    7/288 (Pionier-Kompanie)(mot)
    Nachrichten-Kompanie (mot) 288
    kleine Kraftwagenkolonne (mot) 288
    Sanitäts-Kompanie (mot) 288
    Kraftwagenwerkstatt-Zug 288
    Betriebsstoffuntersuchungs-Trupp (mot) 288

Commander: Oberst Menton

Engagements: Saw action with 90. leichte Division throughout the African campaigns.

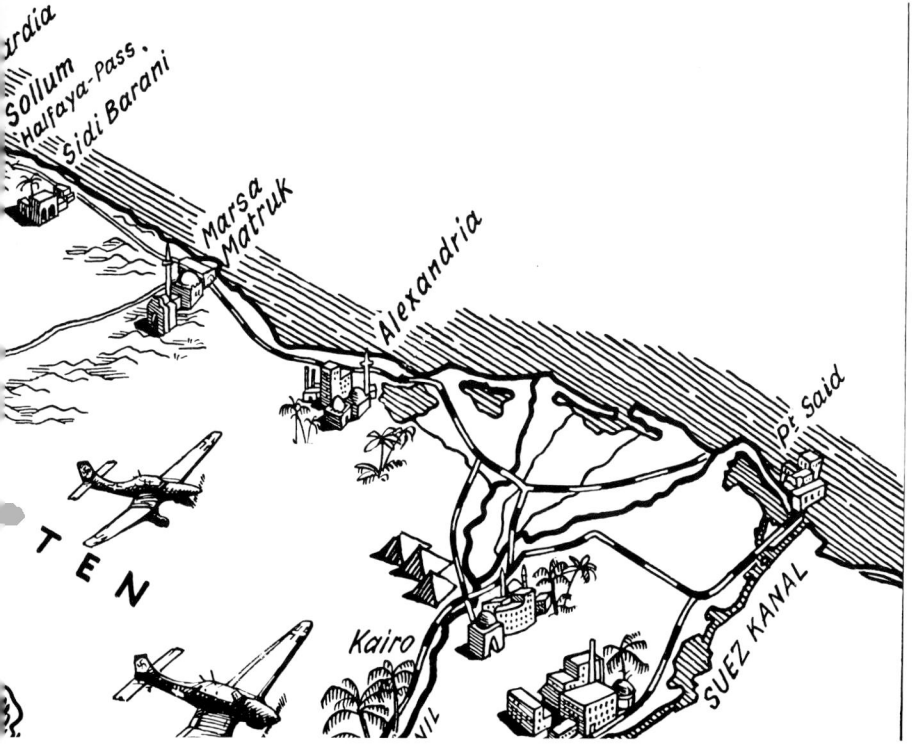

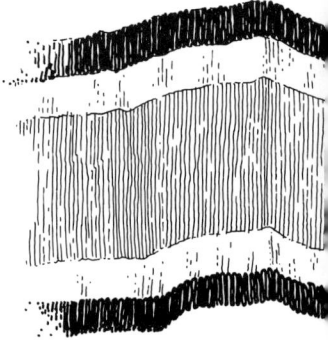

HAUPTMANN KÜMMEL

Knight's Cross Holders:
Africa 1941-1943

The following roster lists all Wehrmacht personnel who actively served in North Africa and who were awarded the Knight's Cross of the Iron Cross during their military career (1939-1945). This list is in alphabetical order with the appropriate rank at the time of receipt, the military position held, and the date of award.

NOTE:

332. Eichenlaub = 332nd individual to be awarded the Oakleaves to the K. C.
50. Schwerter = 50th individual to be awarded the Swords to the K. C.
24. Brillanten = 24th individual to be awarded the Oakleaves and Swords with Brilliants

Ahrendt, Oberfeldwebel Peter		Dec. 4, 1942
von Arnim, Generalleutnant Jürgen	Kdr. 17. Pz. Div.	Sept. 4, 1941
Audorff, Oberstleutnant Paul	Kdr. G.R. 754	May 13, 1943
Baade, Oberst Ernst-Günther	Kdr. S. R. 115	June 27, 1942
	402. Eichenlaub	Feb. 22, 1944
	111. Schwerter	Nov. 16, 1944
Bach, Hauptmann d. R. Wilhelm	Kdr. I/Schtz. Rgt. 104	July 9, 1941
von Barby, Oberstleutnant Hans-Levin	Rgt. Kdr. i. d. Pz.-Gruppe "Afrika"	Dec. 13, 1941
Bayerlein, Oberstleutnant i. G. Fritz	Chef Gen. Stab d. DAK	Dec. 26, 1941
	258. Eichenlaub	July 6, 1943
	81. Schwerter	July 20, 1944
Behr, Oberleutnant Winrich	Kp. Chef i. d. Pz. A. A. 3	May 15, 1941
Beukemann, Oberst Helmut	Rgt. Kdr. (Inf.)	May 14, 1941
von Bismarck, Oberst Georg	Kdr. Schtz. Rgt. 7	Sept. 29, 1940
Boeckmann, Oberst Helmut	Abt. Kdr. im A. R. 187	Aug. 6, 1942
Bolbrinker, Major Ernst	Abt. Kdr. (Pz.)	May 15, 1941
Borowietz, Oberstleutnant Willibald	Rgt. Kdr. (Schütz.)	July 24, 1941
	235. Eichenlaub	May 10, 1943
Bösel, Wachtm. Otto	Geschützfhr. i. d. I/Flak-Rgt. 41 (mot) Afrika	July 5, 1944
Böttcher, Generalmajor Karl	Kdr. 21. Pz. Div.	Dec. 13, 1941
Brenner, Leutnant d. R. Harro	Fhr. e. Inf. Kp.	April 16, 1943
Briel, Major Georg	Btl. Kdr. (Fla.-Afrika)	July 23, 1942
von Broich, Oberst Friedrich Frhr.	Kdr. 24. Pz. Brig.	Aug. 29, 1942

GENERALLEUTNANT VON ARNIM

HAUPTMANN BACH **OBERSTLEUTNANT VON BARBY** **OBERSTLEUTNANT BAYERLEIN**

OBERST FREIHERR VON BROICH

Bruer, Oberst Alfred	Rgt. Kdr. (Pz. Art.)	July 30, 1942
Bürker, Oberst i. G. Ulrich	Ia 10. Pz. Div.	Jan. 19, 1943
Buhse, Oberstleutnant Rudolf	Kdr. I. R. 47	Aug. 17, 1942
Cirener, Oberleutnant Willi	Chef 3./Pi. Btl. 33 (+May 1, 1941)	July 13, 1940
Cramer, Oberstleutnant Hans	Rgt. Kdr. (Pz.)	June 27, 1941
Crasemann, Oberstleutnant Eduard	Rgt. Kdr. (Art.)	Dec. 26, 1941
	683. Eichenlaub	Dec. 18, 1944
Crüwell, Generalmajor Ludwig	Kdr. 11. Pz. Div.	May 14, 1941
	34. Eichenlaub	Sept. 1, 1941
Ehle, Hauptmann Curt	Kp. Fhr. im Krdschtz.-Btl. 15	July 27, 1941
	673. Eichenlaub	Nov. 29, 1944
Everth, Hauptmann Wolfgang	Kp. Chef i. e. Pz.- A. A. 3	July 6, 1942
Ewert, Oberst Herbert	Kdr. Pz. Gren. Rgt. 104	Aug. 18, 1942
Fehn, Oberst Gustav	Kdr. S. R. 33	Aug. 5, 1940
Fenske, Major Günther	Abt. Kdr. im Pz.-Rgt. 8	Dec. 31, 1941
Fischer, Oberst Wolfgang	Kdr. 10. Schtz. Brig.	June 3, 1940
	152. Eichenlaub	Dec. 9, 1942
Frantz, Generalleutnant Gotthard	Kdr. 19. Flak-Div. (mot)	May 18, 1943
Franzisket, Oberleutnant Ludwig	Adj. I./J. G. 27	July 20, 1941
Fröhlich, Generalmajor Stefan	Kdr. K. G. 76	July 4, 1940
Fromm, Hauptmann Walter	Bttr. Chef i. d. I./Flak-Rgt. 33	July 9, 1941
Fullriede, Oberstleutnant Fritz	Rgt. Kdr. (Gren.)	April 11, 1943
	803. Eichenlaub	March 23, 1945
Fürguth, Oberst Helmuth	Kdr. Afrika-Art. Rgt. 1	July 28, 1942
Gause, Generalmajor Alfred	Chef. Gen. Stab Pz.-Gruppe "Afrika"	Dec. 13, 1941
Geissler, Oberst Erich	Kdr. I. R. 200 (mot)	July 29, 1942
Gellert, Oberleutnant Christian	Bttr. Fhr. i.d. I/Flak-Rgt. 43	June 11, 1943
Gierga, Hauptmann Kurt	Chef 5./Pz. Rgt. 5	June 30, 1941
Grün, Hauptmann Werner	Abt. Kdr. im Pz. Gr. Rgt. 5	Feb. 8, 1943
Gürke, Major Ernst	Abt. Kdr. (Flak)	Nov. 12, 1942
Halm, Grenadier Günther	Gren., in einem Pz. Gr. Rgt.	July 29, 1942
Harlinghausen, Major i.g. Martin	Chef Gen. Stab X. Flg. Korps	May 4, 1940
	8. Eichenlaub	Jan. 30, 1941
Hecht, Oberstleutnant Max	Kdr. Flak-Rgt. 135(mot)	March 7, 1942
Hecker, Oberstleutnant Hermann-Hans	Kdr. Pi. Btl. (mot) 29	Aug. 5, 1940
Heintze, Unteroffizier Erich	Geschfhr. (Flak)	March 7, 1942

OBERSTLEUTNANT CRASEMANN AND AN OFFICER OF HIS COMMAND.

GENERAL DER FLIEGER FRÖHLICH

GENERALMAJOR HARLINGHAUSEN

GRENADIER HALM

OBERST VON HERFF

HAUPTMANN EVERTH

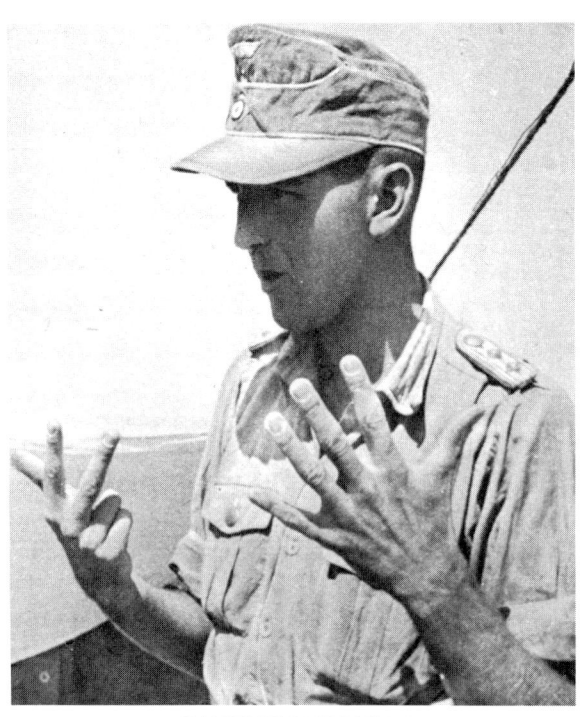

HAUPTMANN FROMM

HAUPTMANN GIERGA

GENERALMAJOR GAUSE

OBERSTLEUTNANT HECKER

von Herff. Oberst Maximilian*	Fhr. e. selbst. Kgru.	June 13, 1941
Heymer, Major Otto	Major, in einer Aufkl. Gr.	April 13, 1941
Hissmann, Major Josef	Major, in e. Fla.-Btl. d. Heeres	May 13, 1943
von Hösslin, Hauptmann Richard	Fhr. Pz. Aufkl, Abt. 33 in Afrika	July 23, 1942
Hoffmann von Waldau, Generallt. Otto	Fliegerfhr. Afrika	June 28, 1942
Homuth, Oberleutnant Gerhard	Staffelkpt. 3./ J. G. 27	June 14, 1941
Hübner, Gefreiter Arnold	Richtkan. (Flak)	March 7, 1942
Hudel, Hauptmann Helmut	Chef 1./Pz. Rgt. 7	May 27, 1942
	219. Eichenlaub	April 2, 1943
Jähnert, Leutnant Erhard	i. d. III./Stuka-Geschw. 3	May 18, 1943
Kesselring, General der Flieger Albert	Chef Luftlotte 1	Sept. 30, 1939
	78. Eichenlaub	Feb. 25, 1942
	15. Schwerter	July 18, 1942
	14. Brillanten	July 19, 1944
Kiehl, Hauptmann Rudolf	Hptm., im DAK Begleitkdo. Rommel	July 6, 1942
Kirchheim, Generalmajor Heinrich	Leiter d. Sonderstelle Lybien	May 14, 1941
Klärmann, Hauptmann Hans	Fhr. II./G. R. 361	Sept. 9, 1942
Kleemann, Oberst Ulrich	Kdr. 3. Schtz. Brig.	Oct. 13, 1941
	304. Eichenlaub	Sept. 16, 1943
Knabe, Oberstleutnant Gustav-Georg	Kdr. Kradschtz.-Btl. 15	June 1, 1941
Koch, Hauptmann Walter	Kdr. Fsch. Jäg. Sturm-Abt. Koch	May 10, 1940
von Koenen, Hauptmann Friedrich	Kdr. III./4. Rgt. "Brandenburg"	Sept. 16, 1943
Körner, Oberleutnant Friedrich	Stffhr. (J. G.)	Sept. 6, 1942
Krause, Oberst Fritz	Kdr. Flak-Rgt. 91 (mot)	Jan. 9, 1943
Kroseberg, Hauptmann Heinz	Stfkpt. in einer Seenotstaffel	June 19, 1942
Kümmel, Oberleutnant Johannes	Kp. Chef (Pz.)	July 9, 1941
	133. Eichenlaub	Oct. 11, 1942
Lang, Oberstleutnant Rudolf	Kdr. Pz. Jäg. Abt. 44	Aug. 23, 1941
Frhr. von Liebenstein, Gen. Maj. Kurt	Kdr. 164. le. Afrika-Division	May 10, 1943
Mahlke, Hauptmann Helmut	Kdr. III./Stuka-Geschw. 1	July 16, 1941
von Manteuffel, Oberst Hasso Freiherr	Kdr. S. R. 6	Dec. 31, 1941
	332. Eichenlaub	Nov. 23, 1943
	50. Schwerter	Feb. 22, 1944
	24. Brillanten	Feb. 18, 1945

*later Chief of "Personalamt der Waffen-SS."

GENERAL DER FLIEGER KESSELRING

OBERLEUTNANT KÜMMEL
"THE LION OF FORT CAPUZZO"

OBERLEUTNANT MARSEILLE

OBERST GERHARD MÜLLER

Marcks, Oberstleutnant Werner	Kdr. Schtz. Rgt. 155 i. d. Pz. Gruppe Afrika	Feb. 2, 1942
	593. Eichenlaub	Sept. 21, 1944
Marseille, Leutnant Hans-Joachim	Flgzgfhr. im J. G. 27 Afrika	Feb. 22, 1942
	97. Eichenlaub	June 6, 1942
	12. Schwerter	June 18, 1942
	4. Brillanten	Sept. 4, 1942
Medicus, Major Franz	Fhr. e. Kampfgr.	April 16, 1943
Melzer, Unteroffizier Reinhard	Geschfrh. i. d. I./Flak-Rgt. 33	June 30, 1941
Menny, Oberst Erwin	Kdr. 15. Schtz. Brig.	Dec. 26, 1941
Mickl, Oberst Johann	Fhr. Schtz. Rgt. 155 i. d. Pz. Gruppe Afrika	Dec. 13, 1941
	205. Eichenlaub	March 6, 1943
Mildebrath, Oberstleutnant Werner	Kdr. Pz. Rgt. 5	Aug. 12, 1942
Müller, Oberst Gerhard	Kdr. Pz. Rgt. 5	Sept. 9, 1942
Müller, Generalmajor Gottlob	Kom. Gen. u. Befelsh. d. Luftgaues Tunis	June 17, 1943

GENERALMAJOR RAMCKE, GREETED BY HITLER AT THE FÜHRERHAUPTQUARTIER ON DECEMBER 1, 1942, SHORTLY AFTER HIS RETURN FROM NORTH AFRICA.

Müller, Hauptmann Klaus	Chef 6./Pz. Rgt. 2	Oct. 7, 1942
Müncheberg, Oberleutnant Joachim	Stfkpt. im J. G. 26 "Schlageter"	Sept. 14, 1940
	12. Eichenlaub	May 7, 1941
	19. Schwerter	Sept. 9, 1942
Musculus, Major d.R. Friedrich-Heinrich	Fhr. Pz. Jäger-Rgt. 111	Feb. 17, 1943

HAUPTMANN MÜNCHEBERG
(HERE AN OBERLEUTNANT)

GENERAL DER PANZERTRUPPE NEHRING

MAJOR d. R. MUSCULUS

GENERALMAJOR NEUFFER

Nehring, Generalmajor Walther K.	Kdr. 18. Pz. Div.	July 24, 1941
	383. Eichenlaub	Feb. 8, 1944
	124. Schwerter	Jan. 22, 1945
Neuffer, Generalmajor Georg	Kdr. 20. Flak-Div.	Aug. 8, 1943
Neumann-Silkow, Oberst Walter	Kdr. 8. Schtz. Brig.	Aug. 5, 1940
Panzenhagen, Oberstleutnant Albert	Kdr. Pz. Gren. Rgt. 361	Oct. 2, 1942
Plinzner, Oberleutnant Peter-Paul	Chef 5./Pz. Rgt. 27	Oct. 20, 1941
Ponath, Oberstleutnant Gustav	Kdr. MG. Btl. 8	April 13, 1941
Ramcke, Generalmajor Bernhard Hermann	Kdr. Fsch. Jäg.-Sturm-Rgt.	Aug. 21, 1941
	145. Eichenlaub	Nov. 13, 1942
	99. Schwerter/20. Brillanten	Sept. 20, 1944
von Ravenstein, Oberst Johann	Kdr. S. R. 4	June 3, 1940
Redlich, Oberleutnant Karl-Wolfgang	Stfkpt. 1./J. G. 27	July 9, 1941
Reissmann, Hauptmann Werner	Btl. Fhr. im Pz. G. R. 104	July 28, 1942
Rettemeier, Hauptmann Josef	Kdr. Pz. Abt. 5	Dec. 5, 1943
	425. Eichenlaub	March 13, 1944
Riepold, Hauptmann Josef	Kp. Chef (Pz. Rgt. 5)	July 29, 1942
Rocholl, Oberleutnant Rolf	Kp. Fhr. im Pz. Rgt. 5	July 28, 1942
	287. Eichenlaub	Aug. 31, 1943
Rödel, Oberleutnant Gustav	Stfkpt. 4./J. G. 27	June 22, 1941
	255. Eichenlaub	June 20, 1943
Rommel, Generalmajor Erwin	Kdr. 7. Pz. Div.	May 27, 1940
	10. Eichenlaub	March 20, 1941
	6. Schwerter	Jan. 20, 1942
	6. Brillanten	March 11, 1943
Ryll, Oberleutnant Wolfgang	Kp. Fhr. im Pz. Rgt. 7	Oct. 13, 1941
Schmid, Generalmajor Josef "Beppo"	Kdr. Div. H. G.	May 21, 1943
Schroer, Leutnant Werner	Stffhr. 8./J. G. 27	Oct. 24, 1942
	268. Eichenlaub	Aug. 2, 1943
	144. Schwerter	April 19, 1945
Schulte-Heuthaus, Oberstleutnant Hermann	Kdr. Kradschtz. Btl. 25	Jan. 23, 1942
Schulz, Oberfeldwebel Otto	Flgzgfhr. i. d. II./J. G. 51	Feb. 22, 1942
Schwabach, Oberleutnant Theodor	Bttr. Chef i. d. I./Flak-Rgt. 33	June 30, 1940
Schweiger, Oberleutnant Franz	Chef 8./Flak. Rgt. 25	Feb. 14, 1942
Graf von Schwerin, Oberst Gerhard	Kdr. I. R. 76 (mot)	Jan. 17, 1942
	240. Eichenlaub	May 17, 1943
	41. Schwerter	Nov. 11, 1943
Seidensticker, Major August	Fhr. Schw. Pz. Abt. 501	July 18, 1943
Senfft von Pilsach, Oberleutnant Ott-Friedrich	Chef 4./Pz. Rgt. 5	June 30, 1941
Sigel, Hauptmann Walter	Kdr. I./Stuka-Geschw. 76	July 21, 1940
	116. Eichenlaub	Sept. 2, 1942

HAUPTMANN ROCHOLL

OBERST GRAF VON SCHWERIN
(HERE A GENERALLEUTNANT)

GENERALFELDMARSCHALL ROMMEL AT THE SPORTSPALAST IN BERLIN ON SEPTEMBER 30, 1942 (NOTE GENERALFELDMARSCHALL KEITEL (CHEF OKW) IN BACKGROUND).

Graf von Sponeck, Oberst Theodor	Kdr. Schtz. Rgt. 11	Sept. 12, 1941
Stahlschmidt, Leutnant Hans-Arnold	Stffhr. (J. G. 27)	Aug. 20, 1942
	365. Eichenlaub	Jan. 3, 1944
Stiefelmayer, Oberleutnant Otto	Chef 1./Pz. Rgt. 8	July 12, 1942
Stolz, Oberstleutnant Harald	Kdr. Kradschtz. Btl. 43	Aug. 28, 1942
Stotten, Leutnant Hans-Günther	Fhr. 1./Pz. Rgt. 3	July 4, 1940
	236. Eichenlaub	May 10, 1943
Streich, Oberst Johannes	Kdr. Pz. Rgt. 15	Jan. 31, 1941
Struckmann, Oberleutnant Rudolf	im Stab d. S. R. 115	Jan. 21, 1942

Stumme, Gen. d. Kav. Georg	Kom. Gen. XXXX. A. K.	July 19, 1940
von Thoma, Generalmajor Wilhelm Ritter	Kdr. 20. Pz. Div.	Dec. 31, 1941
von Vaerst, Oberst Gustav	Kdr. 2. Schtz. Brig.	July 30, 1940
Voigtsberger, Major Heinrich	Kdr. M. G. Btl. 2	July 9, 1941
	351. Eichenlaub	Dec. 9, 1943
Warrelmann, Oberst Heinrich	Kdr. G. R. 502	April 16, 1944
	555. Eichenlaub	Aug. 19, 1944
von Wechmar, Oberstleutnant Irnfried Frhr.	Kdr. Pz. A. A. 3	April 13, 1941
Wendt, Hauptfeldwebel Wilhelm	Kp. Feldw. 5./Pz. Rgt. 5	June 30, 1941
Westphal, Oberst i. G. Siegfried	Ia i. d. deutsch-ital. Pz. Armee	Nov. 29, 1942
Witzig, Oberleutnant Rudolf	i. d. Fsch. Jäg. Sturm-Abt. Koch	May 10, 1940
	662. Eichenlaub	Nov. 25, 1944
Woldenga, Major Bernhard	Kdr. J. G. 77	July 5, 1941
Wolz, Oberst Alwin	Kdr. Flak-Rgt. 135 (mot)	June 4, 1943
Zecherle, Leutnant Konrad	Zugfhr. 1./Pz. Aufkl. Abt. 190	May 10, 1943
Ziegler, Generalleutnant Heinz	Stab H. Gr. Afrika	April 16, 1943

OBERLEUTNANT SENFFT VON PILSACH

HAUPTFELDWEBEL WENDT

HANNY WEBER AND GRETE FOCK, IRON CROSS RECIPIENTS FOR SERVICE IN NORTH AFRICA (NOTE "AFRIKAKORPS" CUFF TITLE).

Special Units in North Africa

Military Field Police

The Military Field Police (Feldgendarmerie) was the equivalent of the British and U.S. Armys' Military Police, whose mission was the supervision and regulation of traffic, the control of ports and air fields, and the discipline of the men located in rear areas. These police units wore the standard tropical-issue uniform in North Africa, but with the following special insignia: an aluminum embroidery on brown "Feldgendarmerie" cuff title, a "Feldgendarmerie" duty gorget (with luminous eagle, bosses and lettering), an orange on olive or tan Police-style arm eagle with black swastika (the eagle was in silver embroidery for officers) and orange Waffenfarbe. When in shirt sleeve dress, only the duty gorget was worn. All Feldgendarmerie personnel had normal Army rank designations.

"FELDGENDARMERIE" CUFF TITLE

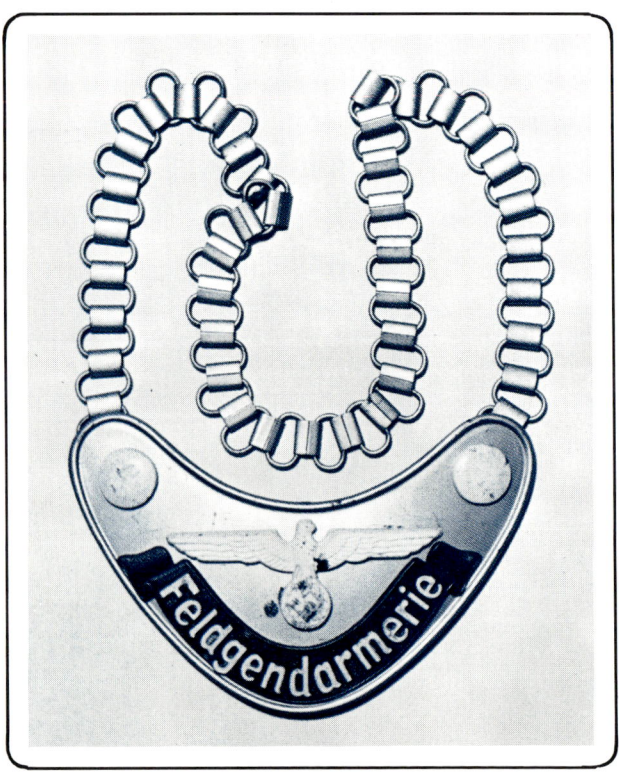

"FELDGENDARMERIE" DUTY GORGET

Secret Field Police

On September 1, 1941, the Secret Field Polize (Geheime Feldpolizei) was set up in the jurisdiction of Panzergruppe Afrika and XXI. italienisches Armeekorps, as a counter-espionage and intelligence agency. As a service branch of the Army, this unit was assigned to Ic/AO (Intelligence Officer - Abwehroffizier) of the Gruppe Staff.

The GFP's principal mission was to prevent sabotage and espionage, graft, damage to Army property and the undermining of morale. It also acted as a fact-finding organ for court-martial trials and aided in the tracing down of deserters. In addition, the GFP worked hand-in-hand with the Feldgendarmerie in carrying out measures designed to maintain discipline.

The GFP officials wore the standard uniform of the Wehrmachtbeamten (the tropical-issue uniform with dark green Waffenfarbe underlay on the shoulder straps and bluish-dark green collar patches), but with a secondary Waffenfarbe of light blue and metalic "GFP" letters in a gold or silver color on the shoulder straps.

While operating in civilian clothing, members of the GFP were required to carry a light green identification card with their affixed photograph. This card plus a service badge, was issued by their command headquarters. Members in plain clothes were only permitted to stop soldiers for their identification. In cases where difficulties arose or an arrest was necessary, a higher ranking official had to be summoned.

NOTE:
THIS RANK WOULD HAVE BEEN ASSIGNED TO OKW OR OKH, AND NOT IN NORTH AFRICA.

FELDPOLIZEICHEF DER WEHRMACHT/ HEERESFELDPOLIZEICHEF

    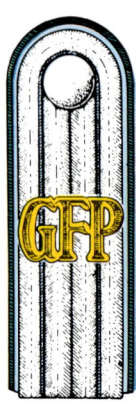

OBERFELDPOLIZEI-DIREKTOR   FELDPOLIZEI-DIREKTOR   FELDPOLIZEI-KOMMISSAR (AFTER FEBRUARY 2, 1944 FELDPOLIZEIINSPEKTOR)   FELDPOLIZEI-OBERSEKRETÄR   FELDPOLIZEI-SEKRETÄR

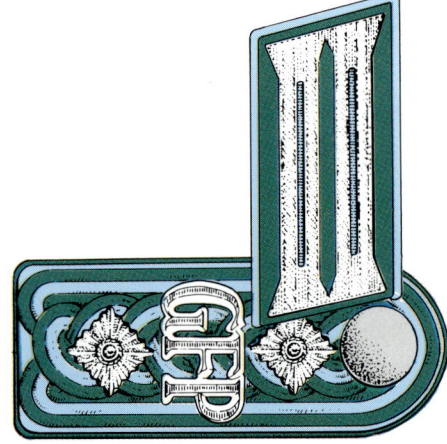

NOTE:
NO NCO COLLAR "TRESSE" WAS WORN WITH THIS RANK.

FELDPOLIZEIASSISTENT (NCO RANK)
(IN EXISTANCE BEFORE JUNE 4, 1943)

SS/SD Einsatz-Kommando Tunis

Although it has long been known that no Waffen-SS combat troops were committed to the North African campaign, it is interesting to note that the SD (Sicherheitsdienst - Security Police) was indeed present on the African continent during the desert war. Little is known of this SS agency stationed in Tunis but its power was far-reaching. SD Einsatz-Kommando Tunis had complete power to direct and inspect the French Police in Tunisia.[1] Their mission was the destruction of North African spy networks, the elimination of black marketeers, the tracking down of subversives, etc. It is most probable that the tropical uniform with SS insignia or civilian clothing was worn during this Tunisian assignment.

NOTE:
SS personnel who fulfilled the stipulations for the "Afrika" cuff title, were permitted to wear it with the SS uniform.

The Brandenburger

The first small Brandenburg unit arrived in Africa in June 1941, with its basic mission being reconnaissance and the collecting of information on known enemy bases and enemy intentions. A Brandenburg company which was designated "Sonderverband 287" was concurrently formed at the Potsdam Ruinenberg-Kaserne, and later trained in desert warfare in southern Greece. The formation of its sister unit, "Sonderverband 288", was completed a short time later and designated as an independent motorized Kampfgruppe. Originally, these two companies were destined for Iraq in early 1942, where they were to make their way to the Suez Canal region and team up with Arab sympathizers. This never came to be, however, for Sonderverband 287 was soon diverted to Greece and Russia to combat the ever increasing partisan activity there, and Sonderverband 288, commanded by Oberst Menton, was transferred directly to Africa.

> NOTE:
> Sonderverband 288 was later to become an official unit of the Wehrmacht for its excellent fighting record in Africa. It fought with the 90. leichte Afrika-Division and officially became Panzergrenadier-Regiment (mot) Afrika on October 31, 1942.

Another tropical company (Tropen-Kompanie Brandenburg) was organized under the command of Oberleutnant Fritz von Koenen, a farmer's son from southwest Africa. This company's personnel were hand-picked by von Koenen and included Germans who had lived abroad and spoke at least one foreign language fluently. The first half of the 300 man company arrived in Africa in October of 1941. Its first missions were the finding of enemy bases, the destruction of important objectives and disruptive activities behind enemy lines.

Originally Rommel had not supported this form of warfare for he respected the chivalry of the British and wished to conduct his campaign in a like manner, but with superior tactics and prowess. It was not till after the attempted British commando operation[2], which called for the capture or death of Rommel and the destruction of his headquarters, that he openly supported the entrance of Brandenburg-style tactics. Numerous small

---

[1] Microfilm Publication T315, roll 416, frame 8731171, and T315, roll 2278, frames 000486 and 000488.

[2] "The Long Range Desert Group", a special British commando unit created for acts of sabotage and intelligence in the desert, was extremely active behind the Afrikakorps lines..... including the blowing up of supplies, the destruction of gasoline transports and surprise raids on airfields. Its German counterpart were the Brandenburger.

commando raids were carried out by both sides in the span of the following year. During their daring missions behind British lines, the Brandenburger penetrated almost to Cairo, disrupted the Allied transportation network, installed listening posts and inflicted heavy casualties. Although they were fierce adversaries, the British and German commandos had the highest respect for the other's ingenuity and courage.

On December 5, 1942, two half companies from I./Regiment 4 Brandenburg were flown to Tunis. Three weeks later, 20 men of this force were flown from the airfield at Bizerta in three cargo gliders, each of which was towed by a Ju 52. Upon landing, they successfully destroyed the railroad bridge at Sidi bou Baker over the Wadi-el-Kbir and escaped. On the same day, another glider with ten Brandenburg commandos landed in southern Tunisia where they were to destroy a major bridge north of Kasserine. This group was captured, however, by French troops shortly after crash-landing. On January 18, 1943, a major supply line was temporarily cut by the destruction of the bridge over the Wadi-el-Melah.... once again, the work of Brandenburg.[3]

The "tropical company" was expanded to battalion strength in January of 1943, and was then designated "Abteilung von Koenen". This unit participated in the last German operational attack in North Africa on February 14, 1943, when it launched an attack against the defensive American line near Sidi-bou-Zid. The Americans were pushed back from their positions leaving behind 27 tanks, 23 pieces of artillery, nearly 100 trucks loaded with munitions, plus other assorted equipment. A total of 700 prisoners was also taken in this last-ditch effort.

"Abteilung von Koenen" did not resign itself to the reality of defeat as "Heeresgruppe Afrika" capitulated in mid-May, 1943. Therefore, with the aid of confiscated fishing boats and rubber dinghies, the Abteilung disembarked from Kap-Bon-Halbinsel and crossed the Mediterranean Sea to southern Italy where they again assembled. After a short recuperation, the Abteilung was once more sent into action, this time in the Balkans against mounting partisan pressure. Oberleutnant Fritz von Koenen, commander of this elite commando unit, was killed in action on August 22, 1944, in Croatia.[4]

NOTE:
When on missions, the Brandenburger wore either his own tropical uniform, a captured British uniform, or any appropriate costume which enabled him to successfully complete his mission.

---

[3] Werner Brockdorff, <u>Geheimkommandos des Zweiten Weltkrieges</u>, (München - Wels: Verlag Welsermühl München, 1967), p. 428.

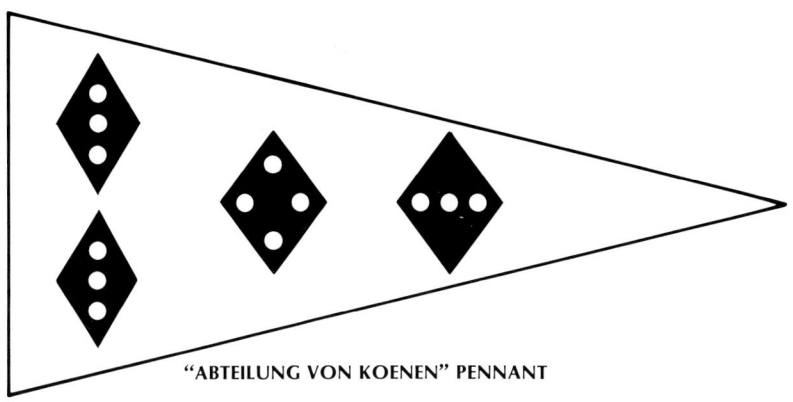
"ABTEILUNG VON KOENEN" PENNANT

The Ramcke Parachute Brigade

With the arrival of autumn 1942, the situation Rommel had wanted to avoid had transpired. ... the Germans were stopped and pinned-down before El Alamein. The British grew increasingly stronger with each passing day as new divisions arrived from Syria, India and Iraq. Simultaneously, however, Rommel received only the 164. leichte Afrika-Division plus Fallschirm-Brigade Ramcke (the Ramcke Parachute Brigade) to bolster his forces, and only one-third of the needed supplies.

The Ramcke Brigade[5] had originally been formed for the planned invasion of Malta, but the situation in Africa soon found it being transferred from Greece to the Libyan desert. On July 15, 1942, Generalmajor Ramcke arrived with the first of his staff and immediately took over command of the few active elements of his Brigade which had arrived some time earlier. Up to this time, they had been assigned to the 15. Panzer-Division. The Brigade's first battalion, under Major Kroh, arrived on August 4; the second, under Major von der Heydte, arrived on August 10; and the third, under Major Hübner, arrived at dusk on August 17. Officially, on August 15, the Brigade was placed directly under Panzerarmee Afrika, and was to serve as the headquarters staff for all future Fallschirmjäger (parachute) units transferred to Africa.[6]

---

[4] Helmuth Spaeter, Die Geschichte des Panzerkorps Grossdeutschland Band III, (Duisburg-Ruhrort: Traditionsverband Grossdeutschland, 1958), pp. 78-79.

[5] At this time, the Brigade consisted of four Jäger-Bataillone, one Artillerie-Abteilung, one Panzerjäger-Kompanie and one Pionier-Kompanie.

[6] KTB, Deutsches Afrikakorps, August 14, 1942.

Because the Brigade was transported to Africa solely by air, it had few vehicles of its own. Therefore, Flak-Regiment 135 was detailed to transport the parachute units, as they arrived, to the front and then use their vehicles to supply the Brigade.[7] As the battalions landed, they were immediately transported to their defensive positions on the El Alamein front. The Brigade was positioned on the southern portion of the front with both the italienische Division "Trento" and the X. italienisches Korps.

ROMMEL VISITING RAMCKE'S POSITIONS ON THE EL ALAMEIN LINE.

The long-awaited British offensive was unleashed on October 23, with a destructive five hour barrage from over one thousand pieces of artillery. Rommel's "Devil's Gardens" (in-depth mine fields) were ploughed up by the heavy concentration of fire and corridors were created through them.

---

[7] KTB Deutsches Afrikakorps, August 19, 1942.

In addition, R.A.F. bombers combined with the artillery to soften up the German-Italian positions. The front cracked and started to crumble under the massive pressure put upon it by Montgomery and his 8th Army.[8] By November 3, the British were advancing all along the front and Rommel was forced to abandon his El Alamein positions and withdraw. The remains of the Panzerarmee retreated through the desert and along the coast to the Fuka positions, sixty miles behind El Alamein. But constant pressure forced Rommel to retreat even further, this time onto Libyan soil.

The German infantryman was the individual to suffer most during this retreat, for little or no transportation was available for him. He was, therefore, left to his own fate. This same situation faced the Italians and even Ramcke's elite Parachute Brigade to the south. In Rommel's headquar-

THE RAMCKE BRIGADE RETREATING TO THE WEST.

ters, it had been reported that the X. italienisches Korps had been over-run and taken prisoner, and it was assumed that the same fate had been shared by Ramcke and his men. This was not to be the case, however, for on November 3, the Brigade had sized up the situation and had begun its march westward, with an artillery detachment covering its retreat. Just before Fuka on November 6, the parachutists observed a British transport column bivouacked for the night. Without firing a shot, they crawled to the vehicles and made off with them. Unknowingly, Ramcke's men had highjacked a complete supply column for a British armored unit, which netted

---

[8]It is estimated that the British had approximately 1,100 tanks with which to destroy Rommel's armored force of 210....a ratio of 5 1/2 to 1. Of these German tanks, only 30 were Panzer IVs; the majority were Panzer IIIs, half of which were equipped with the outmoded short barrel. Of the 300 available Italian tanks, most were decrepit and barely fit for action.

them serviceable trucks plus their precious contents of fuel, water, food and cigarettes. Within a short time, Ramcke and his fully-motorized Brigade rejoined Rommel's retreating Panzerarmee. A total of 200 enemy-infested miles had been covered in this episode. The Brigade was then sent to the rear area for a well-earned rest.

For this remarkable feat of leading his entire Brigade to safety, Ramcke was returned to Germany and awarded the oakleaves to his Knight's Cross of the Iron Cross on November 15.

Another major blow to the German North African campaign was the surprise American landings in Morocco and Algeria. The Germans now had Montgomery pressing them from the east and Eisenhower from the west. They felt that it was now essential that Tunisia be occupied, for its western border offered the best available defensive positions against the Allies advancing through Algeria. It was decided that the fastest way to take Tunisia was with a lightning thrust from the air. Therefore, on November 11, Fallschirmjäger-Regiment 5 under the command of Oberstleutnant Koch, was flown to Tunis from Naples to form a German bridgehead.

KOCH'S PARATROOPERS WERE THE FIRST GERMAN TROOPS IN TUNISIA.

The Barenthin-Regiment, named after its commander, Oberst Walter Barenthin, was hastily formed from various parachute units and also committed to the Tunisian campaign. It was motorized and well-equipped and on November 29, met the Americans at Mateur and Tebourba and repulsed them. The Germans had won the race for Tunis and now had to hold their bridgehead. As the weeks passed, the paratroop regiments were continually called upon to contain Eisenhower's advancing army.

By May 7, it was obvious that Tunis was lost as was the North African campaign, for Armeegruppe Afrika had been totally defeated. All that remained were a few fighting units, among which were remnants of the former Ramcke Parachute Brigade[9] and the Koch-Regiment, which continued to hold their defensive positions north of Mateur. On May 12, Generaloberst von Arnim capitulated on behalf of the staffs of Armeegruppe Afrika and the Afrikakorps. Most of Ramcke's former Brigade who survived the vicious last months of the campaign, marched into captivity on May 13.

NOTE:
The German paratrooper in Africa wore the Luftwaffe tropical tunic, shirt and bloused pants with a large buttoned pocket on the upper left leg. The helmet was painted tan. Both patterns of the camouflage jump smock were worn in the African campaign as well as the tan version (these had originally been destined for use in the invasion of Malta and for operations near the Suez).

Vehicles assigned to the Ramcke Parachute Brigade carried the black on white kite-shaped Brigade symbol at right (sometimes white on black). The small letter at the lower right corner of the symbol indicated the battalion and its commander: "K" - Kroh, "vH" - von der Heydte, "H" - Hübner, "K" again - Kagerer, and "B" - Burkhardt (Fallschirmjäger-Lehrbataillon).

---

[9] At this time, Major von der Heydte was commanding the unit since General Ramcke had remained in Europe to form the 2. Fallschirmjäger-Division.

The German Red Cross Nurse

The German Red Cross nurse in World War II braved aerial bombardment, artillery barrages and countless other hardships during the fulfillment of her duties. In North Africa, some died and a number were wounded and decorated for their bravery under fire. Four nurses were awarded the Iron Cross, 2nd Class, for heroic service. They were Ilse Schulz and Grete Fock (Mutterhaus Kiel) and Hanny Weber and Geolinde Münch (Mutterhaus München).

HANNY WEBER AND GEOLINDE MÜNCH

In addition to the basic nurses' uniform, a tan tropical uniform was issued to the nurses as they prepared for their African assignment. It consisted of a white cotton or linen nurses' cap, a single breasted jacket and a pleated skirt. A tropical helmet, covered with tan gabardine, could be worn directly over the nurses' cap. The gabardine jacket had one row of four buttons and two breast and two side pockets. The side pockets had two buttons each. The jacket's belt was of the same material and color as that of the jacket. A white polo-blouse with short sleeves was worn under the jacket. It could be worn open or closed at the neck, but when worn closed, a Red Cross brooch was worn at the throat. An overcoat was also issued for the cool desert evenings and was of a sand-grey gabardine. It was single breasted and had two breast pockets and two side pockets plus a belt. Long or knee-length grey stockings were worn with brown shoes.

NOTE:
Those Red Cross members who met the requirements were permitted to wear the "Afrikakorps" cuff title and later the "Afrika" campaign decoration.

GRETE FOCK

Field Post Service

Field Post personnel stationed in North Africa wore the standard tropical uniform with distinctive lemon-yellow and dark green collar patches and shoulder straps. They were classified as Wehrmachtbeamten and bore the burden of collecting, transporting and distributing the German military mail.

{ 2 gold pips: Feldoberpostdirektor/Armeefeldpostmeister
1 gold pip: Feldoberpostrat/Armeefeldpostmeister
no pips: Feldpostrat/Armeefeldpostmeister

{ no pips: Feldpostamtsrat/Feldpostamtmann

2 gold pips: Feldpostoberinspektor/Feldpostmeister
1 gold pip: Feldpostinspektor/Feldpostmeister/and later Feldpostobersekretär
no pips: Feldpostobersekretär/and later Feldpostsekretär

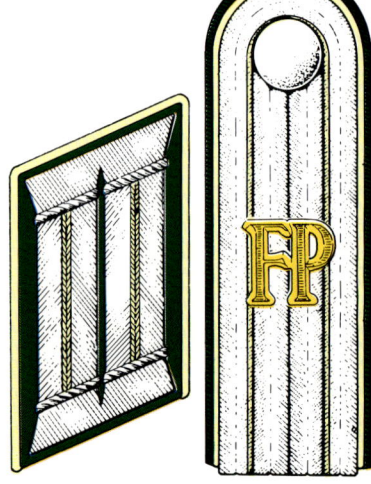

2 silver pips: Feldpostassistent
1 silver pip: Feldpostoberschaffner/ Feldpostschaffner
no pips: Feldpostbote

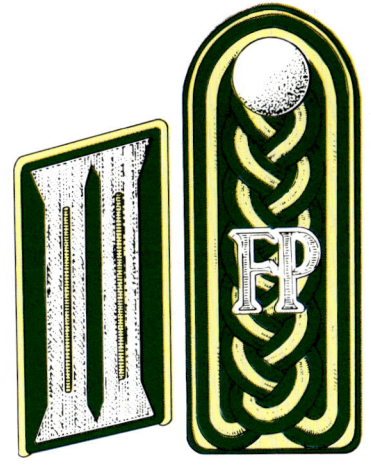

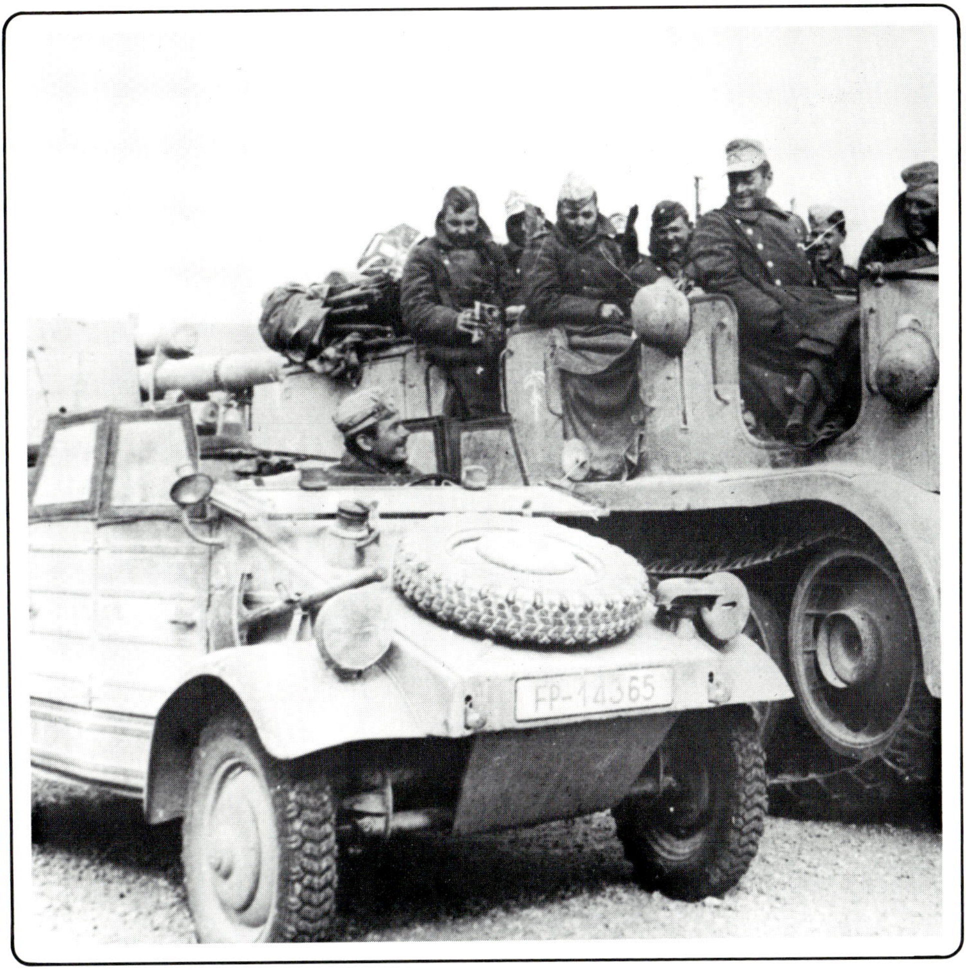

THE NATIONAL ARCHIVES

THE "FP" REGISTRATION PLATE INDICATES THAT THIS VOLKSWAGEN WAS USED BY THE FELDPOST.

GEORGE PETERSEN COLLECTION

Tropical Uniforms and Insignia

The first issues of tropical clothing were supplied through the Chief of the Supply and Administration Office of OKH in late 1940. The basic tropical uniform was the same for all ranks and throughout the campaign, remained quite standardized with few variations. The supply of available uniform parts dwindled from time to time, however, due to disrupted German supply lines... thus inovations. The major source of clothing for the German Army in Africa, other than its own supply system, was either from the Italians or from captured British stores as is indicated in the following Panzergruppe Afrika administration report of August 1, 1942:

> "When Tobruk was captured, a large English clothing depot fell into our hands. The formations passing through, received an enormous amount of clothing from this dump to cover their increasing losses in action. The total amount in the dump was established at about one thousand tons... much of which could be utilized as German clothing with only minor alterations.
>
> Stocks at Tobruk are now sufficient to cover anticipated needs, although these do not include the unforeseen necessity of equipping newly-arrived formations which come to Africa insufficiently or unsuitably equipped for the tropics."

THE FIRST PANZER TROOPS IN TRIPOLI WORE THEIR BLACK PANZER UNIFORM FOR ONLY A FEW DAYS BEFORE EXCHANGING IT FOR THEIR ISSUED TROPICAL UNIFORM.

LIGHTLY WOUNDED MEMBERS OF THE AFRIKAKORPS BOARDING AN ITALIAN HOSPITAL SHIP FOR LEAVE ON THE CONTINENT.

In actual tropical regions, the tropical uniform was worn the year around but when on leave within the recognized borders of Germany, it was authorized for wear between the dates of May 1 and September 30. The tropical uniform parts not permitted to be worn when on leave on the continent were the tropical helmet, tropical shorts and the tropical shirt when worn without the field blouse. They were, however, permitted in Italy. When on leave in Europe between the dates of October 1 and April 30, an individual was authorized to wear the field-grey uniform only. The mixing of tropical and continental uniform parts was forbidden.

During the final stages of the Tunisian campaign, many replacements and new units which arrived in Tunisia continued to wear their woolen "continental" uniform. The tropical uniform was not issued to those personnel because of the wet and cold Tunisian winters and also because of the critical military situation.

> The tropical uniform was designed by professors at the Tropical Institute in Hamburg, and specifically intended and manufactured in 1940 for service in Africa. It proved so popular, however, that it was soon adopted in other tropical regions, such as Crete, Italy, the Crimea, etc.

Tropical Rank Insignia

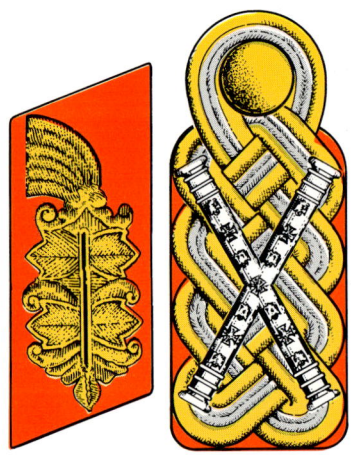

| BEFORE APRIL 3, 1941 | GENERALFELDMARSCHALL | AFTER APRIL 3, 1941 |

NOTES:
1. After April 3, 1941, Generalfeldmarschall shoulder boards had three gold entwined cords instead of gold/silver/gold as worn previously.
2. Continental-style General Officer rank insignia was worn on the tropical uniform.

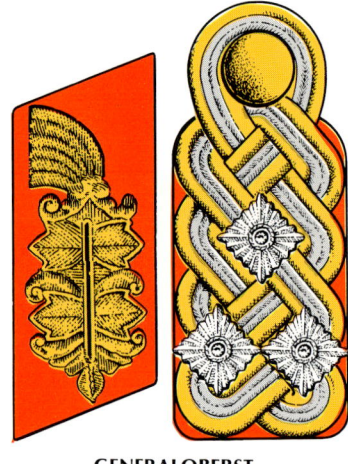

GENERALOBERST

GENERALFELDMARSCHALL ROMMEL WEARING THE PRE-1941 PATTERN COLLAR PATCHES.

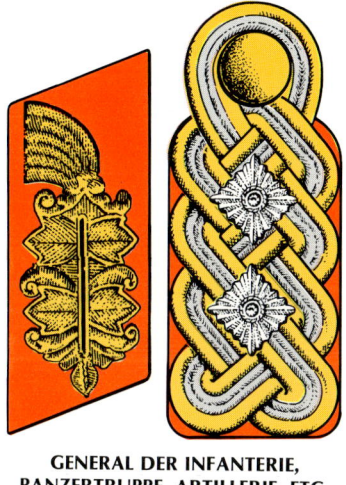

GENERAL DER INFANTERIE, PANZERTRUPPE, ARTILLERIE, ETC.

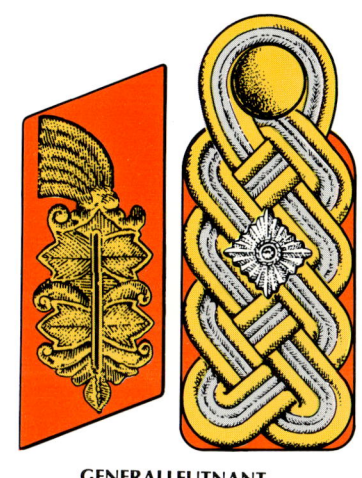

GENERALLEUTNANT

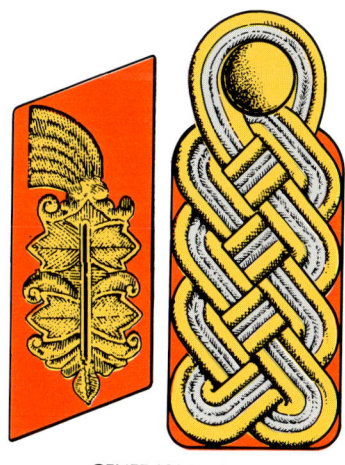

GENERALMAJOR

GENERALMAJOR SCHNARRENBERGER, COMMANDER OF LINES OF COMMUNICATION IN TUNISIA.

JOHN R. ANGOLIA COLLECTION

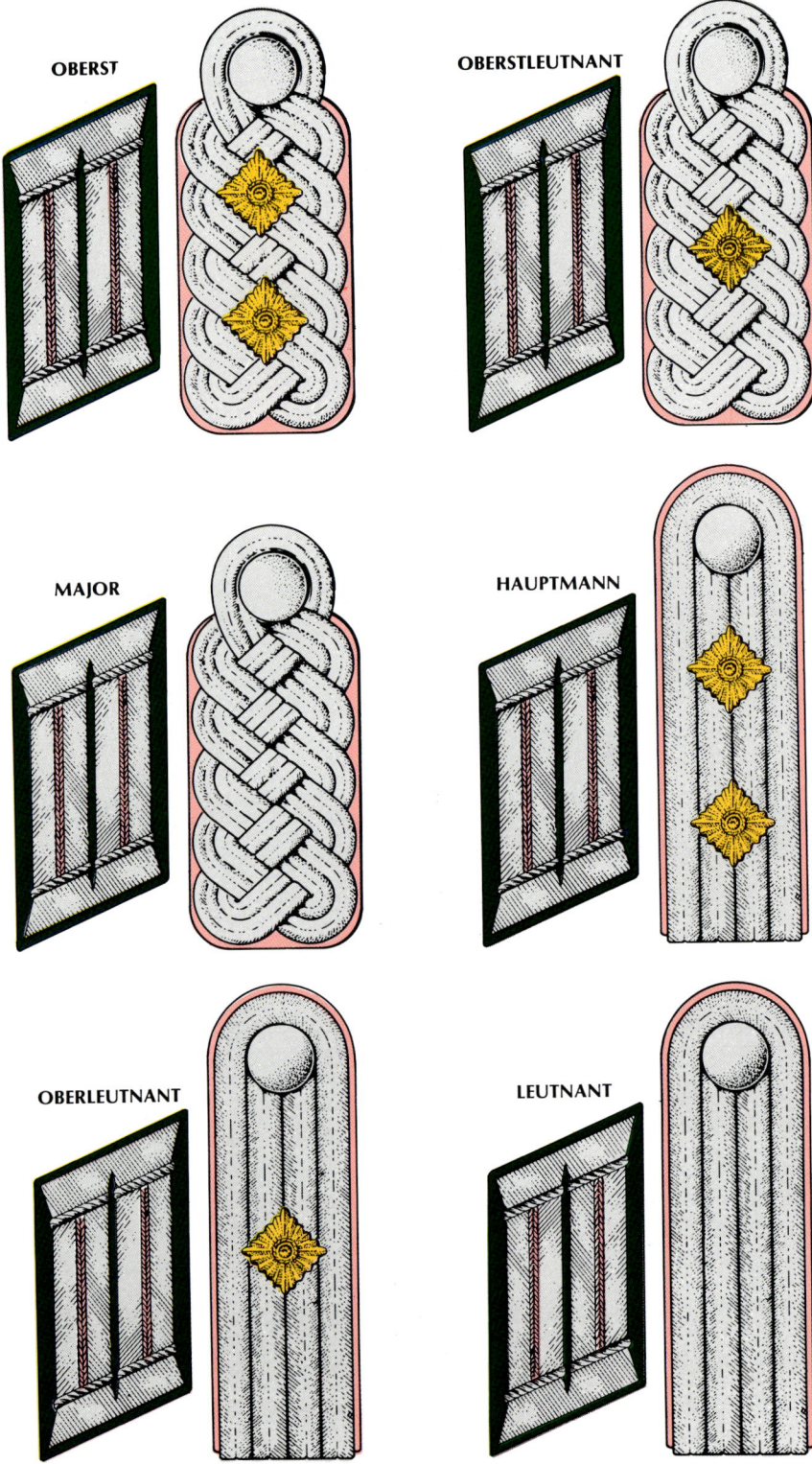

The rank insignia on these and the following pages have pink Waffenfarbe..... indicating Panzertruppe.

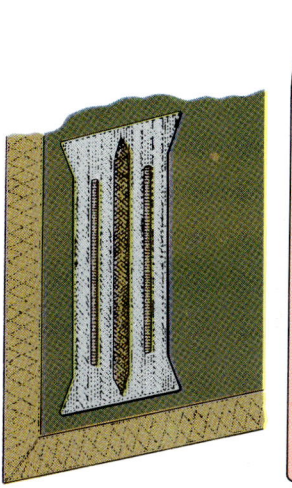

STABSFELDWEBEL/STABSWACHTMEISTER

NOTES:

1. Officers (Leutnant - Oberst) wore continental-issue collar patches which were on a dark green base. The shoulder straps worn were also continental-issue on a Waffenfarbe underlay.

2. The copper-brown Tresse around the collar of the Stabsfeldwebel rank above was worn by all NCOs (except Oberfähnrich and Unterarzt who wore officers' uniforms and peaked caps with aluminum cap cords).

3. Hauptfeldwebel/Hauptwachtmeister ranks were by appointment only and were distinguished by two rings of copper-brown NCO Tresse on both sleeves. When worn with the Afrikakorps cuff title, the cuff title was positioned directly above the Tresse. The slang term for Hauptfeldwebel/Hauptwachtmeister ranks was "der Spiess".

4. The same tropical uniform was issued to all ranks, including high-ranking officers. Many officers retained the tropical breast eagle and collar patches and used the appropriate "continental" shoulder straps, whereas others discarded all of the tropical insignia in preference to "continental" officers' insignia.

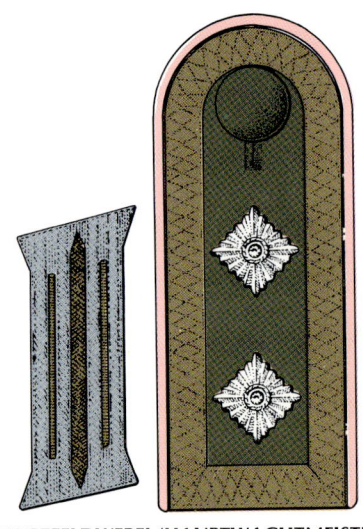

**HAUPTFELDWEBEL/HAUPTWACHTMEISTER/
OBERFELDWEBEL/OBERWACHTMEISTER/
OBERFÄHNRICH**

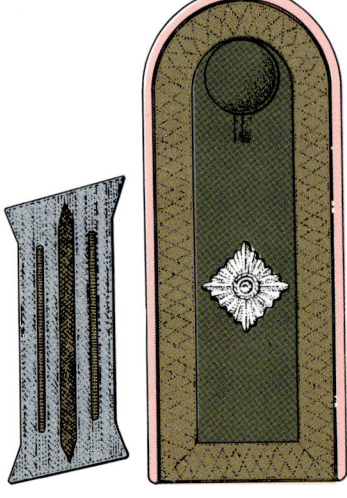

FELDWEBEL/WACHTMEISTER

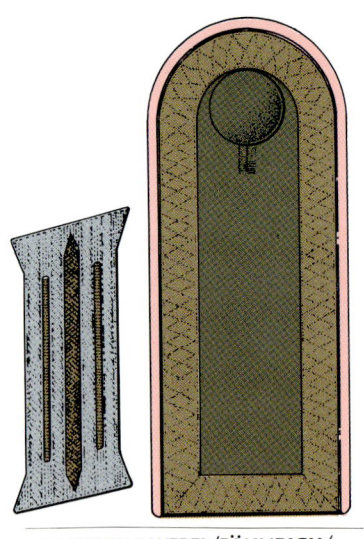

**UNTERFELDWEBEL/FÄHNRICH/
UNTERWACHTMEISTER**

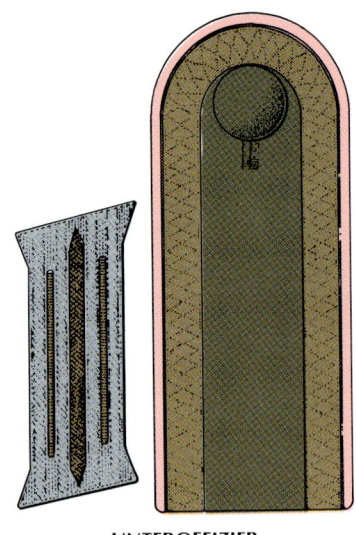

UNTEROFFIZIER

STABSGEFREITER

OBERGEFREITER WITH OVER 6 YEARS' SERVICE

OBERGEFREITER

GEFREITER

NOTE GEFREITER WITH CONTINENTAL-STYLE CHEVRON.

NOTE:
Although regulations prohibited the mixing of tropical and continental uniform parts, it was not uncommon to see continental chevrons and shoulder straps on the tropical uniform.

OBERSCHÜTZE/OBERGRENADIER, ETC.

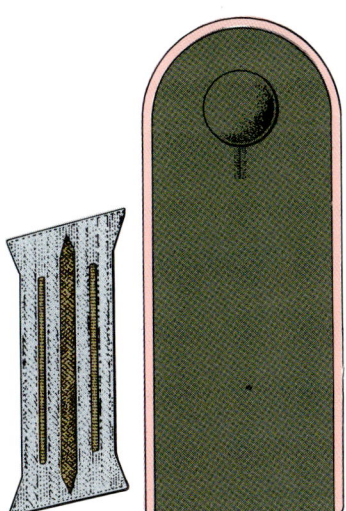

SCHÜTZE/GRENADIER, ETC.

Waffenfarben

Bright Red	- General Officers (Generale)
	- Artillery units (Artillerieeinheiten)
Crimson	- General Staff Officers (Generalstabsoffiziere)
White	- Army Group Commands (Gruppenkommandos)
	- Infantry units (Infanterie/Grenadiereinheiten)
	- Machine-Gun Battalions (Maschinengewehr-Bataillone)
	- Motorcycle units (Kradschützeneinheiten) (also pink or copper-brown)
Golden-Yellow	- Light Division Staffs (Stäbe d. leichten Divisionen)
	- Reconnaissance units (Aufklärungseinheiten)
Lemon-Yellow	- Signals units (Nachrichteneinheiten)
Copper-Brown	- Reconnaissance units, motorized (Aufklärungseinheiten)(mot)
Light Brown	- Construction Engineers (Bautruppe)
Orange	- Field Police (Feldgendarmerie)
Pink	- General Commands, Armored Corps (Generalkommandos der Panzerkorps)
	- Armored Divisional Staffs (Panzerdivisionsstäbe)
	- Armored units (Panzereinheiten)
	- Anti-Tank units (Panzerjägereinheiten)
Grass-Green	- Armored Infantry (Panzergrenadiere)
Black	- Engineer units (Pioniereinheiten)
	- Fortress Engineer units (Festungspioniereinheiten)
	- Armored Engineer units (Panzerpioniereinheiten)
Dark Blue	- Medical units (Sanitätseinheiten)
	- Supply Officer (Nachschubführer)
Light Blue	- Transport units (Kraftfahreinheiten)/Supply Troops (Versorgungstruppen)
Grey-Blue	- Specialist Officers (Sonderführer)
Violet	- Army Clergy (Heeresgeistliche)
Light Grey	- Army Propaganda Troops (Propagandatruppe)
Dark Green	- Army Officials (Wehrmachtbeamte), with the appropriate secondary color... for example:

Lemon-Yellow	- Field Post Service (Feldpostdienst)
Light Blue	- Secret Field Police (Geheime Feldpolizei) and Army Justice Officials (Heeresjustizbeamte)
Crimson	- Weather Service (Wetterdienst)
Light Green	- Pharmacists (Apotheker)
Black	- Technical Service (Technischer Dienst)
White	- Administrative Service (Verwaltungsdienst) and Pay Masters (Zahlmeister)
Bright Red	- Commissariat (Intendantur)

NOTE: The above listing should not be considered as conclusive as it distinguishes only the Waffenfarben more than likely used in Africa, 1941/43.

Shoulder Strap Insignia

Certain services carried distinguishing insignia on their shoulder straps. A few of those most likely worn with the tropical uniform in North Africa were as follows:

    Gothic "A" - Reconnaissance units   "GFP" - Secret Field Police
    Gothic "B" - Artillery Observer units Gothic "K" - Motorcycle units
    Gothic "D" - Divisional Staffs   Gothic "M" - Machine Gun units
    "FP" - Field Post Service   Gothic "P" - Anti-Tank units
          Ornate "HV" - Army Administration Officials

Medical Officers and NCOs with Portepee (Unterärzte)

NOTES OF SHOULDER STRAP INSIGNIA VARIATIONS:

Men and NCOs without Portepee - embroidered in appropriate Waffenfarbe
NCOs with Portepee - white metal
Officers (not including General ranks) - gold metal
Generals - white metal

Specialty Patches

Specialty patches were worn by all qualifying ranks below Leutnant to distinguish a particular military function and to indicate that the individual had achieved proficiency in his field. Those designed to be worn with the tropical uniform were identical to the continental issue except that the base was in olive-green or various shades of brown. It was extremely common, however, to see the continental issue (field-grey base) worn with the tropical uniform. The following are some most likely worn in North Africa.

 1   2   3   4   5   6   7

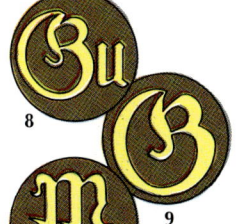

1. Medical Personnel
2. Weapons Ordnance NCO
3. Ordnance Personnel
4. Transport NCO
5. Paymaster Trainee
6. Qualified Radio Operator   } lower right sleeve
7. Signals Personnel*
8. Gas Defense
9. Supply Administration NCO
10. Signals Mechanic

*worn on upper left sleeve, with lightning in appropriate Waffenfarbe (not worn within signals units)

Tropical Uniforms

THE FIELD BLOUSE

The tropical field blouse was of the same basic design as that of the standard Army field blouse and could be worn either open or closed at the neck. It was of a lightweight olive colored cotton, was single breasted with five buttons in front, and had two pleated breast and two pleated side pockets. All of the buttons utilized on this tunic were pebbled and of an olive color. A special tropical breast eagle was worn with this blouse. It was the standard design, but the eagle was in light blue embroidery on a copper-brown base. A number of higher ranking officers, however, removed

the eagle from this uniform and retained the use of their continental-style bullion eagles.

NOTE:
The black Panzer uniform was never intended for use in Africa since it was not appropriate for wear in the tropical regions. Therefore, Panzer troops were also issued the tropical uniform. Besides the wearing of pink Waffenfarbe on shoulder straps and the field cap, they were permitted to affix Panzer skulls onto the lapels of their tropical blouse to further retain their identity as Panzer troops.

THE TROPICAL BREAST EAGLE

GEORGE PETERSEN COLLECTION

(LEFT) A P.O.W. WEARING THE TROPICAL BLOUSE.   (RIGHT) NOTE THE PANZER SKULLS.

THE TROPICAL SHIRT

The tropical shirt was a pullover-style with four small buttons down the front and was in olive colored, cotton drill. It had two pleated breast pockets with grey metal, pebbled buttons and two small buttons per cuff. Detachable shoulder straps were worn by all ranks when the shirt sleeves order was authorized. An olive colored tie could be worn with this shirt and field blouse, but when the shirt was worn alone, its collar was worn open without the tie. An exception to this rule were Knight's Cross holders who wore the collar closed in order to properly display their decoration.

NOTE:
The breast eagle was not permitted to be worn on this shirt. (1)

MEMBERS OF KRAFTWAGEN-KOLONNE 686 IN SHIRT SLEEVES.

---

[1] <u>Heeres-Verordnungsblatt</u>, February 27, 1943, #119.

TROPICAL TROUSERS/BREECHES/SHORTS

Tropical trousers/breeches/shorts were issued to personnel who were stationed in North Africa. They were in olive-colored cotton twill, the same material as the tropical field jacket, and were as follows:

    a. Long Trousers (lange Hose)...worn straight and not bloused at the boots,

    b. Field Trousers (Feldhose)...worn bloused (bloused into the boot tops and allowed to overlap,

    c. Breeches (Stiefelhose)...worn by all ranks in practice with the lace-up tropical boots and the riding boots,

    d. Shorts (kurze Hose)...to be worn with the military shoe or boot and long socks. (2)

NOTES:
1. Army general officers generally wore on their tropical trousers and breeches (also continental issue) a 0.2cm wide red piping sewn into the outer seam. 0.4cm to either side of this piping was positioned a 3.3cm wide red stripe.
2. All tropical trousers/breeches/shorts which were issued to Army personnel had only one unflapped back pocket which was on the right side.

THE NATIONAL ARCHIVES

(RIGHT) FIELD TROUSERS AND BREECHES BEING WORN. MEMBERS OF LUFTWAFFE FLAK REGIMENTS, ASSIGNED TO THE AFRIKAKORPS, WERE ISSUED ARMY TROPICAL UNIFORMS AS IS EVIDENT IN THIS PHOTO.

(LEFT) AN EXCELLENT EXAMPLE OF THE TROPICAL SHORTS BEING WORN.

---

[2]KTB, 164. leichte Afrika-Division, Sanitary Measures dated September 13, 1942. The wearing of shorts was now permissible only between 0800 and 1700, and at all other times long trousers were to be worn. Troops in the front lines were forbidden to wear shorts at any time. If shorts were worn, they were always to be accompanied by some form of leg protection, such as high shoes or boots, puttees, long socks, etc. This ruling was enforced by disciplinary action because of the increasing number of men with sores on their legs which would not heal due to unsuitable clothing being worn.

NOTES: (cont.)

3. The various tropical styles of trousers/breeches/shorts had one item in common besides their color and material... this was their unique hidden belt. It was either of the same material as the trousers/breeches/shorts or of a web material. Note the tropical breeches and shorts below and their different belt and buckle designs.

TROPICAL BREECHES

TROPICAL SHORTS

THE TROPICAL GREATCOAT

The Army pattern tropical Greatcoat was identical in design to that of the continental issue but was in olive colored wool. It did not have, however, the standard blue-green collar and general officers did not have the standard red facings on their lapels. The two rows of six buttons on this double-breasted garment were olive in color, with the exception of Greatcoats worn by generals which were in a gold color. It appears that all ranks, including general officers, wore this pattern Greatcoat with their appropriate rank shoulder straps being the only insignia.*

>*Enlisted ranks from Oberschütze to Stabsgefreiter wore their appropriate rank chevron or star on the upper left sleeve. It should be noted that the "Afrikakorps" cuff title was permitted to be worn 1cm above the cuff, on the lower right sleeve of the Greatcoat.

THE LEATHER GREATCOAT

Generals and high-ranking officers were permitted to purchase fine grain leather Greatcoats for their own use. This practice was followed by a number of officers in North Africa, including Rommel. The only insignia worn were the detachable shoulder straps.

THE MOTORCYCLISTS' PROTECTIVE COAT

This protective coat (Schutzmantel) was an additional garment issued to members of motorcycle units, individual motorcyclists, motorcycle passengers and some Volkswagen drivers. It was of the same design as that of the double-breasted, rubberized motorcyclists' coat but was of an olive colored cotton twill material.[3] Unlike the Luftwaffe protective coat, the Army pattern had accomodations for shoulder straps which were the only insignia worn. Olive colored canvas or cotton mittens were worn with this coat. It was also popular with general officers for wear as a light overcoat.

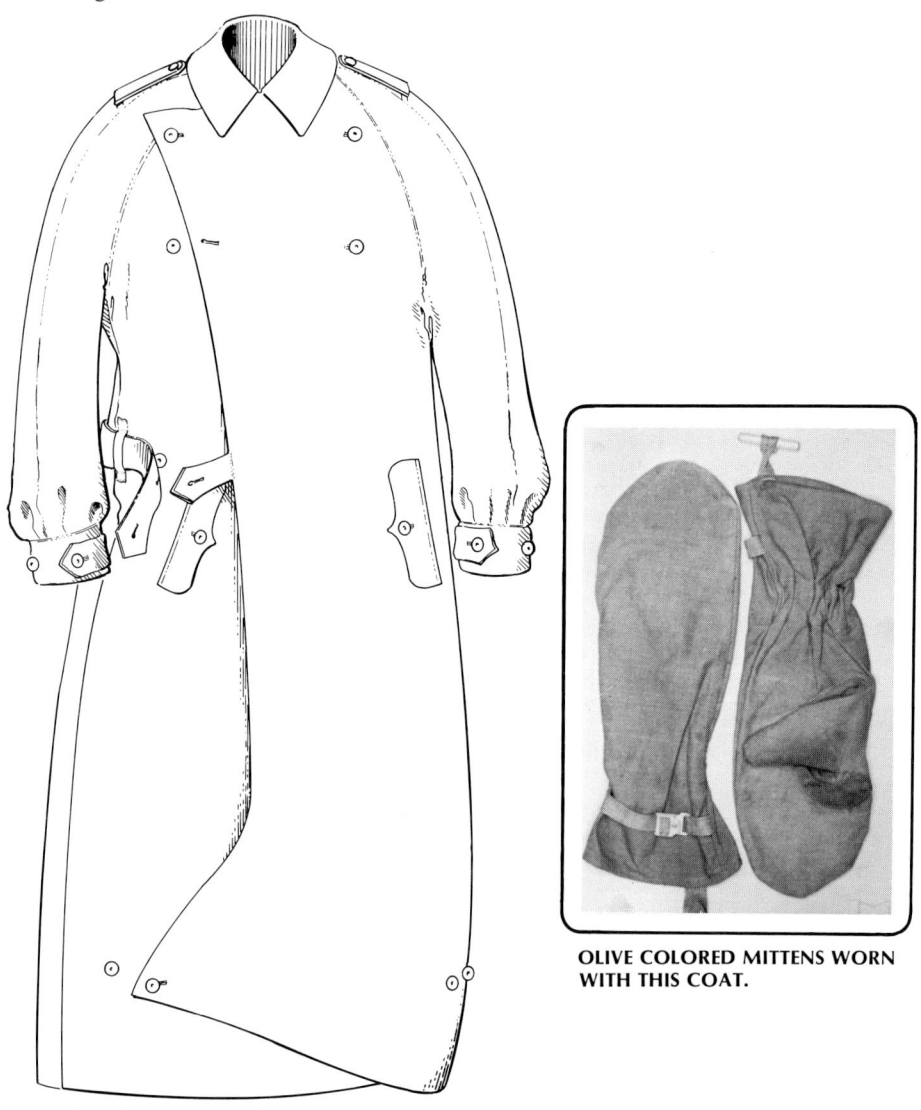

OLIVE COLORED MITTENS WORN WITH THIS COAT.

[3]<u>Uniformen-Markt</u>, May 1, 1941, p. 1.

THE GERMAN PRISONER AT LEFT IS WEARING THE MOTORCYCLISTS' PROTECTIVE COAT.

THE WHITE TROPICAL UNIFORM

It is reported that this uniform was issued to some personnel at permanent garrisons in the tropical areas. It was of the same cut as that of the olive-colored tropical uniform and was in a white cotton material. The uniform parts were as follows:

    a. white field blouse
    b. white shirt with black tie
    c. white trousers
    d. white tropical helmet*

*The white tropical helmet was of the same design as that of the standard olive colored pith helmet, but was without the two metal side shields. The only insignia worn was a large aluminum colored eagle, with spread wings, on the front of the helmet. (4)

MISCELLANEOUS

Several other tropical clothing items were issued to personnel in North Africa. Among the most important were:

    a. the olive or tan scarf (to protect the mouth and nore during sandstorms)
    b. olive colored sweaters (when not available, standard grey sweaters were issued)
    c. olive or grey colored gloves

---

[4]Ibid.

THE OFFICERS' DRESS UNIFORM

Although this uniform was not a tropical issue, it was worn on special occasions in North Africa and has therefore been inserted in this uniform section. Only high-ranking officers could wear their continental dress uniform during specific unit functions, visits by dignitaries, etc. (i.e. General Crüwell, in the photo below, is wearing a Walking-Out Dress uniform for the celebration of his 50th birthday on March 20, 1942, at the DAK bakery).

Tropical Belts and Buckles

Because of the extremely dry climate in North Africa, leather had a tendency to dry and crack. Therefore, all uniform parts and field gear destined for use in Africa, which were normally in leather, were redesigned and constructed of an olive-colored web material. Among those items affected were waist belts. The web belt was issued to enlisted personnel who wore it with the standard Army buckle, which was of an olive color. It was also available to officers who wore it on a limited scale, with either the enlisted mans' buckle or the circular officers' buckle. Most officers and generals, however, preferred the standard brown leather belt with the pebbled double-claw buckle and wore it extensively.

It should be emphasized that from time to time the available stocks of tropical gear became depleated and continental issue items were utilized. This is especially true of the reinforcements and new units which were sent to Africa during the final phases of the campaign, for most of them retained their complete continental uniform.

ENLISTED MAN'S TROPICAL BELT AND BUCKLE (OBVERSE)

(REVERSE)

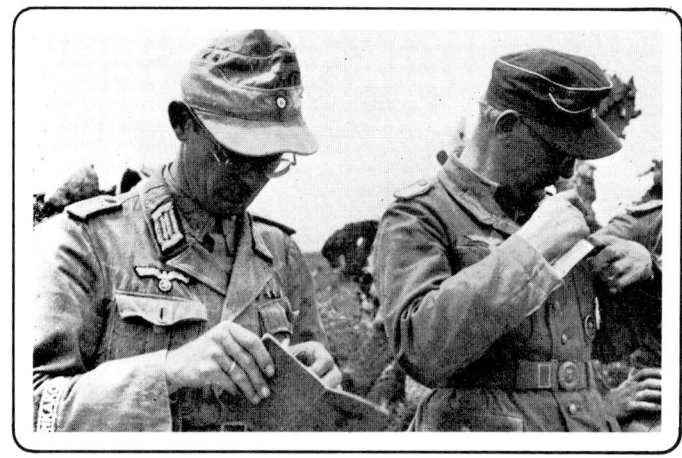

OFFICERS TEARING OUT PAGES FROM THEIR "SOLDBÜCH" SHORTLY BEFORE CAPITULATION IN MAY 1943. NOTE WEB BELT AND CIRCULAR BUCKLE WORN BY OFFICER AT RIGHT.

U.S. ARMY PHOTOGRAPH

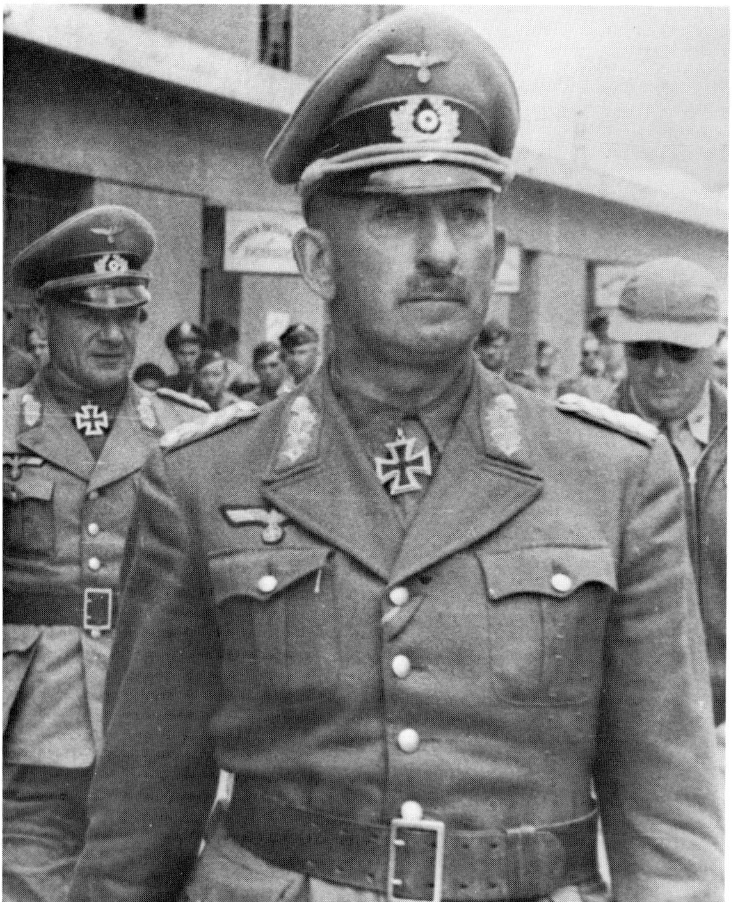

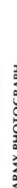

CRAMER AND VON ARNIM SHORTLY AFTER THE CAPITULATION (NOTE BELTS WITH DOUBLE-CLAW BUCKLES).

Tropical Footwear

TROPICAL BOOTS

The canvas and leather, lace-up tropical boot was designed for use in North Africa and saw extensive service in that theater of the war. It was classified as a non-dessicating (i.e. non-drying) boot. The tropical boot was issued in a knee-length and in an ankle-length model, as illustrated below. Olive or grey colored knee- or ankle-length socks were to be worn with the ankle boot.

MEMBERS OF A SIGNALS BATTALION IN MAY 1942.

THE KNEE-LENGTH
TROPICAL BOOT

TRENT PARK PRISONER OF WAR CAMP, ENGLAND, IN NOVEMBER 1943: BACK ROW, L. TO R.—OBERLEUTNANT VON GLASOW, MAJOR BOES, LEUTNANT HUBBUCH, OBERSTLEUTNANT BUHSE (CDR. INF.-RGT. 47), OBERST SCHMIDT, OBERST BORCHERDT. FRONT ROW, L. TO R.—OBERST EGERSDORFF, GENERALLEUTNANT CRÜWELL, GENERALOBERST VON ARNIM, KORVETTENKAPITAN MEIXNER (CHIEF OF THE NAVAL TRANSPORT COMMAND IN TRIPOLI), AND GENERAL-LEUTNANT VON HÜLSEN. (NOTE VARIOUS STYLES OF FOOTWEAR).

German Army personnel wore a wide variety of footwear in North Africa, besides the previously mentioned tropical boot. They were as follows:

    a. black officers' leather riding boots (general and other high-ranking officers)
    b. brown leather lace-up ankle boots* (worn by all ranks)
    c. brown leather lace shoes (worn by high-ranking officers in rear areas)
    d. brown leather sandals for after-hour wear
    e. mountain climbing boots (retained by the few mountain units which were transferred to Africa, generally with issue puttees)
    f. jump boots (worn by paratroop units stationed in North Africa)

*Olive colored canvas and leather reinforced gaiters were issued for wear with the leather lace-up ankle boot, but were introduced quite late in the African campaign. Olive colored issue puttees (a long strip of cloth wound spirally round the leg from the ankle to the knee) were also worn with these ankle boots and the tropical ankle-length boots.

NOTES:
1. The continental jack-boot also saw service, especially in Tunisia, as reinforcements and new units were shipped from Europe without any attempt to issue them tropical gear and equipment.

2. Going barefoot in North Africa was prohibited because of the danger of worm infections. Worm larvae clung to grasses, and so sandals were not sufficient as footwear...therefore, lace-up shoes of a sort were required. (1)

NOTE THAT OFFICER IN BACKGROUND IS WEARING TROPICAL PUTTEES. NEHRING, ROMMEL AND CRÜWELL ARE IN THE FOREGROUND.

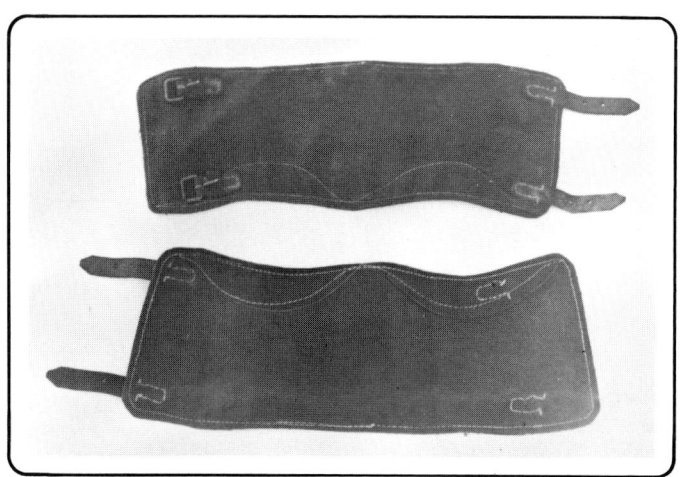

CANVAS AND LEATHER REINFORCED GAITERS.

---

[1]KTB 164. leichte Afrika-Division, July 24, 1942. Subject: Directions re Hygiene in Egypt.

Tropical Headgear

THE TROPICAL OR PITH HELMET

With the initial introduction of German troops into the North African theater, the advent of special tropical uniforms and equipment was made, including the tropical or pith helmet. The first issue was constructed of cork and covered with olive-green colored canvas. A later issue was introduced in 1942 and covered in either olive-green or brown wool. It is doubtful, however, that many second model pith helmets were actually issued in Africa (but were used on Crete and in other tropical regions). Two lightweight metal shields were attached to the sides of the helmet: On the left side was a dull silver Wehrmacht eagle on black, and on the right side, the national colors (black/white/red).

The pith helmet was issued to all ranks, officers and enlisted men alike. It was well designed and served its primary function of keeping the sun off a soldier's head, but was bulky and cumbersome to carry when the steel helmet was required. Thus, the pith helmet was unpopular with most front line troops who preferred the visored field cap which could be folded and carried most anywhere. Although it did not see extensive use near the front, it remained relatively popular in the rear areas throughout the campaign.

Several basic variations were worn by German troops in Africa besides the olive-green issue: They were the standard issue but in tan, plus captured Dutch (with side plates) and occasionally some British models (particularly the South African model).

THE GERMAN PITH HELMET IN SERVICE.

LEFT SIDE

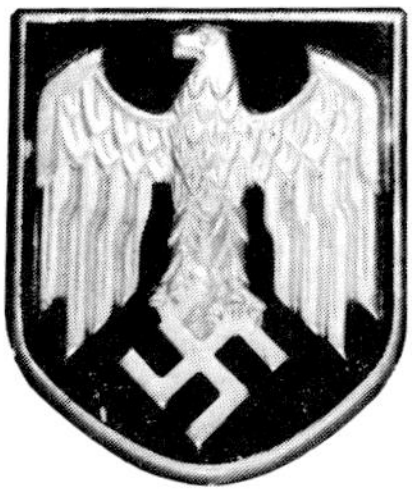

RIGHT SIDE

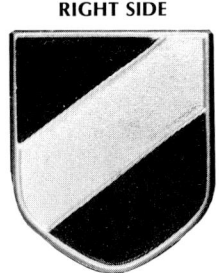

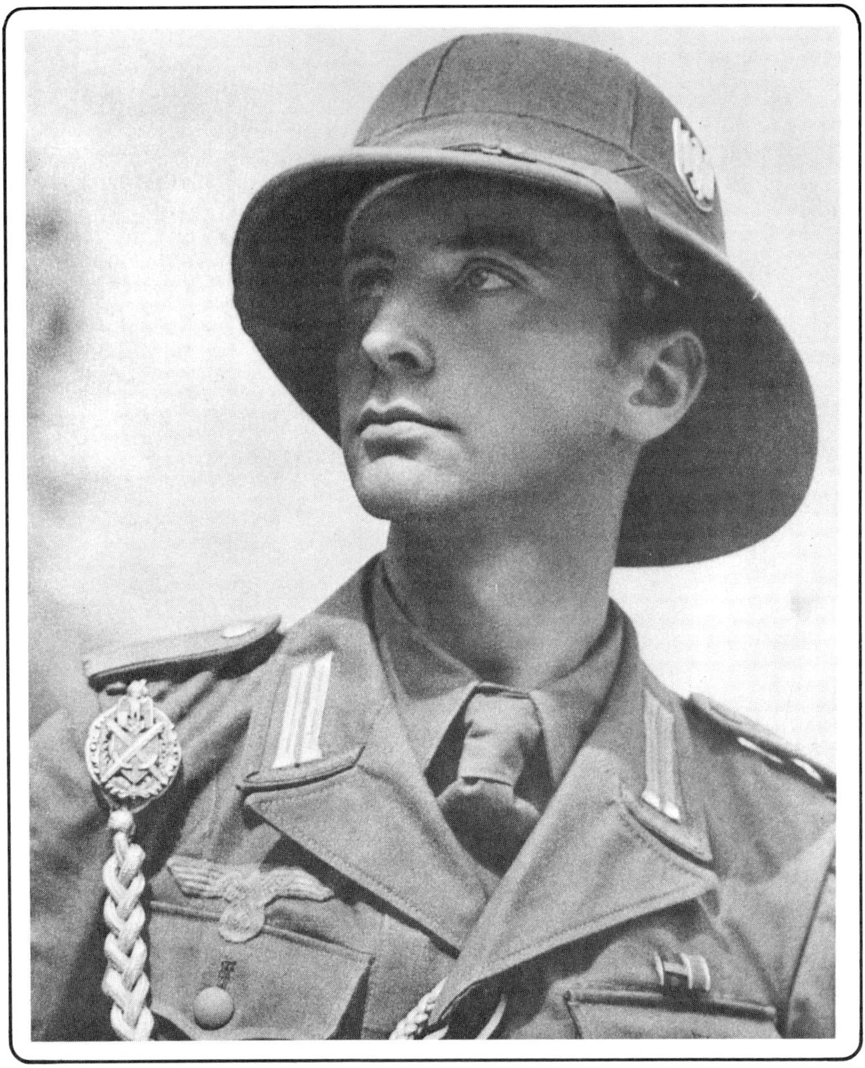

GEORGE PETERSEN COLLECTION

THE STANDARD OLIVE-GREEN ISSUE TROPICAL HELMET

THE DUTCH PITH HELMET WITH GERMAN INSIGNIA.

THE STEEL HELMET

The steel helmet issued to German troops in North Africa was the standard M35 continental helmet. Upon issuance, it was required that these field-grey helmets blend in with the desert terrain, thus a sand-tan paint normally used on vehicles was made available for camouflage purposes. Countless methods of application were followed, a few of which are listed below:

    a. complete paint coverage, including decals,
    b. complete paint coverage, but allowing decals to show,[1]
    c. partial paint coverage, using splotch pattern,
    d. application of sand over wet paint (very popular)

---

[1] Although not rigidly adhered to by all troops in the field, the national colors decal was ordered removed from the right side of the helmet in late 1940, and the Wehrmacht eagle from the left side in 1943.

It should be noted that most helmets were painted by the individual, resulting in excellent to poor paint jobs of any of the above mentioned applications. Rarely, the artistic flair of an Afrikakorps member was expressed by the addition of the Afrikakorps palm tree or a like symbol on his helmet.

Makeshift helmet covers were also used in the North African desert They were generally of available desert-colored material or burlap bags.

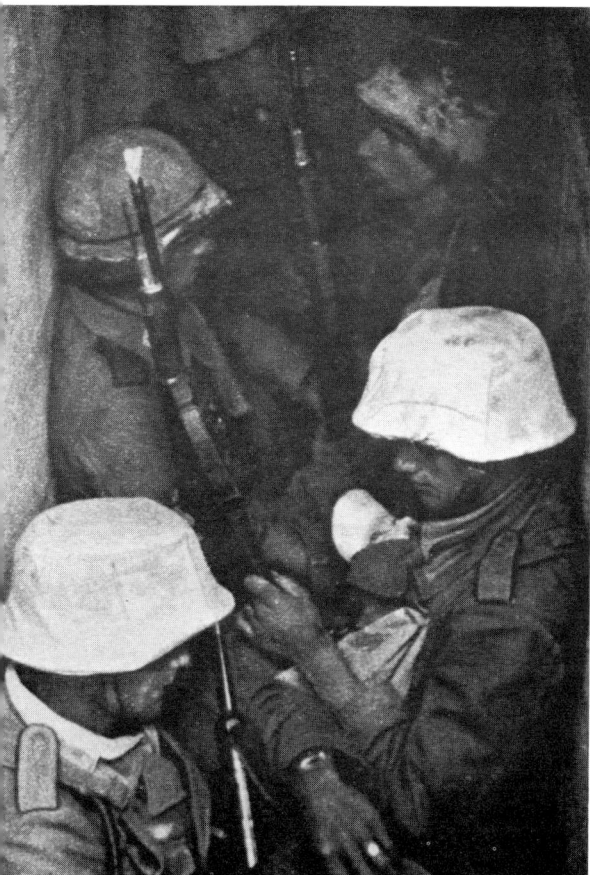

THE CLOTH HELMET COVER WORN OUTSIDE OF TOBRUK.

NOTES:
1. In many instances, no paint of any color was available in the desert, resulting in the use of a strictly continental issue, field-grey helmet.
2. A few examples of German helmets with British chin straps have been observed. It is assumed that these, being more comfortable and flexible than the German chin strap, was obtained from captured stocks and affixed to the helmet.

THE SERVICE OR UNIFORM CAP

The service or uniform peaked cap (Schirmmütze) <u>did not</u> see extensive service in North Africa. Because the visored field cap proved so popular with all ranks, the service cap was worn basically by Rommel and a small number of general and other high-ranking officers.

The service peaked cap worn was the continental model, with a field-grey cover, dark blue-green cap band and a black peak or visor. The crown of the cap always had a 2mm wide piping around it and the cap band had a 2mm wide piping on the top and bottom, thusly:

    a. for officers, NCOs and other ranks - appropriate Waffenfarbe
    b. for all general officers - gold

All NCOs and men wore black leather chin straps with black buttons and the national emblem and oakleaf cluster in white metal. Officers wore the cap described above (usually higher quality) but with aluminum cap cords and aluminum buttons, and white metal or aluminum-embroidered insignia. General officers wore the service cap with gold cap cords, gold buttons, and white metal or aluminum-embroidered insignia. After January 1, 1943, an order stated that gold insignia was to be worn by general officers, but it is doubtful that this order was adhered to at the crumbling Tunisian front.

THE NATIONAL ARCHIVES

ROMMEL, UNKNOWN, NEHRING AND CRÜWELL.

THE VISORED FIELD CAP

The German soldier in Africa was issued a billed field cap (Feldmütze mit grossem Schirm) of olive-green cotton drill material. This model proved to be extremely popular and was worn by all ranks during the campaigns in North Africa. The insignia was tropical issue, and was as follows:

    a. the national emblem was in light blue embroidery on a copper-brown base

    b. the black/white/red cockade was on an olive-green diamond-shaped base

A small inverted chevron (Soutache) in the appropriate Waffenfarbe, which indicated the wearer's branch of service, was positioned directly above the cockade. By an order dated July 10, 1942, however, this practice was ordered to be discontinued.[2]

(RIGHT) FIELD CAP WITH "SOUTACHE" AND (BELOW) FIELD CAP WITHOUT "SOUTACHE".

---

[2] *Allgemeine Heeresmitteilungen*, July 21, 1942. This order was numbered #597, dated July 10, 1942, and effected all field service caps and mountain caps.

Officers and officials of officer rank were authorized to wear the visored field cap with a 3mm aluminum piping around the top edge of the cap and the scalloped portion of the turn-up (gold for general officers).

(ABOVE) NOTE ALUMINUM PIPING ON OFFICER'S TROPICAL, VISORED FIELD CAP. (RIGHT) TROPICAL FIELD CAP WITHOUT VISOR.

NOTE:
A visorless field cap was worn extensively by tank crew members in North Africa. Other than the lack of the visor and the number of vent holes (the visored version had two vent holes per side whereas the unvisored version had one per side), its basic design, color and insignia were identical to that of the visored model above. It was also not uncommon for tank crew members to retain their popular black field caps (Feldmützen (M38)) while wearing the tropical uniform in the desert. The early models also carried the "Soutache".

It should be noted that this, as well as all tropical uniform parts, varied greatly in color due to their exposure to the extreme tropical elements plus the fact that the uniform cloth color varied in shades from olive-green to dark brown. In addition, anti-gas tablets (Losantin) were sometimes used to bleach uniform parts to an almost white color.

THE NATIONAL ARCHIVES

A PzKw III CREW WEARING THE VISORED FIELD CAP WITH "SOUTACHE" AND THE BLACK FIELD CAP. NOTE THE DUTCH PITH HELMET AND DESTRUCTION MARK FOR A BRITISH AIRCRAFT ON THE BARREL.

NOTE:
The black Panzer field cap was introduced for wear on March 27, 1940.

MOSQUITO/FLY NET

An insect net was issued to all Afrikakorps personnel for wear over the head, as protection from flies as well as mosquitos.

Cuff Titles

The first cuff title which was worn by Afrikakorps personnel, was unofficial and saw very limited use. It had "Afrikakorps" in white block letters on a black base and was most probably contracted out to Arab manufacturers in Tripoli, shortly after the German arrival there.

* * *

An order dated July 18, 1941 and signed by Generalfeldmarschall von Brauchitsch, authorized the wearing of an official "Afrikakorps" cuff title by members of the DAK fighting in North Africa.[1] The inscription "Afrikakorps" was in silver thread on a dark green base, which was piped with a 0.3cm wide silver band on top and bottom. The outer edges of the cuff title were in light brown. It was worn on the lower right sleeve as follows:

- a. approximately 15cm from the bottom of the tropical blouse and field blouse sleeve,
- b. approximately 1cm above the cuff of the overcoat,
- c. and approximately 7.5cm above the field-grey tunic's cuff.[2]

A minimum of two month's service in Africa was required before an individual was permitted to wear the "Afrikakorps" cuff title.

* * *

On January 15, 1943, the Führer ordered the introduction of an "Afrika" cuff title which had the status of a campaign decoration (Kampfabzeichen), and was to be the same for all three branches of the Wehrmacht. It was 3.3cm wide and made of khaki-brown camel hair material (Kamelhaarstoff). The piping, plus the inscription "Afrika" flanked by two palm trees, were all in silver colored thread. The cuff title was to be worn on the lower left cuff of the tunic and overcoat as follows:

- a. approximately 16cm above the bottom of the field blouse sleeve for NCOs and men, and 1cm above the overcoat cuff,
- b. approximately 1cm above the cuff of the officers' field blouse and overcoat.

The following conditions were set up by the OKW for the awarding of the cuff title:

- a. at least six months service on African soil was required,
- b. being wounded in combat in the North African theater,
- c. and the contraction of an illness while in the North African theater of the war, which demanded evacuation to the continent. Service was required for at least three months before contraction of the illness, under these circumstances.

---

[1] <u>Allgemeine Heeresmitteilungen</u>, July 28, 1941, #496.

[2] The cuff title was permitted to be worn with this uniform on the continent, when a DAK member was on leave there. He was also permitted to wear his tropical uniform plus cuff title, during the summer months only, when on leave on the continent.

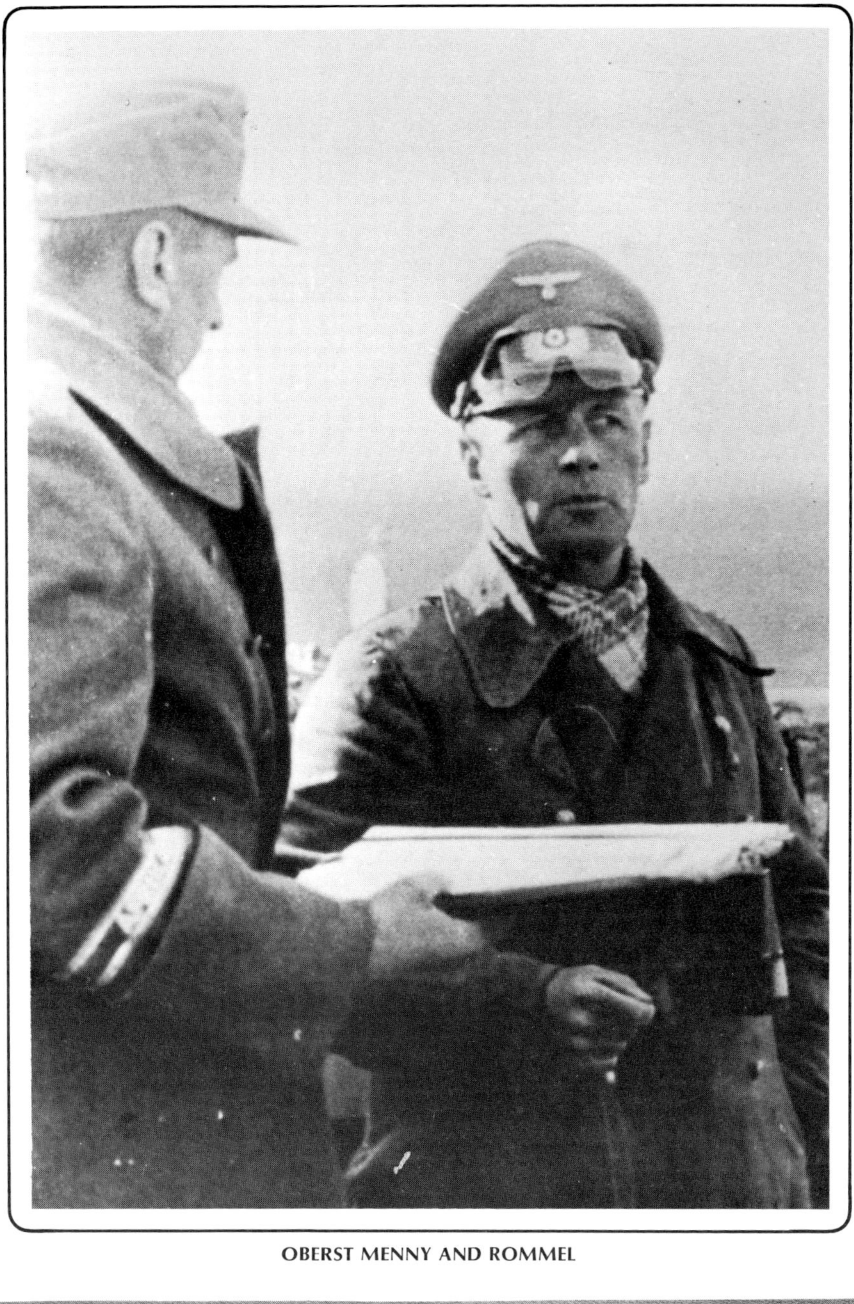

THE NATIONAL ARCHIVES

OBERST MENNY AND ROMMEL

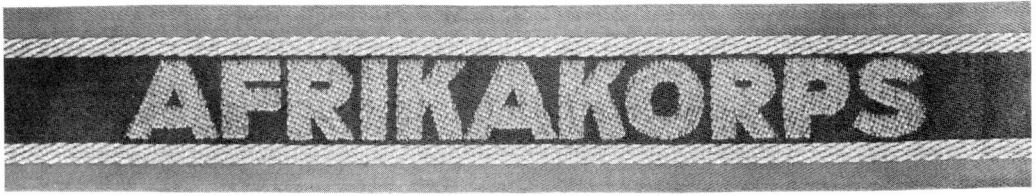

THE "AFRIKAKORPS" CUFF TITLE

THE "AFRIKA" CAMPAIGN DECORATION

Any of the above requirements were considered fulfilled if an individual was killed while on duty in North Africa. In this case, only the award document was presented to his dependents. No foreigner was eligible for the "Afrika" cuff title.[3]

NOTES:
1. As of the January 1943 date of introduction, the "Afrikakorps" cuff title was to be removed from the tunic or overcoat, and replaced by the "Afrika" campaign decoration, if authorized. At this late date in the campaign, it is doubtful that this order was adhered to.
2. A certificate and one cuff title was presented to each awardee. If he wished to purchase an additional cuff title, he had to present the award document to the proper agency. (4)
3. On July 1, 1943, the Führer decreed that members of "Heeresgruppe Afrika" who had fought in the final phases of the African campaign (from May 6, 1943), are eligible for the "Afrika" campaign decoration after four months service instead of six. (5)
4. Those who fought in the African campaign and were awarded the Iron Cross, German Cross in gold or whose name was added to the Honor Roll, were now entitled to the "Afrika" cuff title regardless of service time. (6)
5. As of October 31, 1944, no further "Afrika" cuff titles were to be awarded, except in the case of prisoners of war or those missing in action.... and only then if written requests were filed after their return. (7)

---

[3]Allgemeine Heeresmitteilungen, January 27, 1943, #60.

[4]Uniformen-Markt, No. 3, 1943, p. 21.

[5]Allgemeine Heeresmitteilungen, July 7, 1943, #544.

[6]Ibid, July 1, 1944, #27.

[7]Ibid, October 21, 1944, #576.

GENERALMAJOR HASSO VON MANTEUFFEL AS COMMANDER OF PZ. GREN. DIV. "GROSSDEUTSCHLAND" IN AUGUST 1944. NOTE THE "AFRIKA" CUFF TITLE WORN BELOW THE ARMY DIVISIONAL CUFF TITLE ON THE LOWER RIGHT SLEEVE.

OBERST ZOLLING, WEARING THE "AFRIKA" CAMPAIGN DECORATION IN MAY 1945. (FORMER Ic, PANZERGRUPPE AFRIKA)

Besitzurkunde

Ich verleihe dem

Prüfmeister

das

Ärmelband

~ Afrika ~

Hauptquartier des O.B.S., den 1.5.1943

Der Oberbefehlshaber Süd

Keßelring

Generalfeldmarschall

F. d. R.:

Major

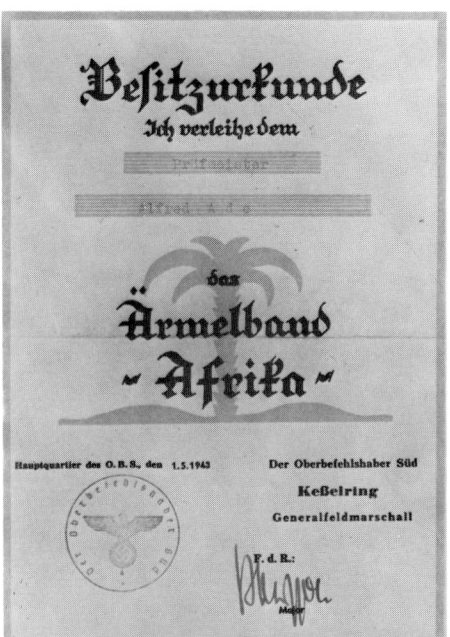

"THE AFRIKA" CUFF TITLE AWARD DOCUMENT WAS IDENTICAL FOR ALL WEHRMACHT RECIPIENTS. (ABOVE IS FOR A LUFTWAFFE PRÜFMEISTER)

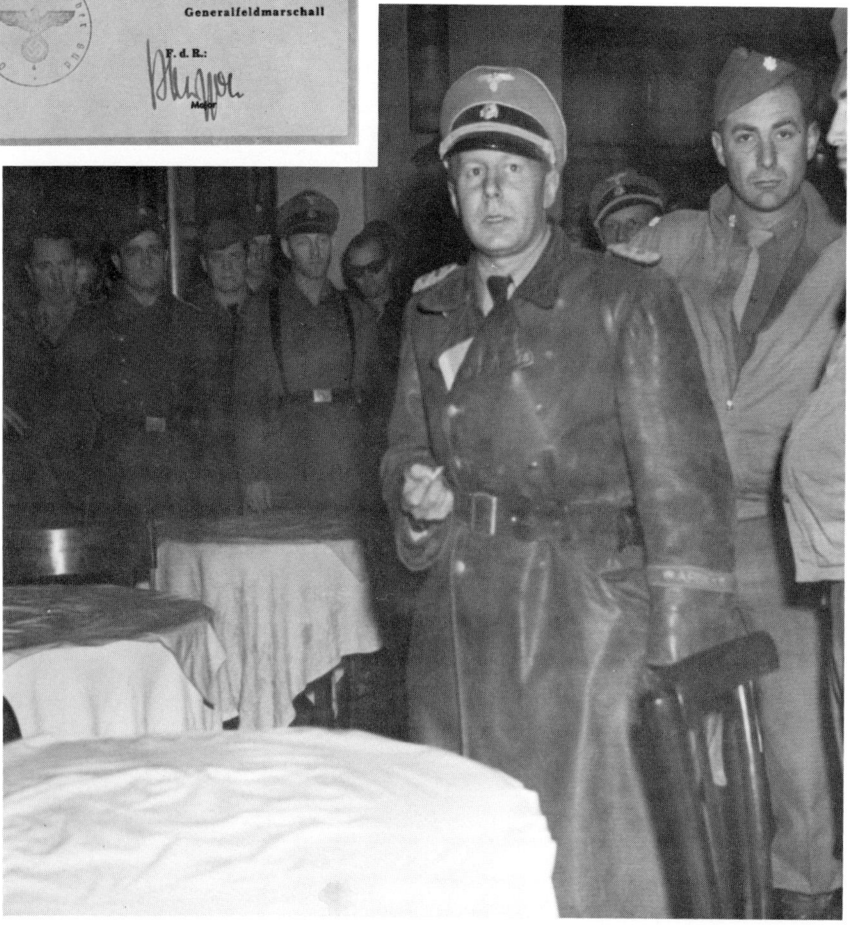

U.S. ARMY PHOTOGRAPH

THE SS OFFICER TELLS HIS MEN THAT THIS IS A BITTER MOMENT AS THEY LAY DOWN THEIR ARMS AND SURRENDER IN MILAN, ITALY, ON APRIL 30, 1945. THIS GARRISON REFUSED TO SURRENDER TO ANYONE EXCEPT THE AMERICANS (NOTE "AFRIKA" CUFF TITLE).

The Italo-German Medal
THE ITALO-GERMAN CAMPAIGN MEDAL IN AFRICA

This decoration was awarded to members of Rommel's command in early 1942. It was a semi-official medal which was awarded by the Italian Military Command and therefore had no prescribed regulations for wear. The German recipients wore the medal in a number of ways, some of which were as follows:

a. mounted on a medal bar (grosse Ordenschnalle),
b. through the button hole of the left breast pocket flap,
c. simply pinned onto the uniform,
d. and through the second button hole of the tunic (the ribbon only-36mm wide), in the same manner as the Iron Cross 2nd Class ribbon was worn.

REICHSORGANISATIONSLEITER DR. LEY WITH A WOUNDED GEFREITER AT THE FESTSPIELHAUS IN BAYREUTH, 1942 (NOTE MANNER IN WHICH THE "AFRIKA" MEDAL IS WORN).

The medal was designed by De Marchis and produced by the firm of F. M. Lorioli and Sons in Milan, initially in bronze, later in a grey (war metal) alloy which was bronze plated, and finally in a war metal which was silver plated. The medal ribbon was 25mm wide and in the German and Italian colors (black/white/red/white/green).[1]

OBVERSE   REVERSE

OBVERSE

An armored German and Italian soldier holding the crocodile's jaws closed (i.e. the crocodile = the British Empire, and the closed jaws = the Suez Canal), plus the designer's and manufacturer's name.

REVERSE

The "Arco dei Feleni", the Italian arch which is on the "Via Balbia" and marks the boundry between Cyrenaica and Tripolitania. It is positioned over the Royal Knot of the House of Savoy and is flanked by the Fasces and the Swastika. The legend, "Italo-German Campaign in Africa", is around the rim of the medal in both the Italian and German languages.

THE "ARCO DEI FELENI" AS SEEN FROM ROMMEL'S AIRCRAFT.

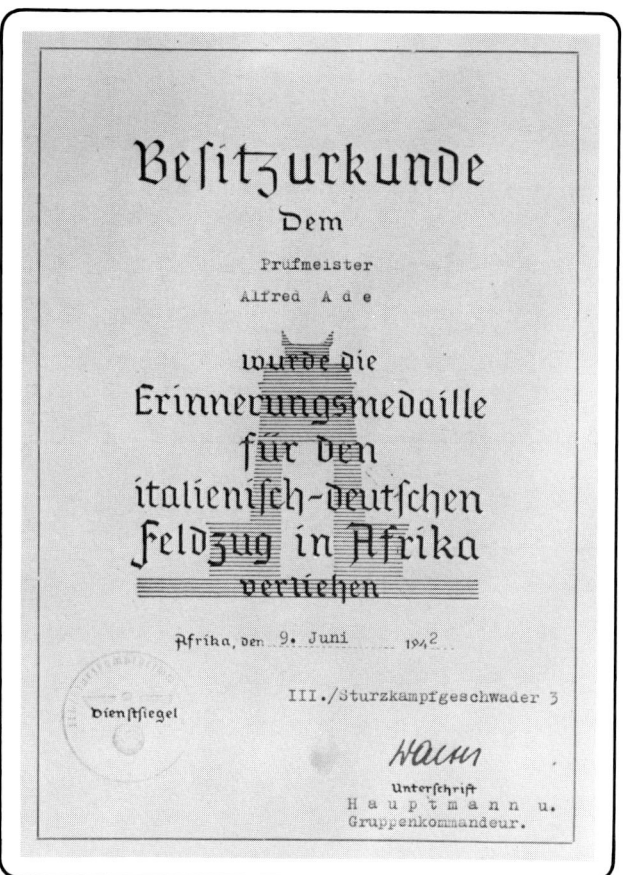

**THE AWARD DOCUMENT WAS IDENTICAL FOR ALL WEHRMACHT RECIPIENTS.
(ABOVE IS FOR A LUFTWAFFE PRÜFMEISTER)**

NOTES:
1. It should be emphasised that no member of the Italian Armed Forces was ever awarded this medal.
2. Several other Italian manufacturers produced small quantities of the bronze plated version of the medal.
3. The manufacturer's name was positioned above the crocodile's left leg on the bronze and bronze plated medals, and directly above the crocodile's right leg on the silvered version.

An order dated March 29, 1944, prohibited the further wearing of any Royal Italian military orders, medals, campaign decorations or combat badges, with the Italo-German Campaign Medal for Africa being specifically mentioned.[2]

---

[1] C. V. Kelly, "The Italo-German Campaign Medal for Africa", The Medal Collecter, Volume 23, No. 7, July 1972.

[2] Allgemeine Heeresmitteilungen, April 8, 1944, order #176.

ON APRIL 8, AFTER THE CAPTURE OF MECHILI, ROMMEL SPOTTED A PAIR OF LARGE BRITISH SUN AND SAND GOGGLES. HE TOOK A FANCY TO THEM. HE GRINNED AND SAID, "BOOTY...PERMISSIBLE EVEN FOR A GENERAL...I WILL TAKE THEM." THESE GOGGLES FOREVER AFTER WERE TO BE THE DISTINGUISHING MARK OF THE DESERT FOX.

WITH ROMMEL IN THE DESERT, **p. 34.**

GENERALFELDMARSCHALL ROMMEL BEING INTERVIEWED BY LUTZ KOCH ON JUNE 20, 1942, GLES WORN BY ROMMEL). KOCH WAS A WAR CORRESPONDENT WITH ROMMEL FROM

TOBRUK (NOTE BRITISH GOG-
1944.

Field Equipment used in North Africa

Because of the climatic conditions in North Africa, field equipment which was destined for service there, was redesigned and constructed in canvas and web material. It should be noted, however, that troops stationed in Africa did not always receive tropical-style field equipment. because of the critical German supply problems. They therefore wore their continental issue as did many troops who were shipped to Africa late in the campaign...the result being a thorough mixture of tropical and continental equipment. The following descriptions are for those basic Army tropical and continental items which were issued to troops stationed in Africa, but do not include the many variations and prototypes.

AMMUNITION POUCHES
(PATRONENTASCHEN)

98K: Constructed of black leather or undyed leather (early), and consisted of three clip compartments (two clips per compartment). Infantrymen were generally issued two pouches, while personnel who did not require much ammunition such as artillerymen, were issued one. It was not uncommon to see K98 pouches painted tan in North Africa.

MP 38 & 40: The "Schmeisser" pouch was available in either black leather or olive-colored canvas and consisted of three magazine compartments (one magazine per compartment). The version, which was specifically designed for service in North Africa, was 100% canvas, with either web or leather reinforcements. These pouches were generally issued in pairs with the left pouch fitted with a small pocket at its base. This pocket contained the MP 38 & 40 loading tool.

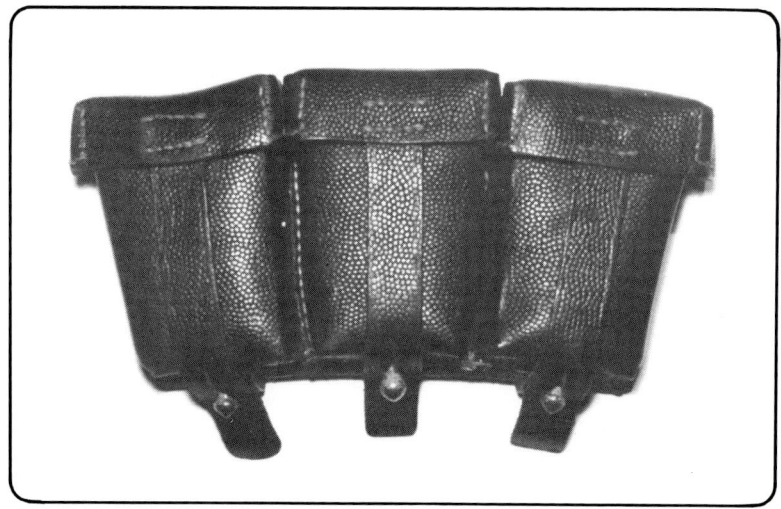

98K THREE-COMPARTMENT POUCH

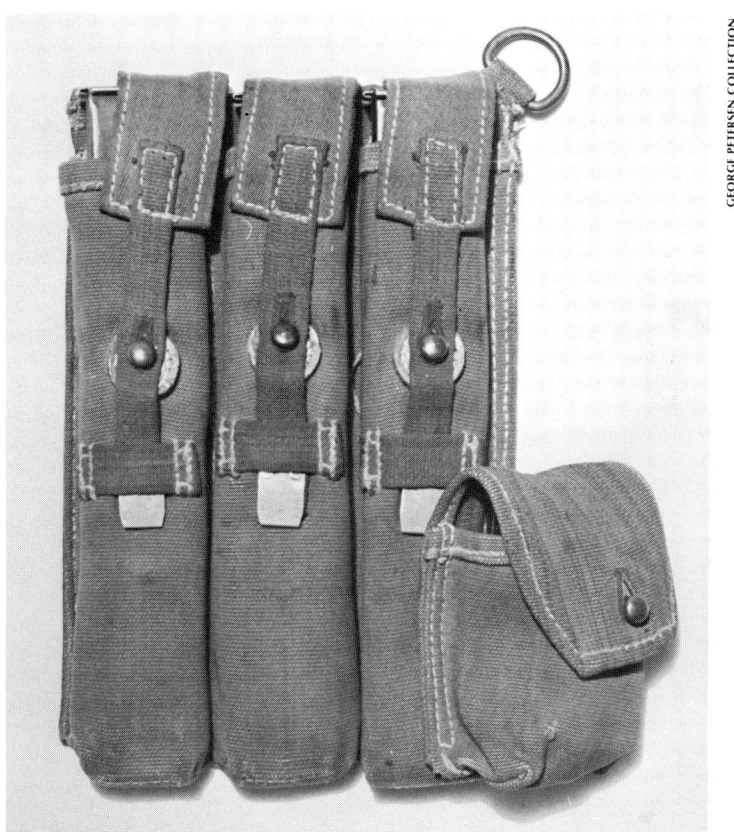

MP 38 & 40 ALL-CANVAS MAGAZINE POUCH

THE BAYONET AND BAYONET FROG
(SEITENGEWEHR UND SEITENGEWEHRTASCHE)

The standard pattern 84/98 bayonet was issued with either wood or bakelite grips, with a blued sheath, and was carried in a black leather or olive-green heavy web frog. The leather frog was available in two basic versions... one for mounted personnel which had a narrow securing strap for the grip and the standard frog for unmounted personnel. All tropical frogs had the securing strap.

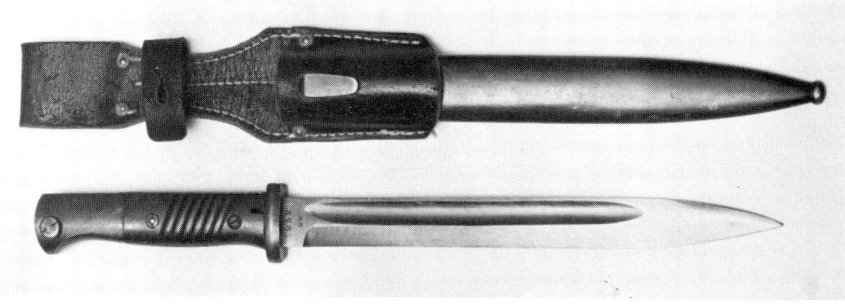

CONTINENTAL-ISSUE 84/98 BAYONET FROG

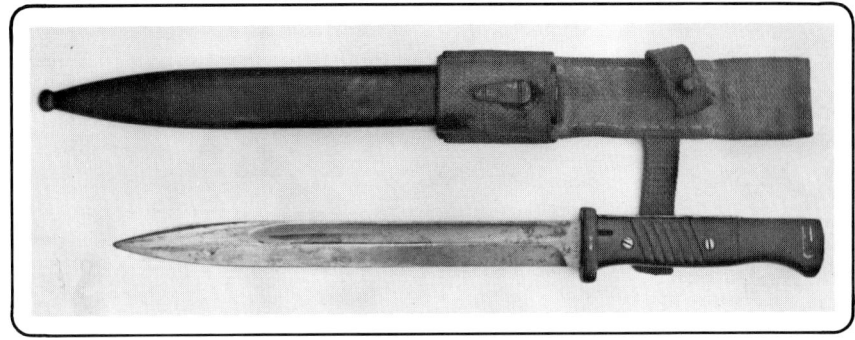

TROPICAL-ISSUE 84/98 BAYONET FROG

THE ENTRENCHING TOOL
(KLEINER SPATEN)

This short-handled shovel was issued with a flat or pointed (Austrian-style) steel blade and was suspended from a black leather or olive-colored canvas carrier, on the left hip. Regulations stated that the bayonet was to be worn attached to the entrenching tool (see illustration). A folding entrenching tool was introduced in 1942, and saw extensive service in North Africa.

STANDARD-ISSUE ENTRENCHING TOOL

THE BREADBAG
(BROTBEUTEL)

The breadbag was made of olive-colored canvas with either web or leather fittings. It was normally worn suspended from the waist belt on the right hip (sewn or buttoned belt loops), but was also issued with a detachable canvas shoulder strap which was most always discarded (see variations illustrated). The breadbag generally contained a wash kit, a field cap when not worn, eating utensils, and rations.

a. Early issue breadbag with sewn belt loops.
b. Breadbag variation with buttoned belt loops.
c. Breadbag with detachable shoulder strap.
d. Breadbag, inside view.

THE CANTEEN AND CUP
(FELDFLASCHE UND TRINKBECHER)

The canteen was initially constructed of aluminum (later enameled steel) and covered with a felt cover (continental) of varying shades (grey, brown, green... all manufacturers' variations). The canteen's capacity was one liquid quart.

The oval canteen cup was also initially constructed of aluminum and painted black (later steel and painted field-grey). The smaller, round cups were generally in black plastic. The drinking cup was positioned upside down over the mouth of the canteen and held in place by a black leather strap (continental) or by a tan, brown or olive-green web strap (tropical). In 1941, an aluminum canteen was introduced with a covering of plastic impregnated wood, which served as insulation in place of the felt cover, and was normally a dark-brown color. It did not, however, see extensive service in North Africa. Canteens which were fitted with shoulder straps were worn basically by officers and medical personnel.

NOTE:
The canteen was suspended from the right D-ring on the breadbag (see illustration).

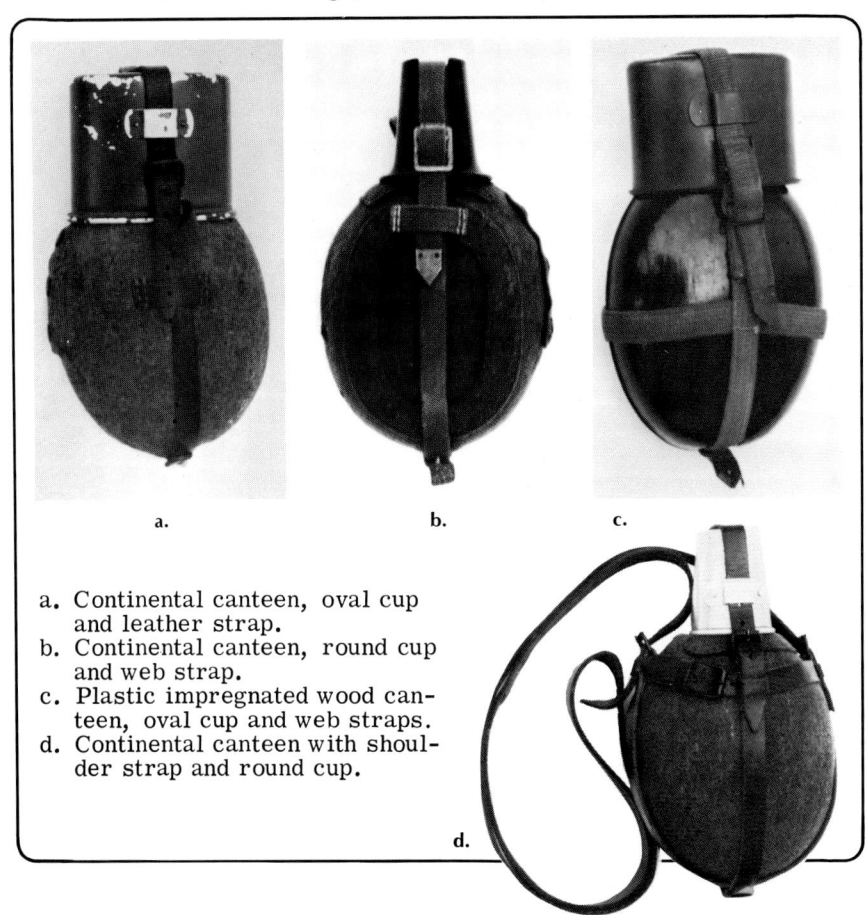

a. Continental canteen, oval cup and leather strap.
b. Continental canteen, round cup and web strap.
c. Plastic impregnated wood canteen, oval cup and web straps.
d. Continental canteen with shoulder strap and round cup.

THE MESS KIT
(KOCHGESCHIRR)

The mess kit was initially constructed of aluminum (later enameled steel) and consisted of a deep pot with a cover which could be utilized as a plate. It was strapped together with either a black leather strap (continental) or an olive-green web strap. The mess kit was normally worn strapped to the assault pack (harness) or suspended from the left D-ring on the breadbag, next to the canteen.

SUPPORT SUSPENDERS/"Y" STRAPS
(KOPPELTRAGGESTELL)

The commonest form of support suspenders were those issued to combat troops in infantry divisions. They were in black leather and designed to support the weight of the belt, ammunition pouches, bread bag, canteen, etc. By the use of two D-rings on the shoulders, various pack arrangements were allowed to be worn. The front straps were clipped onto D-rings which were attached to the back of the ammunition pouches and the single strap in back was attached to the cartridge belt by means of a single broad hook. German troops in Africa were issued thick web support suspenders of the same basic design.

D-RING
(D-RING)

From time-to-time, additional D-rings were required for additional equipment to be worn. To facilitate this need, D-rings on belt loops could be slipped onto the waist belt to whatever position desired. These were available in black leather or olive-colored web material (tropical).

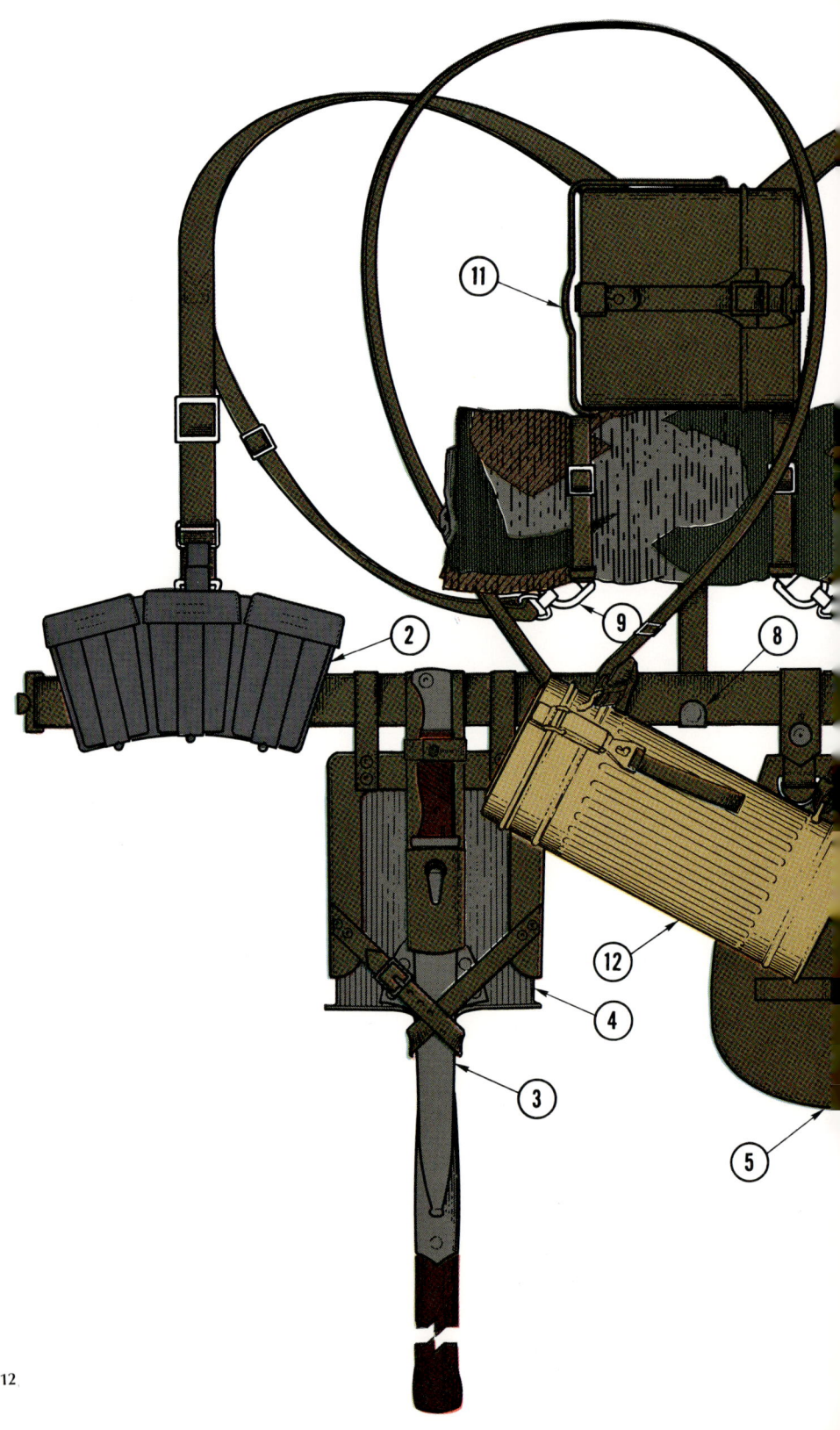

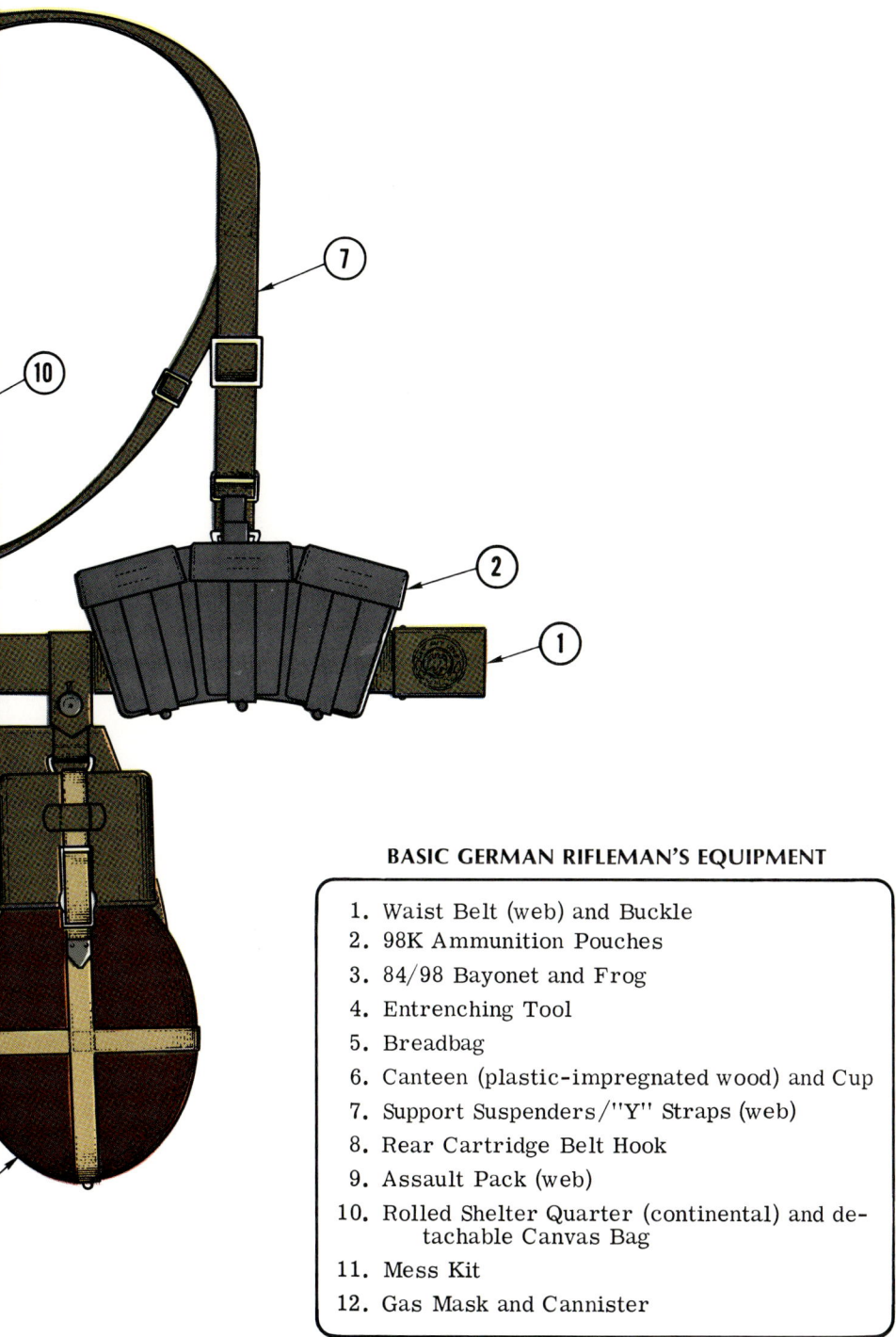

BASIC GERMAN RIFLEMAN'S EQUIPMENT

1. Waist Belt (web) and Buckle
2. 98K Ammunition Pouches
3. 84/98 Bayonet and Frog
4. Entrenching Tool
5. Breadbag
6. Canteen (plastic-impregnated wood) and Cup
7. Support Suspenders/"Y" Straps (web)
8. Rear Cartridge Belt Hook
9. Assault Pack (web)
10. Rolled Shelter Quarter (continental) and detachable Canvas Bag
11. Mess Kit
12. Gas Mask and Cannister

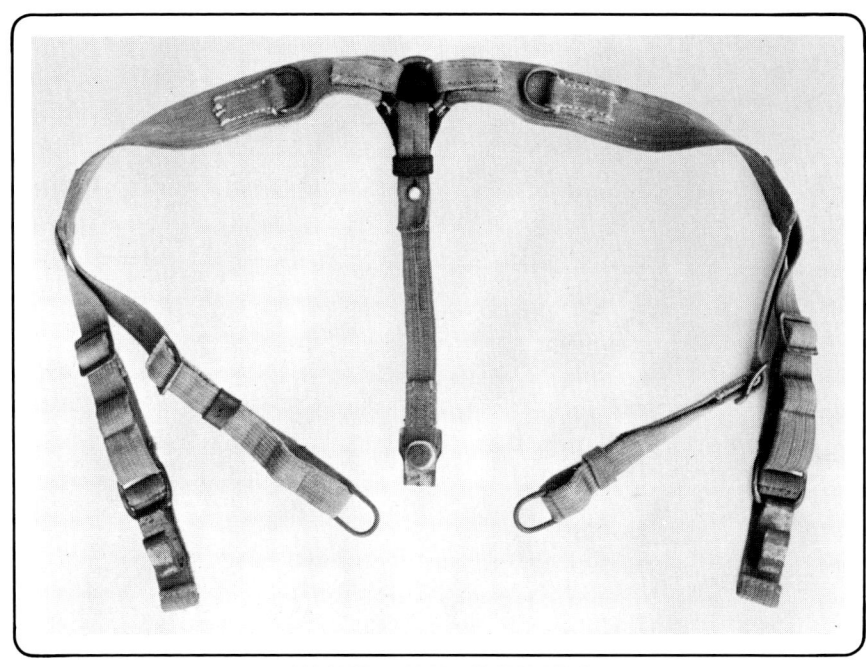

ALL-WEB SUPPORT SUSPENDERS
THE ASSAULT PACK
(STURMGEPÄCK)

The infantrymen's assault pack (harness) was a trapezoid of webbing which attached to the support suspenders. A single web strap was used to attach the mess kit to the top half of the assault pack and two web straps on the bottom were used to hold the shelter quarter tightly rolled and a detachable canvas bag. This bag was designed to hold the rifle cleaning kit, the shelter quarter rope, one day's iron ration (tined meat and Zwieback), and a sweater.

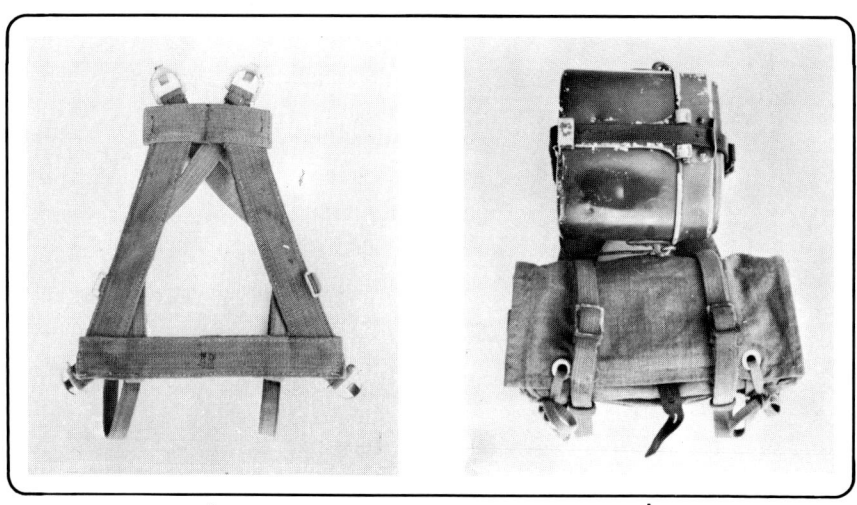

a.   b.

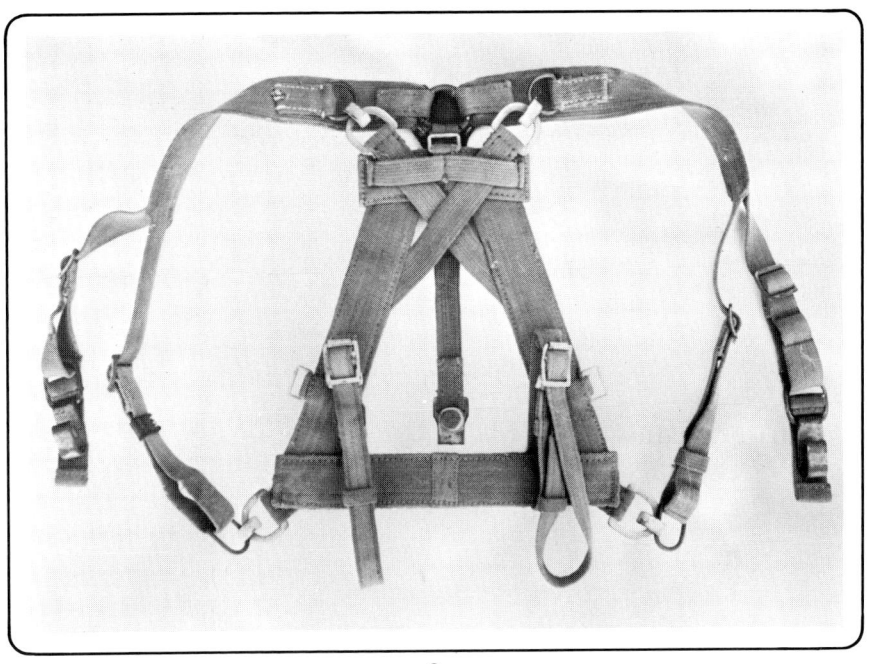

c.

a. Infantrymen's assault pack, rear view.
b. Assault pack with mess kit and small canvas bag attached.
c. Web support suspenders with assault pack attached.

THE RUCKSACK
(RUCKSACK)

The rucksack was in olive-colored canvas with either web or leather fittings. It was issued in addition to the Model 39 pack and held such items as extra clothing items, underclothing, socks, sewing kit, etc.

THE PACK (TORNISTER)

This olive-colored, square-shaped canvas pack (Model 39) was reinforced with leather and had no attached shoulder straps. It could be attached directly to the D-rings on the shoulders of the support suspenders with a cowhide flap. During the war, however, packs were produced in canvas with no fur covered flaps.

A towel, socks, sewing kit and shirt were carried in the flap pocket. The tent pole sections, two tent pegs, service shoes, mess kit, and other necessities could be carried in the pack itself.

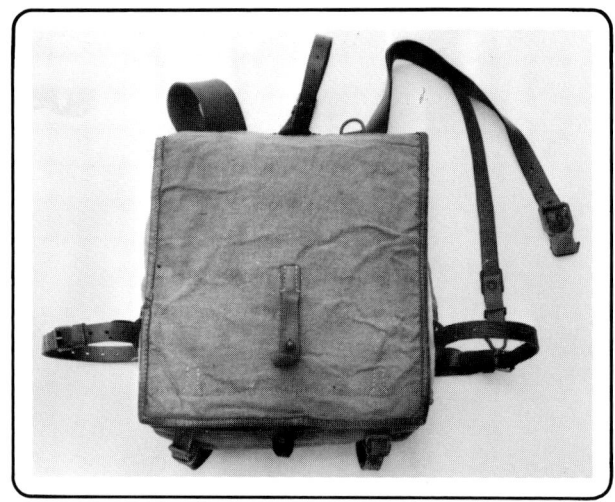

M39 PACK AND SUPPORT SUSPENDERS

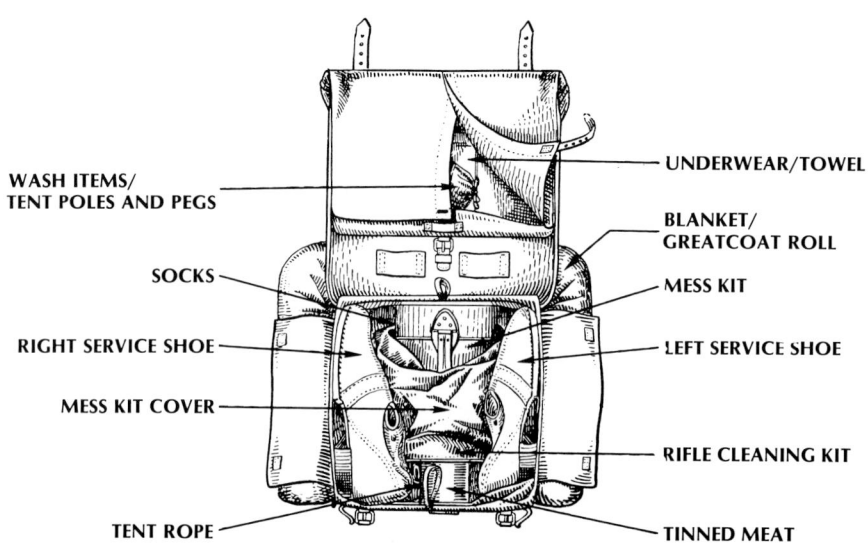

- WASH ITEMS/TENT POLES AND PEGS
- SOCKS
- RIGHT SERVICE SHOE
- MESS KIT COVER
- TENT ROPE
- UNDERWEAR/TOWEL
- BLANKET/GREATCOAT ROLL
- MESS KIT
- LEFT SERVICE SHOE
- RIFLE CLEANING KIT
- TINNED MEAT

NOTE:
When the full-pack was worn, the above contents were carried in the M39 pack.

THE GASMASK AND CANNISTER
(GASMASKE UND TRAGBUCHSE)

German troops were issued this gas mask and cannister and generally wore it suspended from a strap over the right shoulder and resting it on the left hip. It was held in place by an additional small strap and hook which attached onto the waist belt. The Army issue was worn in the African desert, but in many cases, was painted with a tan paint.

TAN-PAINTED GAS MASK CANNISTER

THE SHELTER QUARTER
(ZELTBAHN)

The triangular shelter quarter served as both one quarter of a 4-man tent and as a poncho. It was of a tightly woven, water resistant cotton drill and was in the standard Army "splinter-pattern" camouflage (light on one side and dark on the other). Tan shelter quarters were produced in a limited number for use in North Africa.

MAP OR DISPATCH CASE
(MELDEKARTENTASCHE)

The map or dispatch case, which was in black leather, was suspended by two adjustable straps from the belt. It was worn mainly by platoon and squad leaders, and dispatch riders. Several small pockets were sewn to the front of the case to accomodate pencils, map-reading instruments, rules and other equipment. Officers had the option of privately purchasing better quality cases for their own use. Although no tropical versions were produced, it was not uncommon to see map or dispatch cases in Africa which were painted tan.

SUN AND DUST GOGGLES
(SONNEN- UND STAUB-SCHUTZBRILLE)

Sun and dust goggles, with either clear or amber lenses, were issued to all members of motorized and mechanized units in North Africa. Vehicle drivers and motorcyclists, however, received a heavier model with smoke-colored lenses. Numerous varieties of goggles were issued to personnel in North Africa. Captured British variations were occasionally used by German troops when their own was not available.

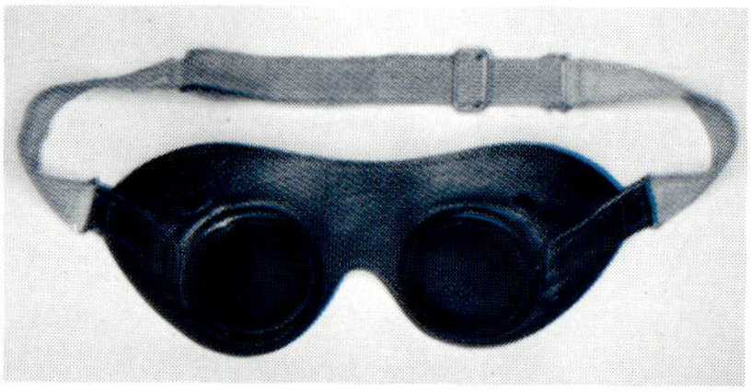

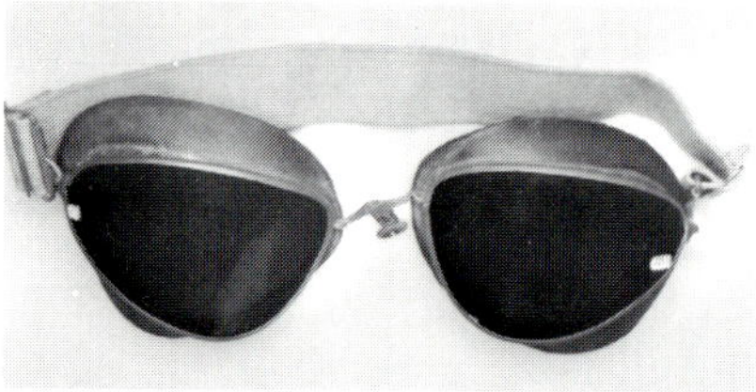

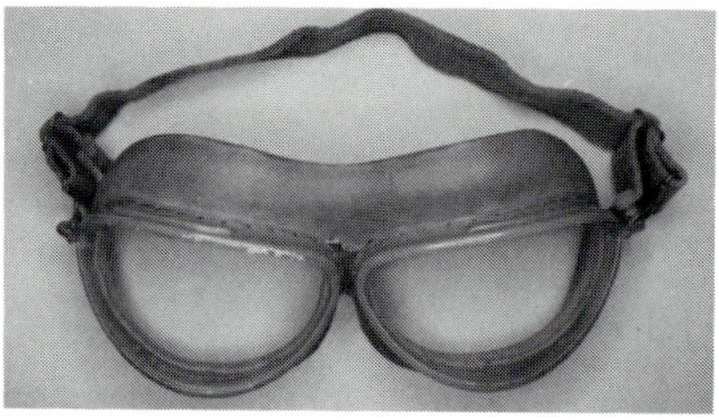

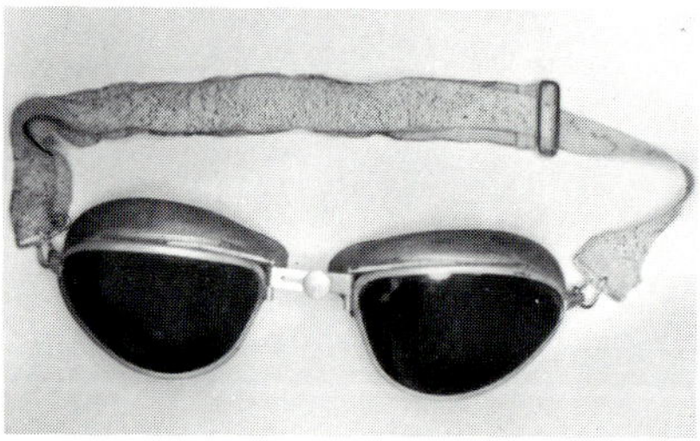

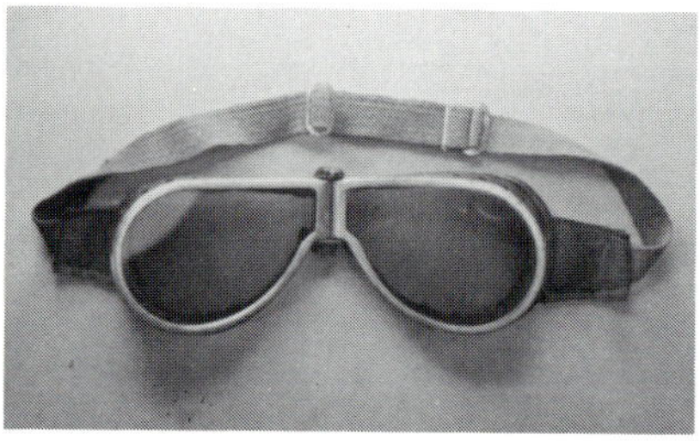

ROMMEL WEARING CAPTURED BRITISH GOGGLES.

HAND-GRENADE BAGS
(HANDGRANATEN SACK)

These olive-green canvas bags were designed for assault troop use and held three stick grenades each. They were hung around the neck and held in place by two smaller adjustable web straps which were around the wearers back.

GEORGE PETERSEN COLLECTION

NOTE:
An item is not necessarily tropical issue just because it is in olive-colored canvas. During the last few years of the war, leather came into short supply, and the already battle-tested canvas substitute soon became an issue material for all fronts.

This section lists only the basic field equipment issued to the German soldier in Africa, both continental and tropical. For that reason, special field equipment such as single and double MG 34 barrel carriers, MG 34 spare parts kits, sniper scopes and cases, hand-held range finders, flare pistols, etc. have not been listed. These items were standard equipment throughout the Wehrmacht, and when used in Africa, were sometimes painted a desert-tan color.

NOTE:
The name "Moritz", on the "Mammoth ("Mammut") below, is from the children's story "Max und Moritz", by Wilhelm Busch. Another captured "Mammoth" was named "Max".

A CAPTURED BRITISH "MAMMUT" NOW DISPLAYING THE BALKENKREUZ, THE AFRIKAKORPS PALM TREE/SWASTIKA SYMBOL, THE CORPS SYMBOL, A BATTALION H.Q. SYMBOL, THE NAME "MORITZ", AND THE REGISTRATION NUMBER.

Army Flags and Pennants
utilized in
North Africa

Command Flags

1

2

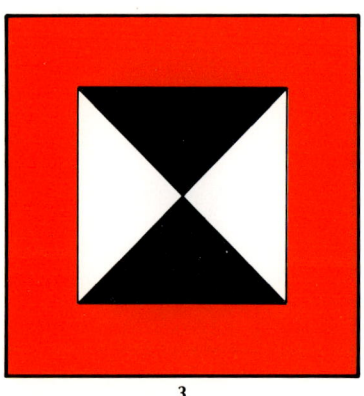
3

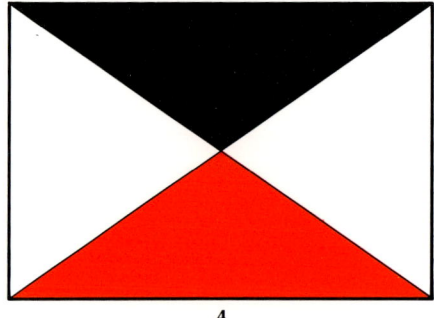
4

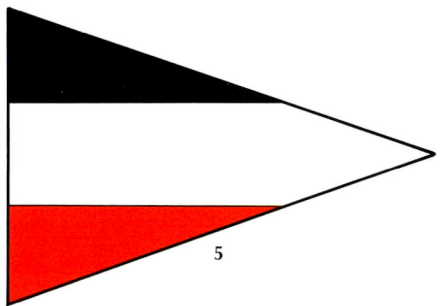

THE REVIEWING OF NEWLY ARRIVED GERMAN TROOPS IN TRIPOLI ON FEBRUARY 27, 1941 (NOTE ROMMEL'S CORPS COMMANDER FLAG). HIS VEHICLE CORPS PENNANT CARRIED THE INSCRIPTION "AFRIKA" ON THE RED FIELD.

1. Command Flag for the "Oberbefehlshaber einer Heeresgruppe" (Commander-in-Chief of an Army Group)
2. Command Flag for the "Oberbefehlshaber eines Armeeoberkommandos" (Commander-in-Chief of an Army)
3. Command Flag for the "Befehlshaber einer Panzergruppe" (Commander of a Panzer Group)(introduced January 25, 1941)
4. Command Flag for the "Kommandierender General eines Armeekorps" (Commanding General of an Army Corps)
5. Command Flag for the "Kommandeur einer Division" (Commander of a Division)

Staff Flags

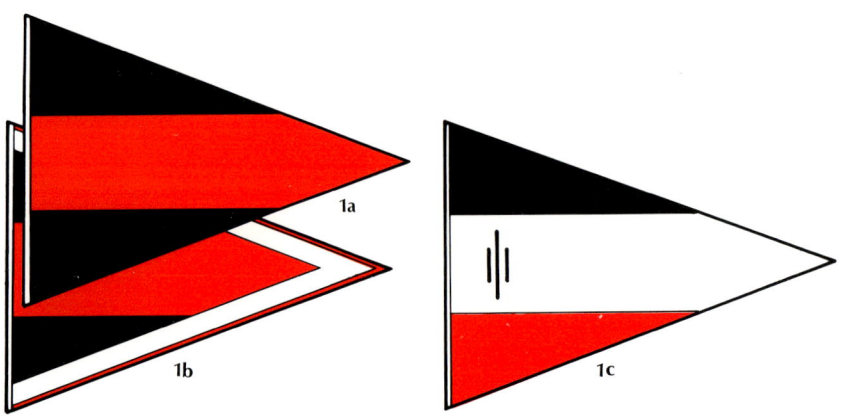

1a. Artillerieführer (in a division)
1b. höherer Artilleriekommandeur (in an army corps) from December 22, 1941 - October 27, 1943
1c. höherer Artilleriekommandeur, after October 27, 1943

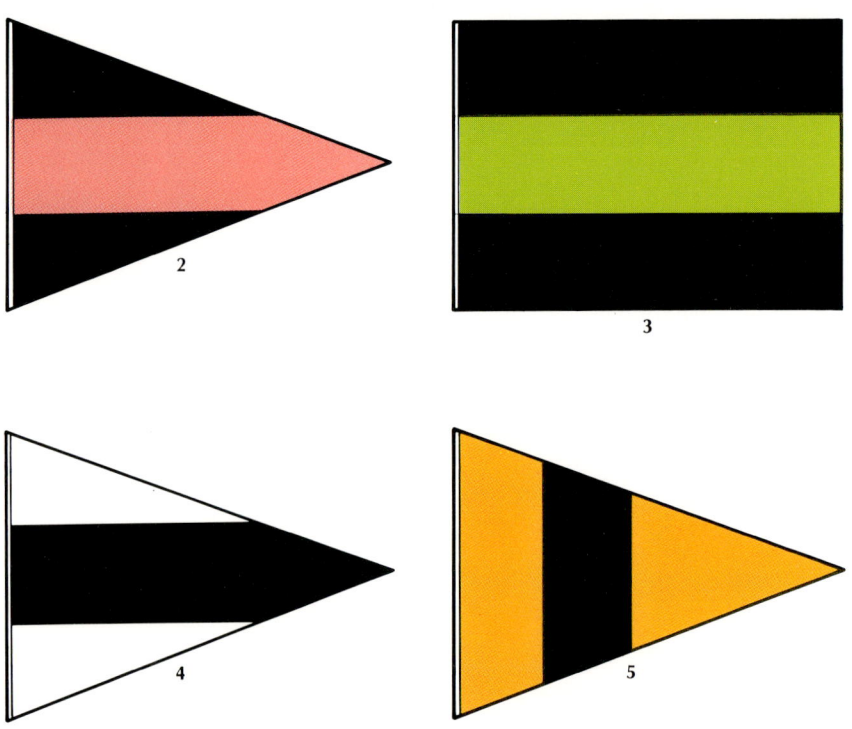

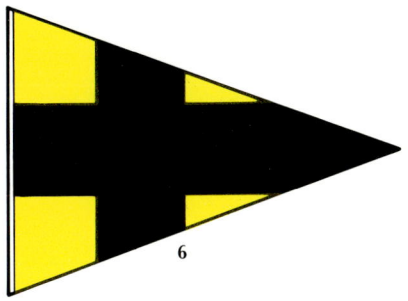

Kommandeur und Stab:
2. einer Panzerbrigade (Panzer-Brigade)
3. eines Schützenregiments/Panzergrenadierregiments (Rifle or Panzer Grenadier Regiment)
4. eines Infanteriebataillons (Infantry Battalion)
5. einer Aufklärungsabteilung einer Infanterie-Division (Infantry Division Reconnaissance Battalion)
6. einer Nachrichtenabteilung (Signals Battalion)

NOTES:
1. Flags and pennants of brigade, regiment and battalion commanders and H.Q. staffs varied in color (Waffenfarbe), according to their specific branch of service (e.g. bright red=artillery, white=infantry, black=engineers, etc.).
2. The battalion flag or pennant, with the black horizontal bar on a Waffenfarbe field (#4), was for a battalion within a regiment and numbered Roman. The battalion flag or pennant, with a black cross on a Waffenfarbe field (#6), was for independent battalions (i.e. outside the regiment) and numbered in Arabic.

Vehicle Pennants

It should be noted that the preceeding command and staff flags, which were used in North Africa, were also utilized in vehicle pennant form (but in half-size). When an authorized officer was uniformed and in his official vehicle, the command or staff flag was displayed on the left front fender and the Army vehicle pennant (yellow eagle for generals and white eagle for other officers) on the right. When he was not present inside his vehicle, however, the pennants were to be covered or removed.

---

[1]Allgemeine Heeresmitteilungen, January 7, 1942, Order #5 which was dated December 22, 1941.

If the officer was not authorized a command or staff flag, but was uniformed and in his official vehicle, the Army vehicle pennant was positioned on the left front fender. When traveling in their personal vehicle, generals/officers and officials and technicians of general or officer rank displayed the appropriate Army vehicle pennant on the right front fender. It should be noted, however, that there were no personal vehicles in North Africa, only official ones.

Reduced versions of the command and staff pennants (usually painted on metal plates) were permitted to be affixed near the front or rear registration plate, as additional recognition (2). On armor-plated vehicles, this pennant was generally painted directly onto the vehicle's surface.

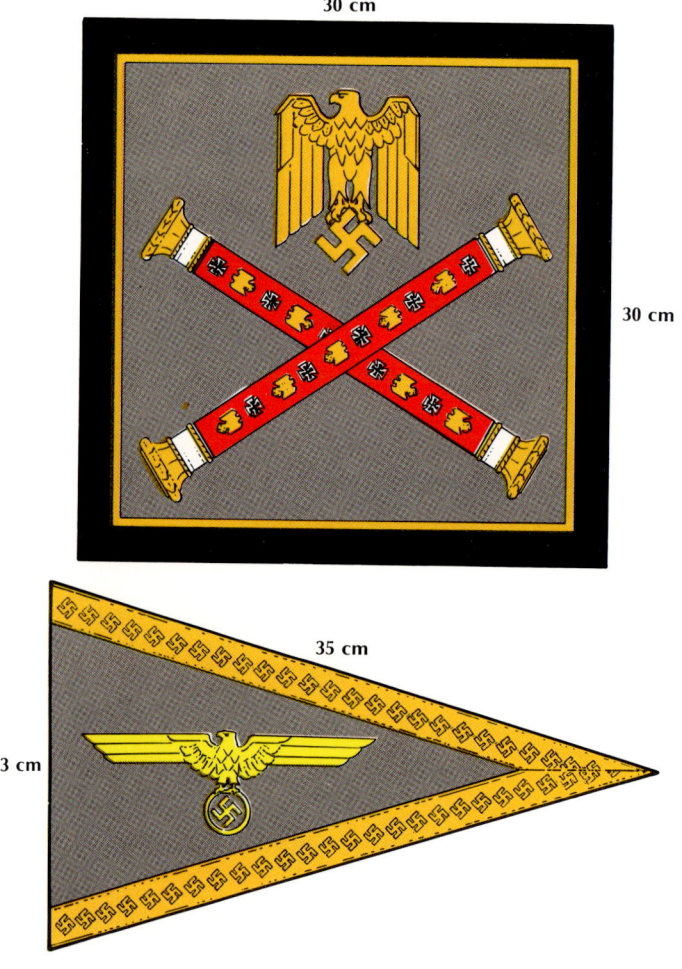

[2] *Allgemeine Heeresmitteilungen*, January 7, 1941, Order #14 which was dated December 30, 1940.

THE NATIONAL ARCHIVES

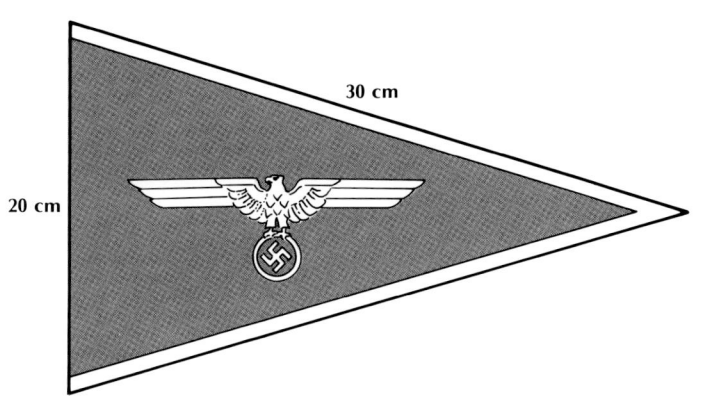

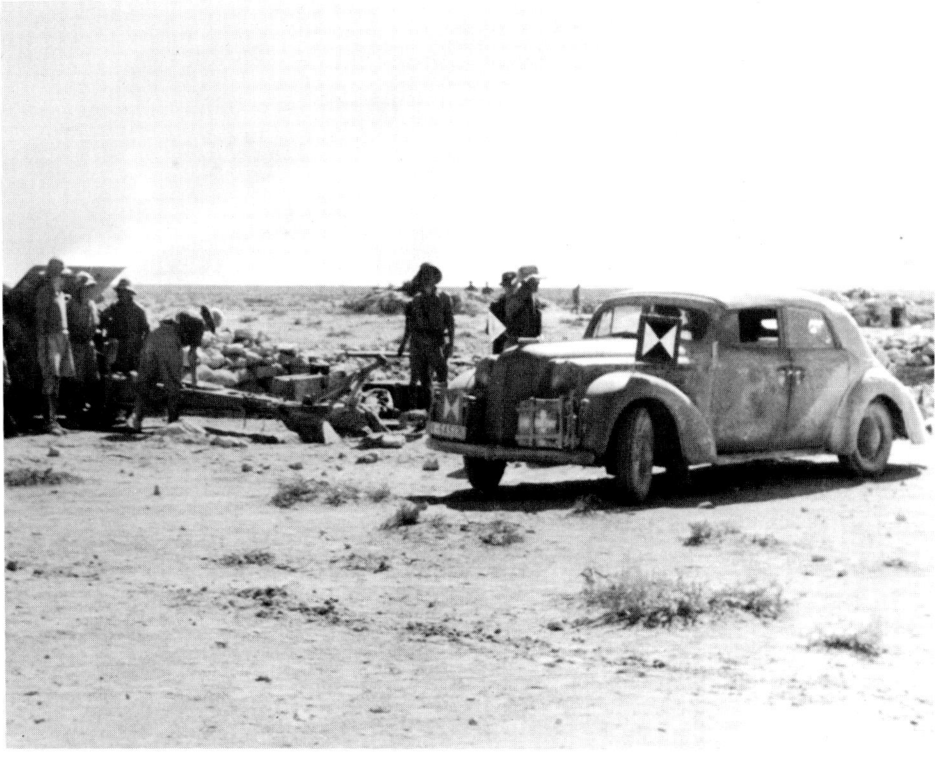

THE DAK COMMANDER VISITING AN ITALIAN ARTILLERY SITE. HIS OFFICIAL VEHICLE DISPLAYS THE CORPS COMMANDER FLAG AND THE GENERALS' VEHICLE PENNANT (NOTE REDUCED CORPS VERSION ABOVE FRONT REGISTRATION PLATE).

Rank Vehicle Pennants for:

1. Generalfeldmarschälle (General Field Marshals) after April 23, 1941
2. Generale (Generals) after April 23, 1941
3. Offiziere und Beamte (Officers and Officials of officer rank) after April 23, 1941)(also for Generals before April 23, 1941)

THE NATIONAL ARCHIVES

Vehicle Markings and Camouflage

Vehicle Markings

THE AFRIKAKORPS SYMBOL

The Afrikakorps symbol (palm/swastika) was carried on most vehicles of the 15. and 21. Panzer-Division (which made up the bulk of the Afrikakorps), including tanks, trucks, reconnaissance vehicles, etc. It was generally in white and was either applied with a frisket or by hand, thus numerous variations were encountered. There seems to have been no set pattern for the symbol's positioning for it varied considerably. The most common positioning on tanks was on:

- a. either of the front fenders
- b. left front hull plate
- c. hull sides
- d. turret sides
- e. rear hull plate
- f. either of the rear fenders

on trucks:
- a. either of the front fenders
- b. one or both doors
- c. either of the rear fenders

on prime movers:
- a. left front bow plate
- b. hood compartment sides
- c. rear access door area

NOTES:
1. A combination of any of the above placements was not uncommon.
2. When a vehicle received a desert camouflage, the palm/swastika symbol was often masked over, leaving a white symbol on an irregular dark-grey base.

MASKED VARIATION PALM/SWASTIKA SYMBOL

THE VARIATION AFRIKAKORPS SYMBOL ON THE TRUCK DOOR WAS APPLIED WITH A FRISKET.

DIVISIONAL VEHICLE SYMBOLS

Divisional vehicle symbols have been covered in their appropriate divisional section. Although originally intended to be in yellow, most division symbols used in Africa were in fact in white, since yellow was not easily distinguishable on a yellow-brown camouflaged vehicle. Black symbols were also utilized to some extent, when on a sand-colored background.

THE BALKENKREUZ

The Balkenkreuz appeared on almost every German vehicle utilized in North Africa. The following are the most encountered variations:

 OR

on tanks:
    a. hull sides
    b. rear hull plate

on prime movers:
    a. hull sides
    b. periodically on hood and rear access door area

VEHICLE IDENTIFICATION NUMBERS

Armored vehicles in North Africa continued to utilize the three digit identification system which had been initiated before the war. This number series, generally on the turret sides (tanks and reconnaissance vehicles) or hull sides (prime movers or personnel carriers), indicated the following:

    1st number - the company number
    2nd number - the platoon number (Zug)
    3rd number - the vehicle's position within its platoon (tank #1 - 5)

These digits were normally black or red, and outlined in white. The red numbers tended to be used with the yellow-brown camouflage color while the black numbers were used with the dark-grey or grey-green colors. This rule was not strictly adhered to, however, for many variations have been encountered. Later in the African campaign, the black or white outline of the numbers was also utilized, with the color of the vehicle showing through.

THIS PzKw IV WAS THE 3rd TANK, IN THE 1st PLATOON, OF THE 8th COMPANY. (NOTE POSITIONING OF THE PALM/SWASTIKA SYMBOL AND THE BALKENKREUZ).

NOTE:
Only the last or last two digits were sometimes utilized on armored vehicles, but they still implied the platoon and vehicle position.

Regimental command vehicles were identified in much the same manner with the following designations:

    R01 - regimental commander
    R02 - regimental adjutant
    R03 - signals officer
    R04 and upwards - other regimental staff vehicles

Abteilung/Bataillon command vehicles:

    I01 - 1st Abteilung/Bataillon commander
    I02 - 1st Abteilung/Bataillon adjutant
    I03 - 1st Abteilung/Bataillon signals officer
    I04 and upwards - other 1st Abteilung/Bataillon staff vehicles

    II01 - 2nd Abteilung/Bataillon commander
    II02 - 2nd Abteilung/Bataillon adjutant
    II03 - 2nd Abteilung/Bataillon signals officer
    II04 and upwards - other 2nd Abteilung/Bataillon staff vehicles

NOTE:
In many cases, the last two digits were quite small in comparision with the "R" or "I".

VEHICLE REGISTRATION PLATES

All wheeled and half-tracked vehicles which were utilized by the German Army were issued registration numbers and plates. These Army registration plates were prefixed with "WH" (Wehrmacht, Heer) and were positioned on the front and rear of the vehicle. Generally, stamped-out metal plates were utilized, with black lettering and numbers on a white base. The plates were also bordered in black. Registration plates were painted directly onto the vehicle's surface when smooth, heavy armor plate or curved surfaces made it difficult to affix the metal plates. An "FP" prefix indicated a Feldpost vehicle.

WH-683 304

FRONT REGISTRATION PLATE
(90mm X 475mm)

**WH
459 658**

REAR REGISTRATION PLATE
(200mm X 320mm)

NOTE HAND-PAINTED REGISTRATION NUMBER
ON REAR OF ROMMEL'S le.S.P.W. (Sd.Kfz. 250/3).

OFFICIAL TACTICAL SYMBOLS

These symbols were generally carried on lightly armed vehicles, weapons, equipment, etc., and characterized the branch of service plus the size of the unit. They were primarily adapted from German military map symbols and were applied in white, normally next to the divisional symbol. Additional numbers and letters could be positioned to the right of the tactical symbol which indicated:

```
R      = Regimental Staff (Regimentsstab)
I      = 1st Battalion Staff (Stab I. Btl.)
II     = 2nd Battalion Staff (Stab II. Btl.)
III    = 3rd Battalion Staff (Stab III. Btl.)
St     = Independent Battalion Staff (Stab einer selbständigen Abt./Btl.)
1-16   = Company, Battery or Squadron (Kp., Bttr., Schwdr.)
K1-11  = Supply train assigned to a Battalion, etc. (Kolonnenbezeich-
         nung K1-11)
B      = Bridge Transport Column (Brückenkolonne)
M      = Engineer Machine Platoon (Pioniermaschinenzug)
W1 & 2 = Workshop Company (Werkstattkompanie, W1, W2)
```

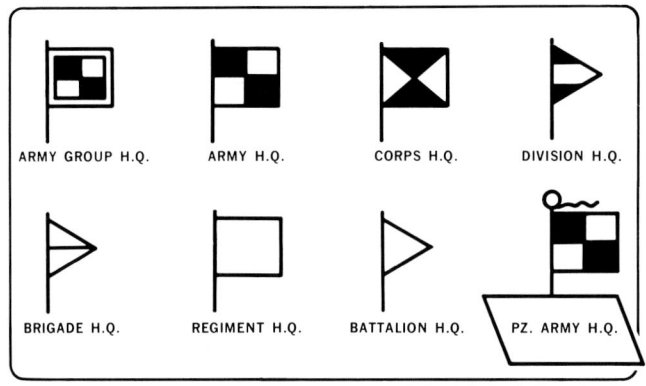

THE ABOVE H.Q. PENNANTS COULD BE ADDED TO BASIC TACTICAL SYMBOLS TO CREATE A UNIT H.Q. OR STAFF SYMBOL.

1. Div. Kdo./Inf.-Div. (mot), later Pz.-Gren.-Div.
2. Infantry Company
3. Infantry Company (partially mot.)
4. Infantry Reg. H.Q. (mot)
5. Armoured Personnel Carrier Company
6. Armoured Personnel Carrier Company (half-tracked)
7. Engineers (Bridge Transport Column)
8. Staff of Engineer Battalion (mot)
9. Staff Signals Battalion, HQ
10. 4th Cavalry Reconnaissance Squadron (mot)
11. 1st Artillery Battalion H.Q.
12. 2nd Artillery Battalion H.Q.
13. 3rd Artillery Battalion H.Q.
14. Light Field Artillery Battery
15. Panzer Artillery Battery (self-propelled)
16. Field Artillery, (mot)(8th Battery)
17. Heavy Field Artillery, 150mm (mot)(10th Battery) } (tracked)
18. Staff of a Flak-Abt. (mot)
19. Flak Battery (mot)
20. Half-Tracked Fla Company ("Fla" referred to 2cm and 3.7cm guns which belonged to the infantry; "Flak" were artillery guns of 7.5 cm or more)

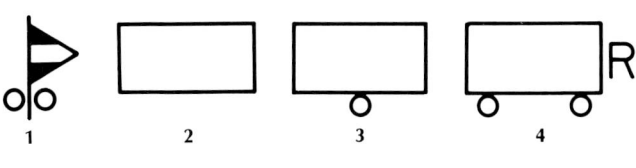

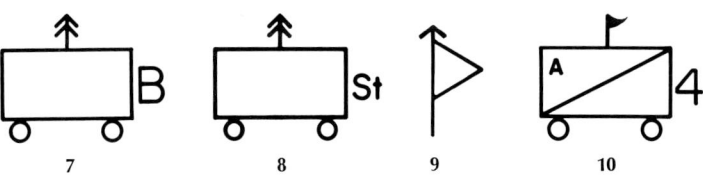

Sd.Kfz. 250/3 OF THE 3rd BATTERY, FIELD ARTILLERY, 21. PANZER-DIVISION.

21. Assault Gun Battery or Company
22. Panzergrenadierdivision H.Q. or Staff
23. Panzergrenadierbrigade H.Q. or Staff
24. Panzer Company
25. Panzer Division H.Q. or Staff
26. Panzer Brigade H.Q. or Staff
27. Staff of a Reconnaissance Battalion
28. Self-Propelled Anti-Tank Company or Zug (equipped with Assault Guns)
29. Anti-Tank Company or Zug (mot)(early)
30. Anti-Tank Company or Zug
31. Anti-Tank Company or Zug (mot)(tracked)
32. Signals Company or Zug (mot)
33. Motorcycle Company or Zug (mot)
34. Technical Services (workshop company)
35. Supply Service
36. Administration Service
    No. 1 - Quartermaster (food)
    No. 2 - Bakery
    No. 3 - Butcher
37. Medical Companies, Platoons or Field Hospitals (No. 3 is the Field Hospital)
38. Field Police Troop
39. Field Post Office
40. War Correspondents' Company Platoon (Kriegsberichter)

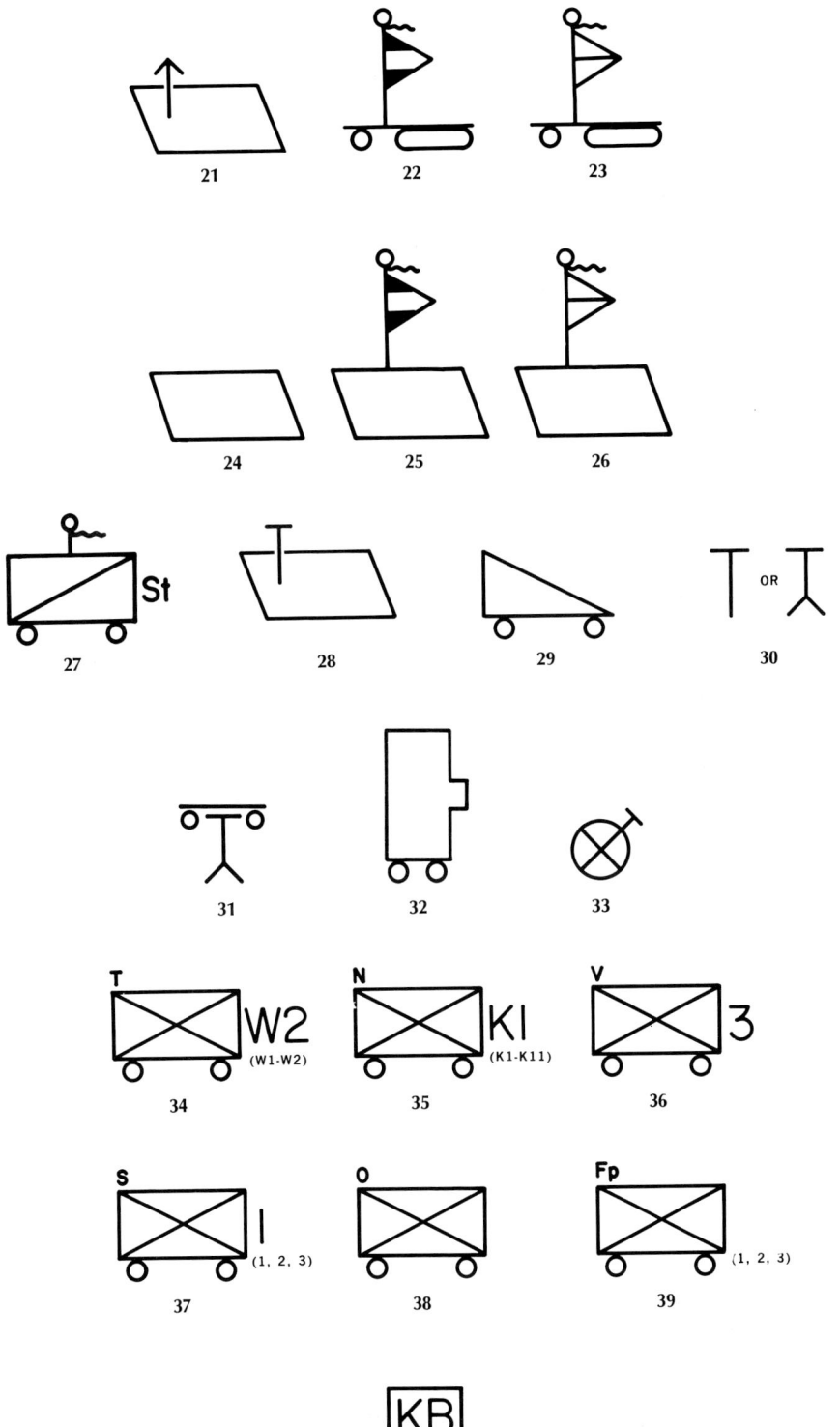

MEDICAL VEHICLE SYMBOLS

Vehicles assigned to medical companies, platoons or field hospitals, carried distinctive insignia as protection against enemy attack. A red cross within a white circle was normally affixed on all four sides of the vehicle plus a red cross on a white flag was sometimes used as additional identification.

THE NATIONAL ARCHIVES

ROMMEL'S COMMAND VEHICLE (le.S.P.W. [SCHÜTZENPANZERWAGEN]) IS AT THE RIGHT OF THIS PHOTO.

AIRCRAFT RECOGNITION FLAG

To ease recognition by German aircraft during combined air/ground operations, a national flag (black swastika within a white circle on a red field) was sometimes tied across the tank turret or across the engine compartment in the rear. Later in the war, a Balkenkreuz replaced the swastika within the white circle. The flag was attached by grommets at each corner.

CAPTURED VEHICLE MARKINGS

A large portion of Rommel's supply columns consisted of captured British vehicles. Once in German hands, this equipment was quickly given a registration number and plates, the proper German markings, and then pressed into service against their former owners. The Balkenkreuz was in either bold white or in black bordered in white, and was distinctively positioned on all captured trucks and tanks.

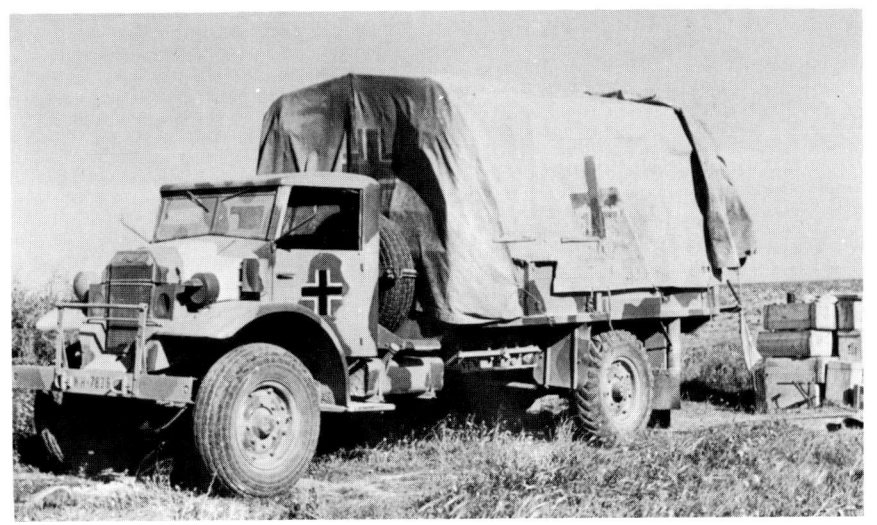

A CAPTURED BRITISH TRUCK (CHEVROLET) WITH THE GERMAN BALKENKREUZ.

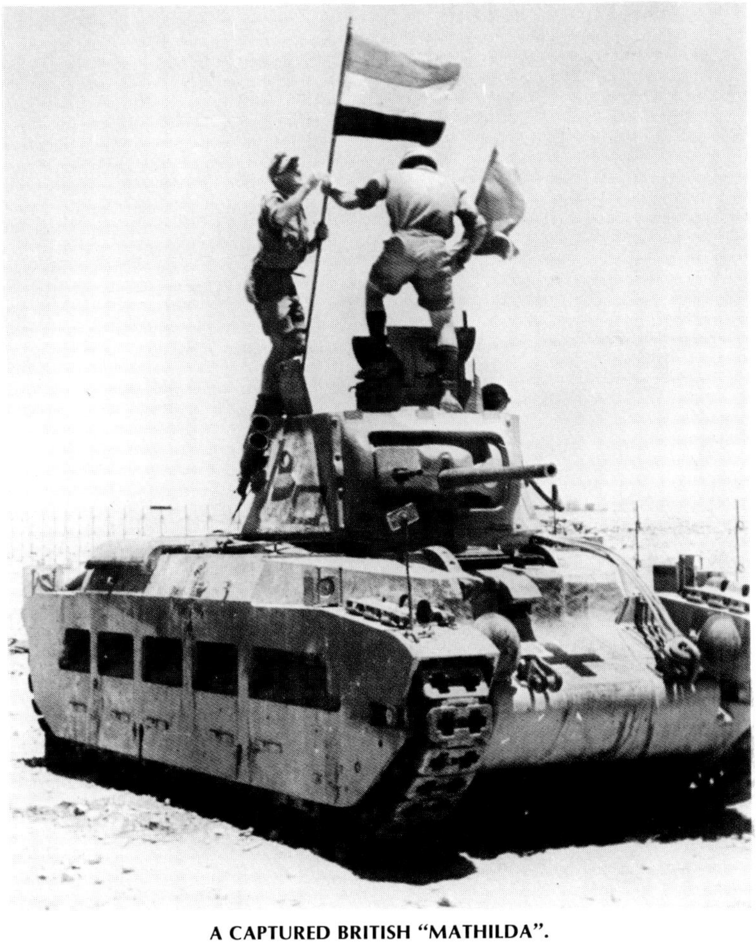

THE NATIONAL ARCHIVES

A CAPTURED BRITISH "MATHILDA".

Vehicle Camouflage

In an effort to keep the destination of the Libyan-bound German troops a secret as long as possible, their vehicles received no special camouflage paint and were therefore left in the dark-grey continental color. The German High Command, in fact, was quite unprepared for the sudden move into Africa in early 1941, and had not even allocated the proper camouflage paint for the vehicles once they had been landed in Tripoli. It was therefore suggested, that until the proper paint was made available, individual crews and drivers should rub their tanks and trucks with oil and then spray them with sand.[1] In this manner, field expediency provided a satisfactory but temporary camouflage which had to be frequently repeated. An order dated March 17, 1941, however, ordered that units destined for Africa were to be supplied with a matt yellow-brown (#RAL 8000) and a matt grey-green (#RAL 7008) paint for vehicles and equipment.[2] These paints were applied, whenever time or circumstance permitted, either by irregular spraying over the original dark-grey color or simply by splotching the paint by brush. Vehicles generally did not receive a complete repaint unless they were in rear or repair areas.

The various desert areas or the different desert seasons required periodic camouflage changes. In some cases, the standard yellow-brown color could be made darker (deep-sand color) by mixing it with the grey-green paint (2 parts yellow-brown/1 part grey-green), or the existing

THE Sd.Kfz. 7 PRIME-MOVER ABOVE WAS GIVEN A CRUDE SPRAY CAMOUFLAGE COVERING.

IN MANY DESERT AREAS, THE BASIC DARK-GREY WAS JUST AS EFFECTIVE AS THE YELLOW-BROWN COLORED CAMOUFLAGE. THE VEHICLE ABOVE, FROM NACHRICHTEN-ABTEILUNG 200, IS CARRYING ACCUMULATED DESERT DUST AND NOT A PARTIAL CAMOUFLAGE PAINT JOB.

sand-brown camouflage could be satisfactorily altered by adding various designs in either dark-grey or grey-green. German tanks and vehicles were painted in many cases with whatever was available, including requisitioned Italian pea-green paint or captured British paint.

An order dated February 1943, introduced three new equipment and vehicle camouflage paints: an olive-green, a redish-brown and a dark yellow.[3] It is doubtful, however, that these were utilized in North Africa except in the case of last-minute replacement equipment from the continent.

---

[1] MS #P-129, "Desert Warfare: German Experience in World War II".

[2] Allgemeine Heeresmitteilungen, March 21, 1941, Order #281.

[3] Allgemeine Heeresmitteilungen, February 22, 1943, Order #181.

Miscellaneous

FIELD NEWSPAPERS

Several field newspapers were produced for German personnel in the African theater, with their contents ranging from unit interest to international matters. It was the responsibility of the Field Post to get them dispersed to their distribution points within the various commands by means of field post numbers (Feldpostnummern). Every unit was issued a field post number, no matter how subordinate, as is indicated below:

    Artillerie-Regiment 115   - F. P. Nr. 09995
    Panzerjäger-Abteilung 605 - F. P. Nr. 03433

Ortskommandeur Misurata - F.P.Nr. 05844
Bäckerei-Kompanie 554 - F.P.Nr. 22174
Wasserfilterkolonne 589 - F.P.Nr. 18217

The most significant of these field newspapers were:
1. The Panzerarmee's "Die Oase", a weekly for all German troops in Africa
2. The X. Fliegerkorps' "Adler von Hellas"
3. "Die Karawane", for German troops in Tunisia

NOTE:
Copies of "Adler von Hellas" were distributed within the Panzerarmee through the Pz.A.O.K. 5, Ic (Chief Intelligence Officer).

ALLIED PROPAGANDA NEWSPAPERS

The "Afrika-Post" was a weekly, Allied propaganda field newspaper which was dropped behind German lines in Tunisia. Its contents were written to demoralize the German soldier by pointing out the failures of the Wehrmacht on all fronts, and not only in North Africa. Some of the searing highlights of the February 8, 1943 edition below, were:

    a. The destruction and capitulation of the 6. Armee at Stalingrad.
    b. Facts about the crumbling home front.
    c. What of the fate of the German soldier in Tunisia? Is Hitler using him to buy time?
    d. English bombers have attacked Berlin on January 30 and 31, in daylight, causing Göring to postpone his scheduled speech for over an hour.

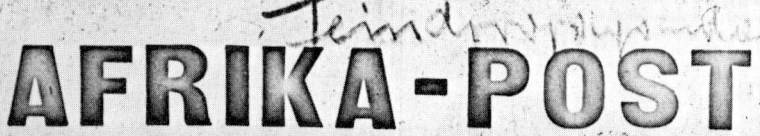

e. Roosevelt and Churchill have met in Morocco to plot the continued offensive against the Axis.
f. The paper points out that since June 1941, three German soldiers have died every minute of the day.
g. It goes on to state that the dead do not come home, but prisoners remain alive and see their homeland again. All German prisoners in Tunisia will be sent to England or America, and after the war, will be sent back to Germany and their loved ones.
h. It concludes with a proposed plan of surrender: Come alone or with other comrades; bring your Greatcoat, mess kit and shaving kit; leave your weapon; and bring, if possible, this newspaper which will assure free passage through English, American and French lines.

AFRIKAKORPS PROVISIONAL STAMP

This provisional stamp was for use on parcel post going from Tunisia to Germany in early 1943. It was lithographed locally by "Die Oase" on a thick porous paper. Perf. 11 1/2.

Color: Red/Brown (light) on cream

DAK SOUVENIR RINGS

One of the favorite mementos of a German soldier's service time in North Africa was a hand-crafted ring displaying the Afrikakorps symbol or some other signifying emblem. Illustrated are two distinct variations which were available in unit canteens or from local merchants.

THIS SYMBOL IS ARABIC FOR "DERNA."

SURRENDER LEAFLETS

GERMAN

Something to make you think!

AMERICAN SOLDIER !   **BRITISH SOLDIER !**

Is your heart in this fight against German troops ? Do you believe in fighting between people so much alike each other ?

We Germans don't ! We know we must fight the Russian enemy to defend our country, our way of living and everything we hold dear, and to make the world safe from Bolshevism.

The majority of the French people in France are today sympathizing with Germany because they too realize that our country and its armed strength is the last barrier to protect Europe against Bolshevism. Even those Frenchmen who were lead to fight on your side in North Africa are beginning to realize their mistake and are coming over to us by the thousand.

Why then should we go on killing each other now — to the 'elight of others ? Are not our affinities far more important than our differences ?

Draw your own conclusions if you agree with this. Do not accept this war in Africa as « one of those things ». Your life is at stake — why waste it in a fight you don't believe in ? You are not endangering your far-away country by saving your life.

We pledge honourable and decent treatment to every American and British soldier who realizes the futility of this struggle on African soil.

> This leaflet shown to a German or Italian soldier assures you free passage through the German or Italian lines.

GILT ALS PASSIERSCHEIN !   **LASCIA PASSARE !**

ALLIED

Generaloberst von Arnim sagt euch:

« VOR UNS DER FEIND ! »
« HINTER UNS DIE SEE ! »
« ES GIBT KEIN ZURUECK MEHR ! »

> Generaloberst von Arnim tells you:
>
>> "Before us the enemy!"
>> "Behind us the sea!"
>> "THERE IS NO WAY BACK"

EUER VERSTAND SAGT EUCH:

« HINTER DEM FEIND : DAS SAMMELLAGER.
« HINTER DEM SAMMELLAGER : DAS GEFANGENENLAGER IN ENGLAND ODER AMERIKA.
« HINTER DEM GEFANGENENLAGER : DIE HEIMAT ! »

« ES GIBT EIN ZURUECK !

> Your mind tells you:
>
>> *Behind the enemy: the detention camp.
>> *Behind the detention camp: the prisoner of war camp in England or America.
>> *Behind the prisoner of war camp: Home!
>> THERE IS A WAY BACK!

The dead do not come home.   But the prisoner remains alive and will see home again.

Bibliography

Agar-Hamilton, J.A.I. and L.C.F. Turner: "THE SIDI REZEG BATTLES 1941", Capetown, Oxford University Press, 1957.

Alman, Karl: "RITTERKREUZTRÄGER DES AFRIKAKORPS", Rastatt, Erich Pabel Verlag, 1968.

"ALLGEMEINE HEERESMITTEILUNGEN", 1940-1943.

"BALKENKREUZ ÜBER WÜSTENLAND", Oldenburg, Gerhard Stalling Verlag, 1943.

Barnett, Correlli: "THE DESERT GENERALS, New York, The Viking Press, 1961.

Braddock, B.A., D.W.: "THE CAMPAIGN IN EGYPT AND LIBYA 1941-1942", Aldershot, Gale Polden Limited, 1964.

Bradford, George R.: "ARMOR, CAMOUFLAGE AND MARKINGS: NORTH AFRICA 1940-1943", Preston, Ontario, Published Privately, 1971.

Brockdorff, Werner: "GEHEIMKOMMANDOS DES ZWEITEN WELTKRIEGES" München-Wels, Verlag Welermühl München, 1967.

Carell, Paul: "THE FOXES OF THE DESERT", New York, E.P. Dutton & Co., Inc., 1961.

Carver, Michael: "EL ALAMEIN", New York, Dufour Editions, 1962.

Carver, Michael: "TOBRUK", Philadelphia, Dufour Editions, 1964.

Ciano, Count Galeazzo: "THE CIANO DIARIES 1939-1943", New York, Doubleday & Company, Inc., 1946.

Davis, Brian L.: "GERMAN ARMY UNIFORMS AND INSIGNIA 1933-1945", New York, The World Publishing Company, 1972.

von Esebeck, Hanns Gert Frhr.: "HELDEN DER WÜSTE", Berlin, Verlag Die Heim Bücherei, 1942.

Freidin, Semour and William Richardson: "THE FATAL DECISIONS", New York, William Sloane Associates, 1956.

"GROSSDEUTSCHLAND IM WELTGESCHEHEN, TAGESBILDBERICHTE 1942", Berlin, Verlag Joh. Kasper & Co., 1943.

Hartmann, Theodor: "WEHRMACHT DIVISIONAL SIGNS 1938-1945", London, Almark Publishing Co., 1970.

Haupt, Werner and Major J.K.W. Bingham: "DER AFRIKA-FELDZUG 1941-1943", Dorheim, Podzun Verlag Dorheim, 1968.

"HEERES-VERORDNUNGSBLATT", 1940-1943.

Howe, George F.: "NORTHWEST AFRICA: SEIZING THE INITIATIVE IN THE WEST", Washington, Office of the Chief of Military History, Dept. of the Army, U.S. Government Printing Office, 1957.

Jacobsen, H.A. and J. Rohwer, Editors: "DECISIVE BATTLES OF WORLD WAR II: THE GERMAN VIEW", New York, G.P. Putnam & Sons, 1965.

Kelly, Clement: "The Italo-German Campaign Medal for Africa", "THE MEDAL COLLECTOR", Vol. 23, No. 7, July 1972.

Kesselring, Generalfeldmarschall a. D. Albert: "KESSELRING: A SOLDIER'S RECORD", New York, William Morrow & Co., 1954.

Law, Richard D.: "DAK: DEUTSCHES AFRIKAKORPS 1941-1943", New Orleans, Trade Mart Reproductions, 1967.

Lewin, Ronald: "ROMMEL AS MILITARY COMMANDER", London, B.T. Batsford, 1968.

Liddell Hart, B.H.: "THE GERMAN GENERALS TALK", New York, William Morrow & Co., 1948.

Liddell Hart, B.H., Editor: "THE ROMMEL PAPERS", New York, Harcourt, Brace and Co., 1968.

Long, Gavin: "TO BENGHAZI", Canberra, Australian War Memorial, 1966.

"LUFTWAFFEN-VERORDNUNGSBLATT", 1940-1943.

Macintyre, Donald: "THE BATTLE FOR THE MEDITERRANEAN", New York, W.W. Norton and Co., 1965.

Macksey, M.C., Maj. K.J.: "AFRIKAKORPS", New York, Ballantine Books, 1968.

"MARSCH UND KAMPF DES DEUTSCHEN AFRIKAKORPS, 1941", Band I, München, Carl Röhrig Verlag, 1943.

Maughan, Barton: "TOBRUK AND EL ALAMEIN", Canberra, Australian War Memorial, 1966.

von Mellenthin, Maj.Gen. F.W.: "PANZER BATTLES", Harman, University of Oklahoma, 1958.

Moorehead, Alan: "THE DESERT WAR", London, Homish-Hamilton Ltd., 1965.

Murphy, W.E.: "THE RELIEF OF TOBRUK", Wellington, Dept. of Internal Affairs, New Zealand, 1961.

Nehring, Walther K.: "DIE GESCHICHTE DER DEUTSCHEN PANZERWAFFE 1916 - 1945", Berlin, Propyläen Verlag, 1969.

Phillips, C.E. Lucas: "ALAMEIN", Boston, Little, Brown and Co., 1962.

Piehl, Hauptmann: "GANZE MÄNNER", Leipzig, Verlagshaus Bong & Co., 1943.

Playfair, C.B., D.S.O., Maj. Gen. I.S.O.: "THE MEDITERRANEAN AND MIDDLE EAST", Her Majesty's Stationery Office.
    Volume I: "EARLY SUCCESSES AGAINST ITALY", London 1954.
    Volume II: "THE GERMANS COME TO THE AID OF THEIR ALLY", London, 1956.
    Volume III: "BRITISH FORTUNES REACH THEIR LOWEST EBB", London, 1960.
    Volume IV: "THE DESTRUCTION OF THE AXIS FORCES IN AFRICA", London, 1966.

Raeder, Erich: "Führer Conferences on Naval Affairs", "BRASSEY'S NAVAL ANNUAL 1948", New York, The Macmillan Co., 1948.

Reibert, Dr. jur. W.: "DER DIENSTUNTERRICHT IM HEERE", Berlin, E.S. Mittler & Sohn, 1940.

Scheibert, H.: "DEUTSCHER PANZERGRENADIER 1939-1945", Dorheim, Podzun Verlag Dorheim, 1966.

Scheibert, H. and C. Wagener: "DIE DEUTSCHE PANZERTRUPPE 1939-1945", Bad Nauheim, Podzun Verlag Bad Nauheim, 1966.

Scoullar, J.L.: "BATTLE FOR EGYPT", Wellington, Dept. of Internal Affairs, New Zealand, 1962.

Schmitt, Heinz Werner: "WITH ROMMEL IN THE DESERT", London, George C. Harrap & Co., 1951.

Schwallach, Günter: "Der Orientfeldzug fand nicht statt: Kampf und Untergang des Sonderverband 288", "DER FRONTSOLDAT ERZÄHLT", Nr. 1, 1956.

"SIGNAL", 1940-1943.

Spaeter, Helmuth: "DIE GESCHICHTE DES PANZERKORPS GROSSDEUTSCHLAND", Band III, Duisburg-Ruhrort, Traditionsverband Grossdeutschland, 1958.

Stevens, Maj. Gen. W. G.: "BARDIA TO ENFIDAVILLE", Wellington, Dept. of Internal Affairs, New Zealand, 1962.

Walker, Ronald: "ALAM HALFA AND ALAMEIN", Wellington, Dept. of Internal Affairs, New Zealand, 1962.

Trevor-Roper, H. R., Editor: "BLITZKRIEG TO DEFEAT", New York, Holt, Rinehart and Winston, 1965.

"UNIFORMEN-MARKT", No. 9, 1941, and No. 3, 1943.

Verney, D. S. O., M. V. O., Maj. Gen. G. L.: "THE DESERT RATS", London, Hutchinson & Co., 1954.

War Department: "HANDBOOK ON GERMAN MILITARY FORCES", War Department Technical Manual TM-E 30-451, Washington, (Sept. 1, 1943, and March 15, 1945).

War Office: "THE EIGHTH ARMY", London, Ministry of Information, 1944.

Warlimont, Walter: "INSIDE HITLER'S HEADQUARTERS 1939-1945", New York, Frederick A. Praeger, 1964.

"DIE WEHRMACHT", 1940-1943.

Young, Desmond: "ROMMEL - THE DESERT FOX", New York, Harper and Brothers, 1960.

FOREIGN MILITARY STUDIES

C-029: "SECRET FIELD POLICE", by Oberst Wilhelm Kirchbaum.

C-065a: "GREINER DIARY NOTES" (Aug. 12, 1942 - Mar. 12, 1943), by Ministerialrat im OKW Dr. Helmuth Greiner.

C-065f: "AFRICA" (1941), by Helmuth Greiner.

D-001: "OPERATIONS OF THE FIFTH PANZER ARMY IN TUNISIA"(1943), by General der Panzertruppe Gustav von Vaerst.

D-046: "STUDIES ON THE MARETH POSITION", by Generalmajor Fritz Krause.

D-070: "REPORT OF ARMY REAR AREA COMMANDER , ARMY OF NORTH AFRICA, PART I", by Generalmajor Ernst Schnarrenberger.

D-072: "REPORT OF MY ACTIVITIES AS COMMANDER OF REAR AREA OF ARMY OF NORTH AFRICA", by Generalmajor Ernst Schnarrenberger.

D-086: "THE FIRST PHASE OF THE ENGAGEMENT IN TUNISIA", by General der Panzertruppe Walther Nehring.

D-120: "THE DEVELOPMENT OF THE SITUATION IN NORTH AFRICA" (Jan. 1 - Feb. 28, 1943), by General der Panzertruppe Walther Nehring.

D-124: "THE DRIVE VIA GAFSA AGAINST KASSERINE PASS", by General Kurt Frhr. von Liebenstein.

D-147: "THE FIRST PHASE OF THE BATTLE OF TUNISIA", by General der Panzertruppe Walther Nehring.

D-173: "BATTLES OF KAMPFGRUPPE LANG IN TUNISIA (10th Panzer-Division)", by Oberst Rudolf Lang.

D-174: "COMMITMENT OF THE 10TH PANZER-DIVISION IN TUNISIA, by Oberst Ulrich Buerker.

D-215: "BATTLES OF 334TH DIVISION AND GROUP WEBER"(End of Dec. 1942 - March 1943), by Generlleutnant Friedrich Weber.

D-325: "XC KORPS", by General der Panzertruppe Walther Nehring.

O-216: "THE OPERATIONS OF MARSHAL GRAZIANI PRIOR TO THE ARRIVAL OF GERMAN TROOPS", by Heinz Hegenreiner.

P-129: "GERMAN EXPERIENCES IN DESERT WARFARE DURING WORLD WAR II", by Generalmajor Alfred Toppe and 9 others.

T-3: "NORTH AFRICAN CAMPAIGN, VOLUME I", by Oberst Rainer Kriebel and 7 others.

T-3-P1: "KESSELRING'S VIEWS OF THE AFRICAN WAR", by Generalfeldmarschall Albert Kesselring.

T-3: "NORTH AFRICAN CAMPAIGN, Volume II (1942)", by General der Panzertruppe Walther Nehring.

MICROFILM

Microfilm Publication T34, Roll 191.

Microfilm Publication T313, Rolls 423, 426, 430, 431, 433, 436, 437, 439, 440, 458, 462.

Microfilm Publication T314, Roll 2.

Microfilm Publication T315, Rolls 570, 666, 1155, 1473, 1474, 2084, 2085, 2086, 2111, 2276, 2277, 2278.

Microfilm Roll 60-15: "ORDER-OF-BATTLE OF THE GERMAN ARMY".

Microfilm Roll 60-106 "ORDER-OF-BATTLE OF THE ITALIAN ARMY".

Microfilm Publication T84, Rolls 273, 276 (The Rommel Photographs).

AIR HISTORICAL BRANCH TRANSLATIONS OF CAPTURED DOCUMENTS

Translations VII/2, 5, 6, 25, 54, 63, 72, 80, 87 (KTB DAK), 88 (KTB DAK), 101 (KTB DAK), 104, 105 (KTB PZ. ARMEE AFRIKA), 106, 108 (KTB PZ. ARMEE AFRIKA), 110 (KTB PZ. ARMEE AFRIKA), 111, 112, 113, 114, 115, 116, 117, 118 (KTB PZ. ARMEE AFRICA), 128, 129.

NEW ZEALAND TRANSLATIONS OF CAPTURED RECORDS PERTAINING TO GERMAN ARMY UNITS PARTICIPATING IN THE NORTH AFRICAN CAMPAIGN FROM AUGUST 1941 TO MAY 1943.

Section 1. Panzergruppe Afrika

Section 2. Deutsches Afrikakorps

Section 3. 10. Panzer-Division

Section 4. 15. Panzer-Division

Section 5. 21. Panzer-Division

Section 6. 90. leichte Division

Section 7. 164. leichte Division

KLINK'S HEROES?

All was quiet, except for the rustling of paper in the prisoners' quarters. The soldiers of the Afrika Korps were busy making, of all things, a kite. The guards at the P.O.W. camp seemed pleased because, as long as they were doing this, they couldn't cause any mischief. The kite seemed strange because it had a small box attached to it and two strings instead of one. These details, however, went unnoticed by the guards. The townspeople, however, would soon find out its purpose since it would make them think that the Germans were invading.

It was a nice, windy day and the P.O.W.'s had no trouble in getting their kite into the air. After it had been up for about 20 minutes, one of the prisoners handed the extra string to one of the guards nearby who had been watching. The prisoner asked the guard to pull it, and, not seeing any harm in it, the guard pulled. As he did, the little box opened and thousands of small swastikas went floating down over the town. The camp commander came running out. He was furious. Having gotten numerous calls from panic-stricken townspeople, he swore heads would roll! He demanded to know who had committed this atrosity and as the prisoners smiled they all pointed at the poor guard. He had been so dumbfounded by the results of his little tug at the string that he was still holding it. The commander stamped back to his office yelling great obscenities at the prisoners, who were now laughing so hard that tears came to their eyes. The nights of cutting out the little swastikas had been worth it.

It was almost two weeks before the prisoners struck again as it took time to steal the materials needed for their next project. Having stolen four sheets, three buckets of paint, a wooden bucket and some coal, the P.O.W.'s now constructed their hot air balloon. Heavy coats of paint were applied to the sheets so the hot air would remain. Soon they were ready. The balloon top was attached to the bucket, the coals lit and a large, homemade Nazi flag, in honor of Adolph Hitler's birthday, was attached to the bottom.

They then took it out of the barracks and up it went before the guards realized what was happening. They had made their balloon better than they had anticipated because it not only sailed over the town of Aliceville, Alabama (where they were imprisoned), as they had intended, but it kept going. After it had flown some 50 miles, the U.S. Air Corps went on one of the strangest missions in its history. Shoot down the balloon, was the order! To add to the pleasure of the Germans, the plane did a victory roll over the camp upon the completion of its mission. Although rations were cut in half, the Germans had never been happier.

Both of these little tales, as bizarre as they might seem, are 100% true. My father, who told me the stories, was one of the P.O.W.'s.

W. Sell